POLITICAL GEOGRAPHY:
RECENT ADVANCES AND FUTURE DIRECTIONS

Political Geography: Recent Advances and Future Directions

EDITED BY
PETER TAYLOR AND JOHN HOUSE

CROOM HELM
London & Sydney
BARNES & NOBLE BOOKS
Totowa, New Jersey

© 1984 P.J. Taylor and J.W. House
Croom Helm Ltd, Provident House, Burrell Row,
Beckenham, Kent BR3 1AT
Croom Helm Australia Pty Ltd, First Floor, 139 King St.,
Sydney, NSW 2001, Australia

British Library Cataloguing in Publication Data

Political geography.
    1. Geography, Political
    I. Taylor, P.J.   II. House, John
    320.1'2   JC319
    ISBN 0-7099-2465-8

First published in the USA 1984 by
Barnes & Noble Books,
81 Adams Drive,
Totowa, New Jersey, 07512

Library of Congress Cataloging in Publication Data

Main entry under title:
Political geography.
    1. Geography, Political–Addresses, essays, lectures.
I. Taylor, Peter John   II. House, John William.
JC319.P588   1984   320.9   84-6493
ISBN 0-389-20493-5

Printed and bound in Great Britain

CONTENTS

Figures and Tables
Contributors
Preface

FIGURES AND TABLES

Figures

Tables

CONTRIBUTORS

BERTHA K. BECKER
  Universidade Federal do Rio de Janeiro, Brazil
STANLEY D. BRUNN
  University of Kentucky, Lexington, Kentucky, U.S.A.
ALAN D. BURNETT
  Portsmouth Polytechnic, Portsmouth, U.K.
PAUL CLAVAL
  University of Paris-Sorbonne, Paris, France
R. J. JOHNSTON
  University of Sheffield, Sheffield, U.K.
DAVID B. KNIGHT
  Carleton University, Ottawa, Canada
BRYAN H. MASSAM
  York University, Downsview, Ontario, Canada
JOHN O'LOUGHLIN
  University of Illinois, Urbana, Illinois, U.S.A.
JURGEN OSSENBRUGGE
  Universität Hamburg, Hamburg, Federal Republic of Germany
G. H. PIRIE
  University of Witwatersrand, Johannesburg, South Africa
PETER J. TAYLOR
  Newcastle University, Newcastle upon Tyne, U.K.
STANLEY WATERMAN
  University of Haifa, Mount Carmel, Haifa, Israel
H. van der WUSTEN
  Universitiet van Amsterdam, Amsterdam, The Netherlands

PREFACE

This collection of essays emanates from a conference of
political geographers held at Oxford in July 1983, which
attracted representatives from eighteen countries. This was
the third such international conference following those at
Lancaster in January 1980 and Haifa in January 1982. The
previous two conferences resulted in books of selected papers
edited by Alan Burnett and Peter Taylor, and Nurit Kliot and
Stanley Waterman, respectively. This is the book of the
Oxford conference but like its predecessors it is not a
conference proceedings. We have selected just thirteen of
the thirty eight papers presented or tabled at Oxford to
bring together in this book. The major criterion of
selection was relevance to our organising principle of
geographical scale. This is discussed in an additional brief
introductory essay below.

    For once editorial duties were clearly demarcated.
John House was responsible for organising the conference,
inviting all the speakers and generally getting this show on
the road. Since the conference Peter Taylor, in consultation
with John House, has undertaken the task of converting the
resulting large batch of papers into what is hopefully a
coherent collection of essays. We have kept to a tight
schedule to enable the book to be published in the summer of
1984 to be available at the Paris International Geographical
Union conference in August 1984. We thank all the authors
for revising their papers promptly to provide us with the
material to make the book a reality so quickly.

    The recent sequence of three international conferences
on political geography is one symptom of the very rigorous
resurgence of our sub-discipline. The purpose of the Oxford
conference was to devise a submission to the IGU for the
establishment of a commission or working party within the
field of political geography. This book is intended as one
small part of the evidence to show that political geography
has emerged from its 'dark age' and is now ready to play its
full role in the development of geographical research and

scholarship. We trust the IGU will recognise that a
geography that neglects its political sub-field will fail to
achieve its potential as one of the most relevant disciplines
of our age.

Peter Taylor and John House, 21.1.84

Chapter One

INTRODUCTION: GEOGRAPHICAL SCALE AND POLITICAL GEOGRAPHY

Peter J. Taylor

It has become commonplace for the subject-matter of
political geography to be organised into three geographical
scales: an international, national and an intra-national
scale. I have previously documented this tendency within
political and welfare geography textbooks since 1975
(Taylor, 1982) and the latest textbook (Short, 1982) also
conforms to this arrangement. Since the scale-organisation
principle lies behind the ordering of chapters below, I have
chosen to introduce this book with a short essay on
geographical scale and political geography. This is
necessary, I feel, because despite the almost ubiquitous
utilization of this principle, adequate discussion of the
reasons why this arrangement is a suitable one for political
geography is most conspicuous by its absence.

POLITICAL GEOGRAPHY'S SCALE PROBLEM

There is a large literature on scale, or more properly
'the scale problem', in modern geography. It is probably
the existence of this literature which has led political
geographers to neglect their own particular consideration of
scale. In fact modern geographical concern for scale has
been in data analysis in the light of the fact that statist-
ical results are not independent of the scale of analysis.
This reduces to either a problem of aggregation (statistics)
or resolution (geography). The political geographer's use of
scale to organise his or her subject-matter is a much more
fundamental issue. By studying activities at three separate
scales political geographers are implying that politics in
some sense exists or at least occurs in three different types
of arena. Of course, the arenas specified pivot about the
essential document of the political geography - the world
political map. What political geographers are saying is that
politics is defined by the state which should be the focus
of attention. This then leads to consideration of the state

itself at the national scale, relations between states at the
international scale and the politics of parts of states at
the intra-national scale. But I would contend that political
geographers still have a scale problem albeit not a data
analysis one.

The problem with the scale principle of organisation is
that it tends to steer discussion into three separate
analyses. Johnston (1973) conceptualizes the three scales as
three distinct spatial systems, for example and Short (1982)
argues that they 'present themselves' as the most distinct
scales of analysis. The implications of this tendency is,
of course, to neglect the inter-relations between the scales.
It is for this reason that I have resisted the temptation to
divide up the chapters below and present them as three
'parts' corresponding to the three scales. All of the papers
below contain important relations beyond the scale on which
they focus. Hence although I am able to order chapters 3 to
13 to approximate an increasing scale of focus, this does not
imply that the papers treat one or other scale exclusively.
For instance, chapters 3, 4, and 5 by Burnett, Massam and
Ossenbrugge, deal with local urban politics but in every case
the subject-matter is related to processes that operate at
least at the state scale and come under the heading 'theory
of the state'. The very term 'local state' implies
relations beyond the local scale. At the other end of the
spectrum chapter 12 and 13 by Wusten and O'Loughlin are
explicitly concerned with the international scale but they
relate inter-state relations in war and peace to the
characteristics of the states themselves. Chapters 6
through to 11 generally focus on the state scale itself but
are particularly adept at moving above and below this
geographical level. Becker (Chapter 6), for instance
relates the crisis of the state to both regional movements
and the current world economic crisis. Similarly Waterman's
discussion of partition (chapter 7) is concerned with state
integrity but has direct relevance to intra-state processes
of separation and the inter-state system if partition
results in an additional member to the international
community of states. Both Taylor and Johnston (chapters 8
and 9) attempt to free electoral geography from its prime
concern with the state scale so as to relate liberal
democracy to a broader world context. Brunn (chapter 10)
discusses the future of the nation-state in the context of
challenges from both 'above' and 'below'. Finally Knight's
discussion of self-determination (chapter 11) deals with the
potential creation of states and its implication for international law. In the initial planning of this book I had
allocated this chapter to the 'Geography of the State' part
and the author wrote to suggest that it fitted best into the
'Geography of International Relations' part. Clearly it
fitted easily into both parts. It was considerations such as

this that led me to abandon the division of the chapters into parts. All of the chapters in their different ways illustrate why geographical scales should be considered in terms of their inter-connections as much as their particular distinctiveness.

This is not another plea for scale-free prescriptions to be developed in political geography as Cox (1979) has advocated. We live in one world and the political processes that operate at the three scales identified above constitute a single politics. Political geographers such as Mackinder were among the first to theorize a one-world situation but as Claval points out in chapter 1, traditional researchers never managed to produce an integrated political geography. Geostrategic studies remained separate from the independent of other political geography to be largely abandoned in the mid-twentieth century. The 'discovery' of the three-scale organisation in the 1970's reflects the birth of an urban political geography along with the rebirth of global concerns in political geography. With such initial disparate themes as the 'distribution of urban public goods' and 'geostrategy in the nuclear era' it is not surprising that these scales became seen as distinct and separate. I trust that the chapters below contribute to a solution to this scale problem in political geography.

The 11 substantive chapters ordered by scale are sandwiched between two more general statements on political geography. As indicated above Claval's concern (chapter 2) is for the 'coherence' of the sub-discipline and he contributes a historical viewpoint which, among other things, traces changes in the scale focus of political geography. This provides a necessary background for the treatment of different scales in subsequent chapters. In the final chapter Pirie identifies the neglect of political philosophy by political geographers as a further problem. Whereas positivist political science and critical political economy provide the basis for the preceeding chapters, the potential contributions of political philosophy are missing. Pirie argues that attention to the modern concerns of philosophy can improve our political geography at all scales.

THE SCOPE OF CONFLICT

It is not enough to identify geographical scale as a useful organising principle. Why is it useful? The three scales do not, of course, 'present' themselves to us, they are made by the men and women who have constructed the institutions of our modern world. And there is nothing neutral about their constructions. 'All organisation is bias' states Schattschneider (1960) and this applies just as much to the scale-organisation principle in political

geography as to other human arrangements. Elsewhere I have
tried to provide a materialist rationale for the dominance of
the three scales in our world-system (Taylor, 1982). The
result is a general framework for studying political
geography; in the remainder of this essay I wish to
supplement this by looking in more detail at the way in which
geographical scale operates within politics. Schattschneider
(1960) presents a conflict model of the political process in
which he introduces the idea of the scope of conflict as a
basic characteristic of all politics. It is this model and
concept which I will use to investigate the role of
geographical scale in politics.

A conflict presupposes two or more opposing interests.
For Schattschneider, however, the outcome of the conflict
will not depend upon the relative power of the competing
interests. Every conflict occurs within a wider context -
an audience - and it is the latter who will normally
determine the outcome. The extent that an audience is
brought into a conflict defines the scope of the conflict.
From this Schattschneider (1960) defines the following
propositions.

1. All conflict is determined by its scope
2. The most important strategy in politics concerns
   the scope of conflict
3. Every extension of the scope will change the
   balance of power in a conflict
4. At any given extent of the scope of a conflict,
   it will be the weaker interest which will
   attempt to broaden the scope

Schattschneider uses these propositions to investigate the
nature of American democracy and the particular way the
politics packages conflict for public consumption.

In essence this model directs attention towards two
fundamentally opposing political strategies - privatisation
versus socialisation of conflicts (Schattschneider, 1960:7).
In the former camp we have ideological justification via
terms such as individualism, laissez faire, free enterprise
and privacy whereas in the latter camp equality, social
justice, civil rights and collectivism are some of the key
words. Two important political conflicts may be briefly
mentioned to illustrate Schattschneider's thesis. First
electoral suffrage reforms have been a process of continual
extension of the scope of national politics. As more and
more of the population are incorporated into elections,
parties and the state itself have had to respond to meet the
new politics. Second the rise of trade unions is an explicit
attempt to widen the scope of industrial conflict. This is
the basic ideology of unionism and it is resisted by keeping
'outsiders' - union officials, pickets, etc. - out of a

'local' dispute. In the last century or so much of the work
of progressive politicians has been to extend the scope of
conflicts, to appeal to a wider public for redress of private
grievances. On the other hand reactionary politicians have
attempted to control conflicts by keeping them private and
therefore almost invisible. But as Schattschneider (1960, 17)
is at pains to emphasize 'there is nothing intrinsically good
or bad about any scope of conflict' - it all depends on what
you want from the politics in question.

In any institutional organisation the scope of politics
will often be closely related to geographical scale. The
classic example in political geography is the rise of the
medium-sized state since about 1500. There was nothing
'natural' about the evolution of an inter-state system
dominated by this particular scale of organisation (Taylor,
1981). In 1500, for example, it is possible to divide up
Europe into three sectors based upon different scales of
political organisation (Rokkan, 1975): In eastern Europe
there were empires, in central Europe city states and only
western Europe was dominated by medium-sized states between
the city and empire scales. Viewing the future from 1500
Tilly argues that the final outcome of sixteenth century
politics, the inter-state system dominated by medium-sized
states, was only one of several possible political scenarios.
This was the successful outcome of the conflicts of this era
because this particular political scale of organisation was
uniquely suited to take advantage of the economic opportunities opening up with the emergence of the capitalist world-
economy (Wallerstein, 1974). So successful was this scale of
organisation that it came to be emulated throughout the world.
Nairn's (1977) interpretation of nationalism is partly as
emulation of the successful medium-size states resulting in
unification in 'city-state Europe' and division of 'empire
Europe'. This advantage seems only to have been eclipsed in
our era by the rise of 'super-powers' which are continental
in scope.

The best example to illustrate the fact that the
emergence of the medium-sized state reflects past patterns of
power can be seen in the case of the political organization
of the 'geographical' unit, the British Isles. How many
'nation-states' exist on these islands? Ignoring for the
moment the Scots and the Welsh, let us consider British-Irish
relations. These can be viewed at three different scales,
each of which produces distinctive outcomes to political
conflicts. At the largest scale, the whole British Isles as
one political unit, there has been a clear British/Protestant/
Unionist majority. This was the popular basis of the British
state before 1921. The subsequent division into three
political units with their own parliaments in London, Dublin
and Belfast produced two British/Protestant politics and a
new Irish/Catholic state. Of course, this was a compromise

solution to avoid a division into two states - Ireland and
Britain - one with an Irish/Catholic majority and the other
with a British/Protestant majority. Cearly the division of
the British Isles into one, two or three political units
changes the scope of political and religious conflict. It is
no wonder that territory has been at the heart of modern
Irish-British conflict.

Geographical scale defining the scope of conflict does
not only operate where the conflict has produced armed
struggle. In all political situations the scale of
resolution will determine political outcomes. For instance
decision-making at different levels of a hierarchy of
government areas will reflect different interests and may well
lead to alternative outcomes. Here are just a few of the
conflicts of current concern to political geographers which
illustrate a geographical interpretation of Schattschneider's
model.

1. The spatial structure of local government. Ward-
    systems versus at-large elections and metropolitan
    government versus community government are both
    classic examples of attempts to resolve conflict
    by spatial engineering.
2. The balance of power in federal states. The whole
    'states rights' or 'province autonomy' issue
    smacks of attempts to keep conflicts relatively
    local and prevent 'national' opinion affecting
    the outcomes.
3. The centralization of the modern state. This
    reflects the past successes of progressive
    politics in adding to the 'public' sphere. But
    it also produces centre-periphery tensions and
    central-local government disputes which are all
    about defining the scope of conflict and hence
    its outcome.
4. The globalization of modern politics. The
    success of nationalization of politics has been
    followed by a globalization at least for the
    super-powers. Concepts such as 'human rights',
    'prevention of counter-revolution', 'protection
    of the free world' are used to broaden
    conflicts beyond territorial sovereignties.

The main advantage of this approach is that it ensures
that instead of merely accepting scale as a principle of
organisation, we are led to question why politics occurs at a
particular scale. There is nothing neutral about the
geographical scale at which any conflict is decided. For
every 'chosen' scale there are other neglected scales which
may have produced alternative outcomes. Hence it is the
relations between scales and the different political meaning

of geographical scales, which are brought to the fore. The chapters below in their many different ways illustrate this basic pattern in modern political geography. Geographical scale _is_ political.

REFERENCES

Cox, K. R. (1979) Location and Public Problems, Maaroufa, Chicago

Johnston, R. J. (1973) Spatial Structures, Methuen, London

Nairn, T. (1977) The Break-up of Britain, New Left Books, London

Rokkan, S. (1975) 'Dimensions of state formation and nation building: a possible paradigm for research on variations within Europe' in C. Tilly (ed) The Formation of Nation States in Western Europe, Princeton U.P.: Princeton, N.J.

Schattschneider, E. E. (1960) The Semi-Sovereign People, Dryden, Hinsdale, Ill

Short, J. R. (1982) An Introduction to Political Geography, Routledge and Kegan Paul, London

Taylor, P. J. (1981) 'Political geography and the world-economy' in A. D. Burnett and P. J. Taylor (eds) Political Studies from Spatial Perspectives, Wiley, Chichester, U.K.

Taylor, P. J. (1982) 'A materialist framework for political geography', Transactions, Institute of British Geographers, NS7, 15-34

Tilly, C. (1975) 'Reflections on the history of European state-making' in C. Tilly (ed) The Formation of Nation States in western Europe, Princeton U.P., Princeton, N.J.

Wallerstein, I. (1974) The Modern World System, Academic, New York.

Chapter Two

THE COHERENCE OF POLITICAL GEOGRAPHY : PERSPECTIVES ON ITS
PAST EVOLUTION AND ITS FUTURE RELEVANCE

Paul Claval

At the present time political geography is fashionable.
This is due to the evolution of our society, to the increase
in international or domestic tension and to the crisis of the
nation state. Geographers hope to contribute to the analysis
of these problems and to the search for solutions. The
internal evolution of the discipline and the opening of new
avenues of research is progressing in this direction. Does
this indicate that contemporary political geography
constitutes a coherent and structured field? This is not how
it appears to us; on the whole we have the impression that
the field has developed in rather a chaotic manner; research
has evolved according to very different points of view, so
much so that different stratas corresponding to the
successive phases of research can still be clearly
identified in it. Coherence, in a subfield of any social
science, is great: (1) when its subject is permanently one of
the most significant for the relevance of the whole
discipline: (2) when its core is relying on the basic
principles developed for the whole field. Neither of these
conditions exist for political geography: (1) political
problems were certainly significant for all geographers
between 1890 and 1945, but they then recessed in the background before a new interest for them grew in the late
1970s: (2) in political geography emphasis was put on the
state at a time when human geography at large devoted more
attention to local and regional phenomena. As a result,
coherence is weakened in order to understand the present
situation it is essential to use a historical viewpoint.
    Three periods can be distinguished (Table 2.1): The
first one, between 1890 and 1950, corresponds to the
discovery and exploration of geographical problems of the
modern state: the second phase, between 1950 and 1970, was a
period in which more attention was paid to the progress of
the young political sociology and to the progress made in
systems theory. The new approach had hardly been elucidated
when people began to question its results: the 1970s are

Table 2.1: The three phases of political geography

		1900 – 1955	1955 – 1970	1970 – 1980
POLITICAL SCIENCES		POLITICAL DOCTRINES CONSTITUTIONAL LAW	POLITICAL SOCIOLOGY	IDEOLOGICAL ANALYSIS THEORY OF JUSTICE MARXIST CRITICISM OF POLITICAL SCIENCES
POLITICAL GEOGRAPHY	Political Geography of States	ECONOMIC BASES OF POWER ORGANISTIC THEORY OF STATE GROWTH → GEOSTRATEGY →		GEOSTRATEGY AS MACRO-SCALE EXTERNALITIES LOCAL EXTERNALITIES and URBAN POLITICS
	Theories of political processes	ELECTORAL STUDIES →	COMMUNICATION PROCESS FEEDBACKS and REGULATIONS →	POLITICAL ARCHITECTURE
	Perceptual problems – Normative Theory	LIVING SPACE →		IDEOLOGIES and SPACE ↑ SOCIAL JUSTICE STATE and FREEDOM
Main characteristics		Mainly macro-scale description	Macro and meso-scale processes	Macro, meso and micro-scale processes Relation between economic, cultural and political processes

9

characterized by the radical demands of a science concerned
with the real problems of modern man.

The great discontinuities which distinguished political
geography did not lead to the elimination of criticized
approaches or to their integration into more wide-ranging
models. It is therefore not possible to cover the evolution
thoroughly in just a few words if one wants to gain a clear
understanding of it - and the very notion of a paradigm,
after Thomas Kuhn's definition, is not appropriate to the
apprehension of a series of transformations which are only
approximations of the revolutions implied by this term.

POLITICAL GEOGRAPHY IN THE FIRST HALF OF THE CENTURY

The Herderian view of history as the root of Ratzel's interest in the State

Many nineteenth century geographers were anxious to elucidate
the problems of the political life of their time. This is
apparent amongst all those who, in the tradition of Carl
Ritter and more fundamentally of Herder, try to explain
history by the location of the peoples who made it (Claval,
1982a, 1982b). Elisee Reclus owes his attempt at a global
interpretation to this inheritance whilst his social and
political involvement and his interest in anarchist principles
directed his research towards the major problems of the
contemporary world. But his approach was such a general one
that he was unable to isolate the political factor from the
others.

Ratzel owes more than is immediately apparent to Ritter
and to Herder's vision of the life of societies and their
evolution. His ethnographic and zoological training
inclined him towards a preference for the idea of a global
society - the small society of the Naturvolker on which much
of his writing was based Ratzel (1885-88), and the state for
modern peoples who thus find the form which suits their
existence and their desire to live together. Ratzel (1897)
invented political geography because what seemed to him to be
the most significant reality in the interpretation of the
modern world was the state. In Germany, at the end of the
nineteenth century, the study of collective agents like
classes or nations held much more interest than the study of
individuals both for him and for many specialists in the
social sciences. That is why political geography first
developed on a different scale to the one which characterized
the other fields of human geography: the latter was interested almost exclusively in lived reality, in "pays" and
regional entities, the former in states. Conceived of in this
way political geography can be seen as a part of human
geography, that which is most typical of a world shaped by

modern bureaucracy. The scale used in Ratzelian political analysis remained the most popular one until the middle of the century.

When political geography was beginning to develop, the political sciences were very different in terms of content than they are today: they presented doctrines, they pointed to the ideal character of an institution rather than describing or explaining its functions. Since the beginning of the seventeenth century and the theories of social contract, since Montesquieu and the doctrine of the separation of powers, this direction had never been questioned: the most significant work in political science at the beginning of the century was the work of legal writers, for example Leon Duguit in France.

Thus geographers interested in political problems did not find anything in the political science of their time that they could use in order to understand the importance of space in the power struggle either of the armed forces or of the administration. They were forced to develop their own thought or, to be more exact, many interpretative frameworks which are referred to in turn.

The organic analogy

The reality of states can be seen today, but it is also helpful to explain their origin. History shows how dynasties of engrossers have succeeded in constructing modern political units through patient work which is often spread over centuries - this is true of the kings of France around Ile-de-France, the Hohenzollern around Brandenburg or the princes of Muscovy from a clearing the Mongols never completely managed to tame. The image which is worth developing into a theory is that of the growth of an organism-this reference to the biological analogy was common at the end of the nineteenth century in the human sciences as they were emerging then. It was used in the Ratzel's (1897) Lebensraum idea - the space needed by the collective social organism to live on.

Geostrategy : introduction of externalities at a macro-scale

States are involved in an international confrontation which dominates their relationship with one another. The arms race is becoming apparent amongst the large industrial nations. Political geography thus becomes world geostrategy: it sets out to measure the strength that each nation owes to its configuration, to its maritime and continental boundaries and to the control that it externally exercised through its naval bases or its colonies. On this theme Mackinder (1904) developed the opposition which soon became a classical example between the possibilities of defense and attack offered by the heartland and the freedom of movement that was created by the

sea to the strength of the <u>rimland</u>. Although the expression
was never used at that time political geography was trying to
decipher the externalities which led to military or naval
strength.

The economic bases for power

The strength of a nation is not solely dependent on the land:
it is a function of the number of its inhabitants, their
resources and their level of education. Since the seventeenth
century, the old statistic, the science of the state in the
etymological sense, that had just been revived in Germany at
the end of the nineteenth century by John's (1884) and
Meitzen's (1886) books (although in France Levasseur (1889)
also referred to their work) sought to evaluate the strength
of princes measuring the wealth reflected in their
possessions, the number of their subjects and the services to
which they had access.

At the beginning of the century political geography again
used these elements in its explanation and sometimes accorded
prime importance to them: this is seen clearly in texts such
as Isaiah Bowman's (1921). Many people confused political
geography with the measurement of the demographic and economic
foundations of a nation's strength. Since the end of the last
century the geography syllabus of the top classes of French
secondary education has been dedicated to the study of the
superpowers: the idea being to warn people of the problems
posed by a world in which competition between nations has been
increasing.

Symbolic dimensions

Ratzel (1897) was well aware of the fact that the analysis of
political events could not stop at the rather barren
considerations of world strategy or listing the economic
factors of power or independence. He introduced an
ideological dimension into political geography by evoking the
privileged relations between people and the space which they
had controlled and moulded but he did this by using a dynamic
image that was so ambitious that it could be used to justify
all political ambitions - something which was proved in the
following years. The idea of <u>Lebensraum</u> was built partly on
the above mentioned organicist model but it was conducive to
an awareness of psychological and symbolic dimensions of the
state.

Meso- or micro-scale interests: the geography of frontiers and boundaries

The core of political geography in the nineteen hundreds and
in the first half of the century lacked a unified theoretical

foundation: there was hardly any connection between the organisation involved in the formation of national territories, the understanding of external influences generated by military strength, an inventory of the economic bases of strength or the evolution of the psychological dimension of the relations between people and space. Chapters were written whose relationship to this central core was even more tenuous : this was true or frontiers and boundaries. Their practical interest is clear and this is one of the fields in which geographers can be considered experts - the negotiations for the treaty of Versailles prove this - but the knowledge mustered up on this occasion had little connection with political science. In order to designate a border or to decide whether those in existence are in the right place it is necessary to be familiar with the history of the disputed region, the settlement limits of the different groups which occupy it and the strategic value of the rivers, mountains and passes which characterize it: briefly this is the store of knowledge that regional geography allows one to use. Is this why the geography of frontiers and boundaries has been one of the favourite fields of political geography for a long time?

Meso- and micro-scale interests : electoral geography

The studies of electoral geography are even more tenuously linked to the rest of political geography than the geography of boundaries. The work was begun by André Siegfried (1913, 1949) who was a geographer, historian, political scientist and a sociologist. It announced the time when political geography would cease to be isolated from the other social sciences - this area might also interest historians as much as sociologists and political scientists. But due to their scale and the fact that they were revealing processes within the nation, this research was marginal to the main-stream of political geography conceived of as the analysis of states.

At the beginning of the century political geography was so varied that it was able to highlight all the political problems of the moment. Geographers were eager witnesses to the changes of their time. Demangeon (1920, 1923), for example, was one of the first people to stress the decline of Europe and also one of the first people to question the rationale of the great colonial Empires, particularly the British Empire.

Interest fades when we pass from monographs to the text-books which deal with the entire field: the lack of theoretical coherence, which is not apparent at the level of concrete problems, becomes very obvious in insipid textbooks containing nothing but common sense.

The insufficient elaboration of principles undoubtedly

explains at least as much of the decline in political
geography in the 1950s and 1960s as the unfortunate encounter
with Geopolitik. Numerous work still expounds upon the
economic and strategic foundations of power, on the questions
of boundaries or on the base of electoral geography, but
these ignore a large number of the problems which are
becoming important issues, those of the Third World, the
political instability of certain long-established nations, or
the competition between East and West.

THE THEORETICAL WORK OF THE 1950s AND THE 1960s

The role of political sociology

The academic context in which political geography developed
in the 1950s and 1960s was completely different to that which
prevailed at the beginning of the century. The normative
direction which strongly characterized political science has
declined – it was a time when people were proclaiming the end
of ideologies. Instead of concerning itself with the
depiction of the institutions of a just government – a
democratic government – attention was focused on the
functioning of those in existence – that is how the study of
the geography of elections had heralded political sociology
which then came to dominate research (Duverger, 1973).
Researchers endeavoured to show the workings of power, of
authority and of influence, according to the clues that
already existed in Max Weber's sociology, the relevance of
which was shown by the analyses of political anthropology.
In modern states the crucial problem is the gap between
institutions, statements of the official line and the real
interplay of social and economic forces. The new political
sciences spoke in terms of classes, organisations, pressure
groups, unions and parties. It enabled one to grasp, to use
a term coined by Robert Dahl (1963), the difference between
the polyarchies that one sees and the democracies which
constitutions have tried to set up.

The movement away from simple doctrine to political
sociology entailed a change of scale. There was of course a
sociology of international relations, a sociology of war and
peace which interested those people concerned with understanding the balance between states, but the essential part
of research developed by the new political sociology had a
bearing on the type of representation and on the
administrative organisation – it dealt with the local or
regional scale where power was nurtured and exercised at
least as much as at a national scale.

Systems theory, political feed-backs, information and space

Amongst the new approaches, some are devoted to attracting
geographers' attention: particularly those which regard the
political organisation of a country as a system: this is
analysed by measuring the flows that affect it, the demands
coming from the society on the one hand, corrective and
stabilizing actions coming from the government on the other.
Electoral geography ceases to be a marginal sector of the
discipline: it describes one of the feed-backs through which
political control is achieved.

Since the early 1960s, geographers such as Douglas
Jackson (1964) have realized the applications of David Easton
(1953) or Karl Deutsch's (1953) work. They learnt to pose the
problem of political geography in terms of the exchange of
information, of transactions between groups of varied
strengths and of the regulation of social life. They felt
that it would be possible to grasp the spatial dimensions of
political operations through the understanding of news and
orders which are part of political life. Karl Deutsch's
research is on these lines exactly and Edward Soja (1968)
started with this work when he wanted to assess the real
control of governments instated by the decolonization of
Africa. He reconstructed the changing surface of modern-
ization expressed by the progressive integration of groups
and regions into new states. The methods used cannot go
beyond this crude evaluation of the growing impact of state
machinery on social groups.

The new theory developed by political geography was too
concerned with quantitative methods to pay attention to
qualitative factors without which thought cannot pass beyond
the state of trivial generalizations in which it had been
until then.

Economic explanation vs. political approaches

In the 1950s and 1960s the world scene and the destiny of
peoples and states seemed to be increasingly explained in
terms of the processes of economic growth than by the
operation of political domination. Were we not taking part
in rapid decolonization at the time? Did we not also witness
the same or the increasing dependency of the Third World
countries on developed countries? Did this not mean that
Marxists or liberal economists were right in ascertaining
that the basic problem of the present world were those of
production, and that the rest is nothing but an ideological
veil?

Iconography, symbolism, perception

Nevertheless theoretical thought of a classical nature
undoubtedly progressed. The relationship between man and his

home environment was henceforth analysed with more
satisfactory tools than Geopolitik and the notion of
Lebensraum. Jean Gottmann (1952) drew attention to the
symbolic aspect of the events of political geography. He was
the first person to show an interest in political iconography
and in the agency which links the citizen to his native land.
There arose a new direction which was sensitive to the
strength of territorial ideology (Gottmann, 1973) to the
diverse nature of their motivations and to their role in
social regulation. The research into territoriality which
attracted ethnologists led in the same direction. Does not
the interest in perception problems which was shown in many
works bear witness to the need to increase research in this
field?

THE 1970s : A CRITICAL DECADE

The shortcomings of behaviourist theory
The reaction against the work of political sociology in the
1950s and 1960s was quick to develop and gained support in
the 1970s. What is there to reproach then in Easton and
Deutsch's work, and even in the work of people influenced by
Talcott Parson's thought in the USA? Their inclination is to
study only balanced phenomena and to rub out from social and
political life all those tensions which cannot be reduced to
conflicts over economic interest with the result that the
feedback game can go ahead undeterred and without profound
social disturbance. The world in which we live is a world of
competition between ideologies and systems of society to the
point of death, and people claim to understand it by using
models which ignore violence, disturbances, changes and
precisely what constitutes history! The age criticizes those
people who ignore the power of ideologies.
    The world changes quickly. The role of the economy is
very strong in the life of contemporary societies but how can
one consider it without taking into account the political
aspect in an age of OPEC and high oil prices? The geography
of social life is shaken by power struggles on all levels :
it is not just a case of the international arena becoming
politicized once again but also the politicization of
regional and urban life.

Back to traditional approaches
In the 1970s political geography witnessed the increased
strength of traditional interpretations: even if their
theoretical justification is unsatisfactory they had the
advantage of reflecting the power struggle or ideologies.
Never before had so much space been given to the analysis of

the economic basis of power: does the oil crisis not indicate
the relevance of this approach?

Geo-strategy strengthens its hold when we are concerned
with the competition between superpowers and with the local
conflicts through which they oppose each other or through
which new territorial units try to make their mark in the
world arena. Research is abandoning the rather restricted
framework of traditional wars : it has bearing on the balance
of power and on the geographical forms of revolutionary
movements and querilla actions. Some of the people who are
encroaching on this area feel that they are altering
traditional approaches in a radical manner when they are in
fact rediscovering approaches that staff officers and
geographers often cultivated in the first decade of this
century (Lacoste, 1976).

There has been some renewed interest in the study of
boundaries and frontiers - to the extent that the increased
mobility has shaken conditions of life at the points of
contact between two or more societies - these form an
important part of the surface of all countries like
Switzerland, the Netherlands and Belgium. The exploitation
of offshore resources and the problem of the destruction of
shoals of fish by uncontrolled onslaughts leads one to
conceive of new ways of dividing ocean beds which call upon
the many skills of the geographer in the defining of new
boundaries for territorial waters as it did in the first
world war.

Political geography in the 1970s, despite its radical
stance, was much nearer to traditional principles than it
seemed. It hardly furthered the coherence of the field and
abandoned the efforts made in the 1960s.

New problems to tackle with
On a national scale, particular attention should be directed
to the analysis of the ideological factors of political life:
why are the oldest and most consolidated nations often
subjected to the demands for the autonomy of new and
unforeseen groups? Is it not necessary to consider the
attention given to all collective protests and to feelings of
territorial belongings (Agnew, 1981; Knight, 1982).

Research devoted to urban problems is multiplying :
conflicts are emerging, struggles for influence are
developing - and their violence does not yield anything to
the one which is present in international relations. In the
early 1970s geographical works learnt to look behind the
tension and to read into the externalities which are causing
them (Harvey, 1973; Cox, 1973, 1978; Cox and Johnston, 1982).
The field of inquiry open to the discipline grew wider and
more specific at the same time: amongst other displays of
power and influence geographers were particularly interested

in all those that betrayed externalities - strategic
externalities in the field of international relations,
economic forces linked to overspill effects in urban
environments.

The importation of economic theory in political geography

In this decade most progress was made by borrowing from
economic understanding. Many of the conflicts which
developed within nations were due to the unequal accessibility
to services: not everyone had access to the same conditions
of public welfare and it was often the case of not having
access to any at all (Burnett, 1981). A good administrative
structure will correct this fault by offering people public
services where they are accessible to the greatest number of
families. A theory of local government can also be
elaborated on economic grounds (Dear, 1981). If one
considers, and one frequently does now, following Rawls (1971)
that the role of the state is to ensure the equality of every
citizen, it is possible to elaborate a normative political
geography: was this not one of the ambitions of all the
radical movements of the 1970s?

Despite some undeniable successes like this one,
geography in the 1970s has not been able to turn political
geography into a coherent field. To date, the restructuring
that has taken place has not been very extensive - the
inclusion of electoral geography in the larger sphere of the
analysis of information systems and feed-backs from political
institutions, the inclusion of externalities as the sources of
many forms of influence at different scales and in different
settings. All this is preparing the way for a more universal
theoretical construction: we have now to suggest some major
themes around which it can be built.

PERSPECTIVES : STRUCTURING THE DISCIPLINE AROUND THE POWER CONCEPT

When one tries to understand contemporary political
geography one realises that it is linked to the attempt to
solve pertinent questions rather than to thought avowed to
encapsulating methodology. This explains the many frameworks
of analysis and their imperfect agreement. Contemporary
reflexion has dealt mainly with the economic aspects of
political relations. In order to probe more deeply and to
introduce more coherence it becomes necessary to consider the
basic mechanisms of power.

Basic Principles : Power and Communication

Any relationship can be defined as political when power is brought into play and is imposed on the whole group bestowing both unity and efficiency upon it.

By matching the decisions and behaviour of individuals, groups and organisations, political action enables one to define the benefits which fall to the community and/or governors and authorities. The system is only a viable one when the costs of its functioning are less than the advantages which it generates.

Any political relationship involves the exchange of information between governors and the people who are governed. There are many different kinds of these exchanges - but they are always important and quasi-permanent.

Oral communication, face to face, with the physical presence of the parties, is the richest and incur the least loss through encoding and decoding. As it is instantaneous it does not suffer delays due to the transmission and return of information.

The king could not always reign in council and hand out justice under an oak tree or listen to the demands of his subjects at the same time. The functioning of a large and complex society demands means of communication tested by time and space. There is thus a political geography whose roots must partly lie with these problems. 1960s theoricists were right in dealing with information problems, but their basic concepts were too crude to cover the whole field.

Basic Principles : Communication, Networks, Territories and Political Organisation

The efficiency of the political system is primarily a function of the way in which one transmits orders and information that one wants to use. A parallel can be drawn between the extent and strength of political construct and the communication techniques which they are able to use (Innis, 1952). Printing has allowed the birth of the modern state, the telegraph and the railway the birth of the large colonial empires of the nineteenth century (Eisenstadt, 1963). The intensity of present relations allows the omnipresence of the welfare state in the life of the citizen - but the dream of a world government seems paradoxically to be becoming more distant.

In every instance, the economy and efficiency of communications involve: (1) an organisation of communication routes in a hierarchical sense around central nodes which allows the exchange between partners to be carried out at a minimal cost; (2) a territorial division with limits to areas and well-defined frontiers.

There is an organic link between the appearance and development of complex societies, the emergence of a regulatory political function and the birth of the <u>polis</u>.

A network of towns allows a body of a relatively small number of civil servants, speaking the same precise and concise language of administration, united by a system of routes and messengers, to insure the transmission of orders and the dispatching of return information - and all that with relative economy and over large distances.

The need to limit the territory is linked to the necessity of efficiently controlling the population at the lowest cost (Sack, 1983). That also allows the restriction of the powers of those people who receive a delegation of responsibility from central powers.

The layout of the ideal prison, of Bentham's <u>panopticon</u>, is central to an understanding of the spatial structures which are fundamental to all political organization (Foucault, 1975). A number of wardens at the centre of an enclosed circular area which is internally divided but also transparent, with paths radiating from the observation points, allows the observation and control of hundreds of prisoners to be maintained.

If this scheme is transferred to the field of territorial organisation one can understand the need to enclose all policed states in a network of divisions centred on the areas in which the representatives of government lives. The respect for law and order can also be ensured. Beyond the boundary is the land of outlaws and anarchy. But it is obvious that the analogy with Bentham's prison is very formal. The purely technical conditions of the flow of information are not enough for an understanding of the insertion of space into the political system.

Basic Principles : Power, Authority, Influence and the Diversity of Political Architecture

<u>Pure power</u> (Claval, 1978) asserting itself through physical constraint, terror, continual supervision, can only work at such great information cost that it rapidly exhausts its strength.

<u>Authority</u>. If power is tolerated, or even better, if it is largely accepted, the cost of supervision and information flow, such as that necessitated by the elimination of deviance, are considerably reduced. One can appreciate the important role which is open to <u>ideologies</u>: the strength of a system of thought which is so convincing that no-one manages to evade its logic might prove to be superior to a system based on weapons.

<u>Influence and the civil society</u>. Societies are not made up of isolated individuals, on whom armies of civil servants and policemen are imposed. A number of complex relations structure the <u>civil society</u> in the form of small groups or larger collectives, according to egalitarian principles of

exchange or association or according to the hierarchical
principle (Maquet, 1970). The latter is often based on one's
status at birth.

Authority or influence help to hold groups together.
Custom and acculturation give social relations a major role
in the formation of social architectures.

The political system takes part, to reduce the
communication costs, of everything which helps to structure
the civil society and to organise space - but it has to be
constantly alert because local power is always on the point
of emerging. It is born within groups and private
organisations, it is linked to the possible control of
communicating routes or networks for the exchange of
information or it can be the result of the excessive autonomy
of the agents of central power who turn their authority to
their own ends. Mistrust and good information networks are
not sufficient to avoid the increase in centrifugal
tendencies : the exercise of power is only easy when it can
set resources aside and use them when the need arises. The
monetarization of the economies and the taxes payed are
indispensable to the creation of really workable political
systems. They can thus create state bureaucracies which
assure the respect for the law in every way and ensure the
equality of everyone inside the largest countries
(Eisenstadt, 1963).

PERSPECTIVES : OTHER ORIENTATIONS AND APPLICATIONS

From spatial power theory to other aspects of political
geography
The advantage, for political geography, in starting with a
spatial theory of the exercise of power, stems from the
possibilities which then arise to arrange most of the former
approaches into one body of knowledge. Power, authority and
influence are consubstantial aspects of all social life
within a defined area: they stem from the unequal distribution of resources, the existence of strategic positions,
advantages conferred by transport and communication services
and all types of exchange. In a punctual society, that is a
frictionless one, it is always possible to dream of
unconstrained relations; geography teaches that space
introduces always constraints - but it also shows how
political systems, by accepting the necessity of relationships where force, threats and coercion play a part,
substitute larger or smaller area regulated by the same
responsible people, under the same constitution and with the
same motivations for the disorderly explosion of local
tyrannies. Ideologies, institutions and spatial
configurations are then linked in coherent systems. The

study of externalities, whose strength we have shown in urban
or international contexts, describes the spontaneous
emergence of constraint; the analysis of representative
systems describes one of the types of political architecture
which assures a global self-regulation by indicating to those
in charge the emergence of the needs of civil society. We
can at least envisage a political geography with coherent
theoretical foundations.

The role of political economy

The success of economic explanations in political geography
stems from three facts: (1) the overspill aspects of social
and economic life are an important form of influence; (2)
the state is providing imperfect public goods, so that it has
to look for an equitable distribution of them; (3) transactions in economic life have two aspects; some of them are
concerned with the exchange of goods and services; the other
are fixing the rules of negotiations (Lapage, 1978; Alchian
and Demsetz, 1972; North and Thomas, 1973).

The two first aspects are useful to improve minor
aspects of spatial political theory. The third aspect is
more controversial.

One of the main advances of economic theory during the
last 20 years concerns the study of decisions regarding the
whole social organisation: their logic could be illuminated
by adopting an economic perspective (Buchanan and Tullock,
1962). Collective choice theory is certainly excellent for
exploring the logic of macro-scale social systems and of
their political components, but they are relevant only as
long as partners are trying to maximize some economic value.

Economic explanations are certainly useful in political
geography, but they are unable to cover all the aspects of
present-day situations. As long as the aim of political life
is to maximize and then divide between different categories
the benefits of order and security, the modern generalized
economic theory is relevant. When the logic of institutions
and of behaviours is to maximize the control exercized by
some categories, or when it is not to achieve prosperity, but
global power, we have to rely on more classical political
analysis. Political economy is only a part of the conceptual
apparatus needed by modern political geography.

Applied political geography : equality, segregation, security and freedom

Partly because of its economic assumptions, the political
geography of the 1970s has been mainly interested in problems
of equality and equity: the question has been studied at the
local scale as well as at the national and international
scale.

Is equality the most important social good? Yes, as soon as the first condition of justice as defined by Rawls (1971) - that is the procedural freedom condition - is provided for. Geographers have accepted Rawl's views without inquiring into the first condition: the spatial requisite for procedural equality are costly and there is in them some measure of contradiction with what is needed for distributive equality. Some form of segregation may be helpful to build effective security and real freedom.

The normative political geography of positive discrimination is theoretically weak. Political geographers have certainly to improve this part of the discipline to be able to advise better spatial organization.

REFERENCES

Agnew, J. A. (1981) Structural and dialectical theories of political regionalism' in A. D. Burnett and P. J. Taylor (eds.), <u>Political Studies from Spatial Perspectives</u>, John Wiley, Chichester, U.K., pp. 275-89

Alchian, A. A. and Demsetz, H. (1972) 'Production information costs and economic organization', <u>American Economic Review</u>, <u>62</u>, 777-95

Bowman, I. (1921) <u>The New World</u>, World Books, New York

Buchanan, J. M. and Tullock, G. (1962) <u>The Calculus of Consent</u>, University of Michigan Press, Ann Arbor

Burnett, A. D. (1981) 'The distribution of local political outputs and outcomes in British and North American cities' in A. D. Burnett and P. J. Taylor (eds.) <u>Political Studies from Spatial Perspectives</u>, John Wiley, Chichester, U.K. 201-36

Claval, P. (1978) <u>Espace et Pouvoir</u>, PUF, Paris

Claval, P. (1982a) 'Les grandes coupures de l'histoire de la geographie', <u>Herodote</u>, <u>25</u>, 129-56

Claval, P. (1982b) 'Methodology and geography', Progress in <u>Human Geography</u>, <u>6</u>, 449-554

Cox, K. R. (1973) <u>Conflict, Power and Politics in the City</u>, McGraw Hill, New York

Cox, K. R. (1978) <u>Urbanization and Conflict in Market Societies</u>, Maaroufa Press, Chicago

Cox, K. R. and Johnston, R. J. (1982) <u>Conflict, Politics and the Urban Scene</u>, Longman, London

Dahl, R. (1963) <u>Modern Political Analysis</u>, Prentice Hall, Englewood Cliffs, N.J.

Dear, M. (1981) 'A theory of the local state' in A. D. Burnett and P. J. Taylor (eds.) <u>Political Studies from Spatial Perspectives</u>, 183-200

Demangeon, A. (1920) <u>Le Déclin de l'Europe</u>, Payot, Paris

Demangeon, A. (1923) <u>L'Empire Britannique. Etude de Geographie Coloniale</u>, A. Colin, Paris

Deutch, K. W. (1953) Nationalism and Social Communication,
    M.I.T. Press, Cambridge, Ma.
Duverger, M. (1973) Sociologie de la Politique, PUF, Paris
Easton, D. (1953) The Political System, Knopf, New York
Eisenstadt, S. N. (1963) The Political Systems of Empires,
    The Free Press, New York
Foucault, M. (1975) Surveiller et Punir, Gallimard, Paris
Gottmann, J. (1952) La Politique des Etats et leur
    Geographie, A. Colin, Paris
Gottmann, J. (1973) The Significance of Territory, University
    Press of Virginia, Charlottsville
Harvey, D. (1973) Social Justice and the City, Arnold,
    London
Innis, H. (1952) Empire and Communication, University of
    Toronto Press, Toronto
Jackson, W. A. D. (1964) Politics and Geographic Relation-
    ships, Prentice Hall, Englewood Cliffs, N.J.
John, V. (1884) Geschichte der Statistik, F. Enke, Stuttgart
Knight, D. B. (1982) 'Identity and territory : geographical
    perspectives on nationalism and regionalism', Annals,
    Association of American Geographers, 72, 514-31
Lacoste, Y. (1976) La Géographie, ça Sert, d'Abord, à Faire
    la Guerra, Maspéro, Paris
Lepage, J. (1978) Demain, le Capitalisme, Librairie Generale
    Francaise, Paris
Levasseur, E. (1889) La Population Française, Rousseau, Paris
Mackinder, H. J. (1904) 'The geographical pivot of history',
    Geographical Journal, 23, 421-37
Maquet, J. (1970) Pouvoir et Société en Afrique, Hachette,
    Paris
Meitzen, A. (1886) Geschichte und Technik der Statistik,
    Berlin
North, D. C. and Thomas, R. P. (1973) The Rise of the
    Western World, Cambridge University Press, Cambridge,
    U.K.
Ratzel, F. (1885-88) Völkerkunde, Bibliog. Inst., Leipzig
Ratzel, F. (1897) Politische Geographie, Oldenburg, Munich
    and Leizig
Rawls, J. (1971) A Theory of Justice, Harvard University
    Press, Cambridge, Ma.
Sack, R. (1983) 'Human territoriality : a theory', Annals,
    Association of American Geographers, 73, 55-74
Seigried, A. (1913) Tableau Politique de la France de l'Ouest
    sous la III Republique, A. Colin, Paris
Seigfried, A. (1949) Géographie Électorale de l'Ardeche sous
    la III° République, A. Colin, Paris
Soja, E. W. (1968) 'Communications and territorial
    integration in East Africa', East Lakes Geographer, 4,
    39-67

Chapter Three

THE APPLICATION OF ALTERNATIVE THEORIES IN POLITICAL
GEOGRAPHY : THE CASE OF POLITICAL PARTICIPATION

Alan D. Burnett

Whatever other strengths and weaknesses the sub-
discipline of political geography may have had in the past, it
has undoubtedly suffered from inadequacy in theorisation.
Theory from other social sciences and other branches of human
geography has largely been eschewed; deemed as an unnecessary
diversion from the 'realities' of empirical research.
However, there is now evidence that this neglect is being
rectified. Increasingly, it is being realised that there is
great potential for advance in theoretical, methodological and
empirical studies. As Reynolds (1981:91) states:

> like any sub field of social science, the future
> vitality of political geography is dependent on the
> ability of its practitioners to develop theory
> which is rich both in concepts and application.

Of course, there are differences of opinion as to the need for
theory, and what approaches should guide the range of research
currently being undertaken under the auspices of political
geography. Can theories be labelled as 'traditional' or
'critical'? Is it possible for certain to be classed as
'outdated', and others characterised as having been applied
and found wanting? Are middle range theories of more
practical value than 'grand' ones? What are the merits and
demerits of individual approaches? Should empirical research
start off on the basis of a single theoretical stance, and if
not, how can contrasted paradigms be integrated? These key
questions are unlikely to generate unanimity of response
amongst political/human geographers. In this paper, a
selection of paradigms are discussed with particular
reference to the theme of local collective political
participation and demand-making. At the outset, however, a
number of general points are made about the intrinsic value
and empirical use of theories.

IN PRAISE OF THEORETICAL ECLECTICISM

Clearly, there are dangers in taking on board the multiplicity of theoretical stances which can be found in the social science and geographical literature. As Paddison has observed recently, eclecticism may undermine the potential for integration in political geography (Paddison, 1983). Likewise Couclelis and Golledge (1983:331) graphically portray the difficulties encountered by 'the brave ones who dare challenge the dividing abyss, miserably foundering on the shoals of eclecticism, relativism and sheer ignorant confusionism'.

Given that different paradigms are based on different assumptions, are focused on different levels of analysis, and employ contrasted means of validation, there are bound to be problems in trying to evaluate, integrate and apply such a theoretical 'smorgasbord'.

> There appears to be an assumption that these 'approaches' are in some way alternatives; that we can select this concept from one approach, that method from another ... unfortunately, this desire for eclecticism rests on the false assumption that these approaches are, above all, techniques for analysis rather than epistemologies (Eyles and Lee, 1982:117)

Then there are those who would argue that one particular approach is inherently superior in providing a starting point for political geographical analysis in general or a specific theme such as the study of the state. For example, Fincher (1983) argues that the practice of sampling Marxist categories and combining them with concepts from other theories cannot be sustained epistemologically (or politically).

Nonetheless, these mono-theoretical arguments can be countered by points in favour of 'careful' eclecticism. Selecting approaches, concepts and techniques from a variety of paradigms in a 'principled' rather than ad hoc arbitrary way, can overcome the dangers stated by Lee (1979:87)

> The available theory is used as a toolbox, or perhaps more accurately as a bran tub in which the analyst rummages and finds pieces of theory that may be modified to provide ... a basis for analysis ... underlying assumptions ... are ignored in the anxiety to find, unwrap and remove the bit of theory selected for use!

A 'catholic' acceptance of the insights provided by several paradigms is preferable to a blinkered outlook for, as

Saunders (1979) has stated, the last thing that is wanted is a
strait-jacket of theoretical methodology which is applied
uniformly to a wide range of problems. Given the variety of
political themes being currently studied by geographers - the
state, locational and territorial conflict, re-districting and
voting, regionalism and ethnic separatism - to name but a few,
there is every likelihood that alternative theories will be
resorted to in the search for analytical guidance. Many may
feel intuitively that no one approach has a monopoly of
wisdom

> To take the two extremes, at one pole are the jumbo
> marxists seemingly condemned to an endless re-run of
> capital, but now with space added in; at the other
> pole are the humanists who seem equally blinkered,
> still thinking that the explanation of individual
> action resides in the individual ... (Thrift, 1982:
> 1283)

Using only one approach can incur the danger that research
will find out only what a given theoretical perspective has
encouraged the researcher to look for (Hain, 1981).
Furthermore, there is now available in the social science and
human geography literature, an impressive, not to say
bewildering, array of theories which await synthesis and
application in politico-geographical studies. As Couclelis
and Golledge (1983:337) state 'we may draw from these
insights, with the care and caution that is due, to make
geography the powerful, enlightened, self-critical human
science that we would like to see'.

THEORIES FOR SPECIFIC THEMES

While the question of merits and demerits of different
paradigms for political geography as a whole is an intriguing
one, it may be more fruitful to consider the opportunities for
theory building and application in relation to specific
empirical topics. One such attempt has recently been made by
Paddison (1983). He considers a variety of approaches which
he believes can help to examine the problem of public
facility location. The list includes the following
approaches - community elite, pluralist, functional fiefdoms
(urban bureaucrat), political ecology, and neo-Marxist. The
sources of each model are noted, and their basic characteristics and some key questions posed by each are cited, and
briefly explained. Other geographers have attempted a
similar exercise though often in a more limited and implicit
manner. Of the numerous attempts to structure the diverse
theories of the state, Dear and Clark's (1978) framework is
commendable. Likewise, in relation to political separatism

(regional and/or ethnic), Williams (1981) and Agnew (1981) have outlined theories and used them.

In terms of local urban political participation, or what Cox (1983) calls neighbourhood activism, similar theorisation can and should be attempted. The case for studying political participation between elections with an individual and group referent and the reason for its neglect in favour of studies of voting behaviour has been outlined elsewhere (Burnett, Cole and Moon, 1983). Here, dimensions of political demand-making attempts by citizens to influence public policies and political decisions are highlighted. Political participation needs to be viewed from below from a citizen's perspective, and also from the standpoint of those in authority and power. If possible, the causes, characteristics <u>and</u> consequences of neighbourhood political involvement in the city should be studied. While the socio-spatial distribution of political participation is likely to be a major focus, it is by no means the only aspects that is open to investigation. Motives <u>and</u> constraints should be involved in an analysis of patterns of participation and non-participation. Different modes of participation are available for analysis in terms of who is involved where, and to what effect. The complex nature of <u>issues</u> and outcomes is to be classified and explained. Finally, light can be shed on the several <u>functions</u> of citizen participation - as a means of mobilizing support for a policy or its implementation; communicating the wishes and preferences of the population to local councillors and officials in the form of demand diverting dissent into manageable channels, and exerting social control in the interests of the status quo and private capital accumulation. If the form <u>and</u> functions of local political involvement are to be fully understood it is unlikely that any one paradigm alone is adequate for the task.

What, then, are the major approaches which provide competing or complementary bases for empirical work in urban political participation? The ones which will be reviewed in this chapter include pluralist theory, managerialism, public goods theory, locational theory, the neo-Marxist political economy approach, systems and behavioural theories. If all of these diverse theories are relevant how, then, can they be employed? If, as has already been suggested, an eclectic approach is desirable, what strategy can be devised to achieve a synthesis and an integrated framework for any investigation? One possible tactic, which only partly acknowledges the possible contradictory/incompatability of different approaches, is to apply different theoretical standpoints. However, this begs the question of what sort of data ought to be gathered in the first place. A more promising method is to subsume frameworks within each other, ie. a 'multi level' approach to analysis favoured, amongst others, by Herbert (1979). Later in the chapter a model will be constructed which develops

links between different aspects of the political participation
and a range of paradigms. Before that, individual approaches
are briefly outlined.

PLURALIST THEORY

Perhaps the most influential perspective on (local urban)
politics is the pluralist model. As seen from this
perspective the policy-making process is one of governments
weighing and sifting the diverse demands of citizens. The
pressure group system is representative of differential
societal interests and responsive to the changing concerns and
needs of groups of citizens.
    According to Dunleavy (1977) pluralist accounts of urban
politics have three themes: (1) urban governments are
controlled by politicians who are primarily concerned in
gaining or staying in power by means of the electoral system
and are, thus, responsive to external influences from the
community; (2) individual preferences expressed reflect
people's interests; and (3) these interests will be reflected
in political action.

> Since people who become politically active are those
> with an interest in the decision and since the 'weak'
> politician is responsive to external pressure, the
> outcome will faithfully reflect the balance of
> interests in the community (Dunleavy, 1977:195).

Urban politics has also been referred to in terms of 'street-
fighting pluralism' - a pattern of unstructured, multi-
lateral conflict in which many different combatants 'fight'
with one another over a variety of issues. Conflict can arise
within and between neighbourhoods and between citizens,
elected representatives and officials. The following
characteristics are in evidence - diversity of interests which
are often sharply defined and locality specific; variability
in complexity of conflicts; instability of conflicts (the
players, demands, and problems constantly change) and the
interdependence of conflicts. According to this model, policy
makers are highly reactive to a continuous and highly
changeable barrage of diverse demands from groups of citizens.
Elected representatives play a crucial role in aggregating and
evaluating or occasionally ignoring political demands that
emanate from below. Public opinion will play a decisive role
in securing changes in public policy either directly through
making demands by a variety of channels between elections or
ultimately through the ballot box.
    Pluralism as a theory and analytical framework has been
criticised as unrealistic (Manley, 1983). Dominant groups, it
is argued, are better equipped to win in zero-sum conflicts,

and the ruling elite are able to prevent the accurate
perception of interests by the powerless, can inhibit
mobilization by those whose interests threaten them, and
control the agenda of urban politics by preventing certain
issues from being raised at all. The pluralist model
provides useful insights into, for example, the strategies of
interest groups once mobilized and explaining why some succeed
and others fail. Some well established models such as those
involving 'vote buying' and 'pork-barrelling' have been
formulated and tested. On the other hand, hypotheses
concerning the differential perception and evaluation of
neighbourhood demands by councillors have yet to be examined
empirically.

PUBLIC GOODS THEORY

The public goods theory of interest groups has developed a
framework by which collective political participation can be
analysed on the basis of individual calculations of the costs
and benefits. It has been operationalised in relation to
neighbourhood mobilization and the formation and durability of
neighbourhood associations by Henig (1982), Rich (1980) and
O'Brien (1976).
    This paradigm assumes that individual citizens will act
'rationally' in their own interests and that of their
families. It is based on the attributes of collective or
public goods - anything provided to any individual within a
specified group that cannot, within practical limits, be
withheld from individuals in that group. There is a basic
tension between the interests of the individual and those of
the group. The individual may decide to sit back and let
others do all the hard work since he or she will benefit from
collective action even without having contributed to it. Thus
those activists leading groups or organisations are faced by
the 'free rider' problem, and have in some way to find
incentives to persuade all those potentially affected to
participate.
    This dilema is considered by O'Brien in relation to poor
urban neighbourhoods. He suggests that, while residents of
such areas do have a latent or potential base for common
interest by virtue of their residence, they will act
primarily as individuals trying to cope with the everyday
problems which confront them. However,

    the principle which defines the latent common
    interests of neighbourhood residents is found in
    the nature of public service delivery systems ...
    a host of public services ... are delivered to
    neighbourhoods. Since the quantity and quality of
    these services varies considerably from one

neighbourhood to another ... since all
individuals within a particular neighbourhood are
similarly affected by the quantity of services the
neighbourhood receives, they have a latent or
potential basis of common interest. This does not
mean that residents of a neighbourhood are
necessarily aware of their common interests or that
they will see collective action as a reasonable
course of action, but it is safe to say that if the
quantity or quality of services in a neighbourhood
are improved, all the residents will benefit
(O'Brien, 1976:9).

The public goods dilemma faced by organisers of collective
action is, therefore, that the benefits of collective action
will accrue to all regardless of whether or not individuals
participated. It is clear that some people, at least, in a
neighbourhood may be unlikely to participate because they can
automatically benefit from the involvement of others. O'Brien
suggests that the poor should be viewed as purposeful actors -
the nature of their lives and environment 'forces' them to
spend most of their time and energy on non-political
activities. Life is a daily struggle to make ends meet, and
they are unable to afford the 'luxury' of engaging in
political activities which promise only to yield results
sometime in the future (if at all). They also feel powerless
and indeed they are powerless vis-a-vis the forces that
control their lives; their experience leads them to doubt the
efficacy of such involvement. If they are to be politically
involved they may feel that _individual_ action is more
relevant to their needs. That is unless incentives,
sanctions or pressure can be brought to bear on them. There
is also the suggestion that the face-to-face relationships
involved in small groups may, in some cases, provide such an
incentive to join in collective action:

> The free rider problem is less troublesome in small
> groups where each individual has a proportionally
> larger stake, and informal mechanisms for ensuring
> individual co-operation can be employed
> (Henig, 1982:44).

Rich has focused on neighbourhood organisations from what he
idiosyncratically calls a 'political economy' approach.
(Because it involves costs and resources.) The fundamental
question, he believes, is if and how the cost/benefit
calculations of potential members are swayed in favour of
participation in a given neighbourhood:

> Whether residents will form organisations depends
> theoretically on the costs and benefits they

31

associate with such organisation to secure
collective goods for their neighbourhoods
(Rich, 1980:564).

Such resources and costs vary between neighbourhoods as do the
extent of demands for collective goods. Low resource areas
are frequently characterised as having high demands for public
services. Rich postulates that the combination of resources
and demands which are optimal for the formation of neighbourhood organisations is most likely to occur in middle class
communities - in others either resources or demands are
lacking. The same author states that middle and upper class
citizens generally feel more personally efficacious with
regard to government and are more likely to have had
experience with organised effort: also the cost of
satisfying the demand for publicly provided collective goods
are likely to be lower in affluent areas than in poor areas,
since it is easier to secure marginal changes in service
delivery than fundamentally to re-allocate public resources
among services or geographic areas. The service needs of poor
neighbourhoods are often so extensive as to be costly to
satisfy, they have few indigenous resources and the costs of
gaining political access are likely to be high (Rich, 1981:
572).

Leaders in different sorts of areas will, therefore, not
face the same difficulty in terms of persuading residents to
act together. Thus, the resource/demand ratio, and costs/
benefits associated with co-operative activity will vary in
different socio-political settings. Social sanctions and
pressure may have to be applied in such small scale locales,
and selective incentives (for example, a newsletter or
organisational help with an individual grievance), may have to
be provided before individuals will be prepared to get
involved.

Based, therefore, on the assumption that 'rational' and
'self-interested' individuals weigh up the costs, benefits and
probable outcomes associated with participation or non-
participation, the public theory provides a framework to
analyse collective and neighbourhood mobilization.

Critics would point out that people do not always behave
as atomistic 'profit-seeking' beings. Furthermore, not all
the issues which form the agenda of neighbourhood associations
involve collective goods. In addition, political action may,
for some individuals, be motivated by 'expressive', ie.
non-material goals. Whatever its limitations, the approach
and its derivative 'exit or voice' model does provide
significant insights into the individual basis of collective
action. It follows that permanent or powerful neighbourhood
associations are unlikely to be established in poor areas or
those characterised by a fragmented, heterogeneous or highly
mobile population. The theory also suggests that certain

modes of political participation will be more frequently
employed in relation to public goods issues; for example,
petition signing requires little or no effort on the part of
citizens (apart from that of the organiser(s). It helps to
understand what sort of areas political activity is likely to
occur in and where it is not; also the link between types of
issues and probable political responses. It also provides a
significant antidote to pluralist assumption that groups will
automatically emerge to contest issues which affect them. The
approach has been used by Rich, O'Brien and Henig to study
neighbourhood organisations in American cities.

MANAGERIALIST THEORY

In contrast to the paradigms discussed above, the managerialist thesis focuses on officials in public bureaucracies who,
acting as 'gatekeepers' in relation to citizen demands, will
largely determine the form and outcome of political
participation. Urban managers, with their own ideologies and
interests, will mobilize support for their own interests and
policies by manipulating citizen involvement. Thus, insights
may be given about why some political demands fail and others
succeed, and the functions of public involvement from the
perspective of those in official positions is highlighted.
Indeed, Hain suggests that little real understanding of the
process of participation and its significance is possible
without an examination of the role of officers, the
constraints in which they work and the control they exercise
over the citizen participants. The degree of autonomy
enjoyed by urban managers in their allocative and distr-
butional decision-making and adjudication between the demands
of urban residents, has been the subject of some debate. That
they are influenced by the organisations in which they
operate, as well as wider structural constraints, is accepted
in more recent formulations of the managerialist thesis
(Williams, 1982). It is now widely recognised that though
planners, housing officials, engineers and educational
officers and the like, do have considerable discretion, they
also are subject to guidelines, decision rules and practices
which operate within the agencies which employ them. All
impose their goals and values on citizen participants in the
urban political system but they themselves are subjected to
organisational and structural constraints.

Thus, in his work on local government in the London
Borough of Croydon, Saunders (1979) pinpoints three sets of
limitations operating to restrict the autonomy of urban
managers - ecological forces, central government, and
dependence on the process of capital accumulation.

Whatever the opportunities and controls which
characterise the role of officials in urban bureaucracies,

there is little doubt that they do play a central role in evaluating political demands and converting them into decisions, plans and policies. Once authorative decisions have been made by elected representatives, it is officers who implement them.

The managerialist perspective has been operationalised in British and American housing studies, notably by Nivola (1978), and also applied to local authority planners by Knox and Cullen (1981). Bassett and Short (1980:52) suggest that there are three broad recurring questions in such research:

> Who are the individuals and which are the institutions which supply and allocate housing? What rules and precedents do they use to allocate housing? What are the effects of their rules and consequent actions on different types of households?

Urban managerialism has not been explicitly used to explain how citizen demands are evaluated and if, when, and why they are converted into outputs. But, clearly, it provides insights into the conversion process which must be a key element in any analysis of the factors which determine whether or not citizen participation is effective in achieving any tangible aims. If public demands are in accordance with the goals, values and interests of managers and their organisations, then it would appear they should stand a fair chance of success. This perspective also suggests that instigating certain modes of participation is sometimes a strategy to gain support and win acceptance for established official policies and proposals.

At the same time, one must be alert to the criticism of this approach levelled by Dunleavy (1981:42) who maintains that:

> the built-in forms of mediating institutions ... thus generates a possibility of seriously misleading conclusions in which broader structural constraints and determinants of the local or regional policies are lost sight of and excessively individualistic and voluntaristic accounts of urban management are given on a one-off, non-cumulative basis.

Recent managerialist writing has strayed onto the fringes of the political economy approach which stresses the dependence of local officials on structural conditions surrounding the local state in which they operate.

LOCATIONAL THEORY

Many human geographers have been content to use theories
developed in politics and sociology to provide a framework to
study political issues. However, over the last decade a
series of spatial models of political life have been
constructed which include those concerned with jurisdictional
structure, locational conflict, the neighbourhood effect on
voting, the impact of noxious facilities, correlates of local
political activism and vote buying. Together, these
constitute a middle range body of theory which can shed light
on spatial aspects of urban politics and, in particular, on
the causes and consequences of political participation.

This approach has been termed 'political ecology' by
political scientists though geographers, for the most part, do
not use this term. Some critics, such as Elkin (1974) and
Dunleavy (1981), have expressed scepticism as to the validity
of considering spatial location as an independent variable.
They argue that an adequate account of the spatial factor
necessitates analysing all social processes involved and the
allocation of space emerges as a derivative consequence of a
whole range of social, economic and political factors
(Dunleavy, 1981:39). Nonetheless, geographical variations in
the distribution of political inputs and outputs still remain
to be plotted; residential location may, in conjunction with
other causal factors, exert an influence on political
involvement; what have been called 'ecological uncontroll-
ables', ie. the fixed nature of the built environment, may
constrain policy outputs; and land-use and the location of
public facilities constitute major stakes in the 'game' of
urban politics.

The basic assumption of these models is that spatial
location is a significant explanatory variable. Where one
lives may influence whether or not one is politically
involved and how. Distance from an unwanted intrusion in the
living space will influence the distribution of participation,
with a distance decay mechanism operating. The neighbourhood
may act as a secondary or, in the context of friends and
neighbours, as a primary reference group. What Cox (1983)
has called 'turf politics' is concerned with organisations
trying (1) to attract into their turfs that which its
members regard as utility-enhancing, or beneficial, and (2)
to keep out what members regard as utility-detracting, or
harmful. Not only can spatial patterns of conflict be
identified but geographical explanations (amongst others) are
tested in relation to participants, issues and outcomes.

In terms of specific hypotheses, it is possible that
certain types of neighbourhoods (those, for example,
physically bounded) are likely to generate higher levels of
neighbourhood political involvement; contrasted ecological
zones within the city generate different sorts of issues;

those living close to actual or proposed noxious facilities will be (all things being equal) more likely to mobilize and make political demands. Furthermore, the ability of different groups to persuade or force the authorities to respond to their demands, may be influenced by the electoral character of the area (for example, its marginality) as well as the scale of the demands being made. Geographers are, of course, well aware that the spatial variable is only one of several important dimensions to be explored and that analysis has to be integrated into political processes and economic structure (Kirby, 1983). Nonetheless, the statement by Elkin (1974:297) that

> there may be aspects of political behaviour that
> are crucially influenced by the spatial context in
> which they take place but research presently
> available to this writer does not inspire
> confidence ...

remains to be thoroughly explored.

ECOLOGICAL AND BEHAVIOURAL MODELS OF CONTACTING

Under the umbrella of the pluralist interpretation of politics, considerable research has examined (1) the ecological/socio-economic correlates of individual participation and, (2) political involvement as a behavioural process. A body of theory and concepts has been formulated which not only seeks to explain which sort of people are politically involved and in what sort of areas but also examines the response to demands made on the part of bureaucratic organisations in terms of the speed and salience of official action. This middle range theory clearly can be integrated with the managerialist paradigm already discussed and also behavioural and organisational approaches which are noted below. Citizen-initiated contacts with government officials in American cities have been investigated by Jones et al. (1977), Vedlitz et al. (1980), Cox and McCarthy (1980), and Brown (1982). These analyses have focused on the relationship between socio-economic status and contacting, and their findings have varied considerably (Sharp, 1982). It is important to note that these studies are on an areal aggregate basis and that the researchers have used different methods of measuring areal social well-being, looked at contrasted types of service contacts directed at different municipal agencies, and in different cities. The citizen contact municipal response model suggests that several factors explain the variation in political outcomes. The volume of demands from an area, the 'cost' of acceding to them, whether they accord with bureaucratic decision rules and technical-rational criteria employed by officials in allocating resources, and pressure from elected councillors are all important. These studies conclude that it is not so much the sort of people who are making demands which determines how they are treated, but what precisely is being demanded and the implications of acceding to the demand on the part of the authorities.

The second approach adopted in this corpus of research is a behavioural one. Individual and group participants deciding whether or not they are going to take political action, when, how and towards which agencies. Unlike the areal/aggregate approach adopted by the researchers noted above, several authors have focused on the stages by which people with a grievance consider what to do about it (if anything). Although the models and detailed research findings vary as between, for example, Cornelius (1974) and Nelson (1980), both identify a series of stages in the demand-making process. These include consideration of the 'problem' itself (is it sufficiently serious? Is it the fault of the government? Do others feel the same way about it?); the likelihood of political action being successful (including a sense of efficacy born in some cases out of previous experience); perception of channels to make the contact or demand. It is clear that a number of key factors are important when political action is being considered. In the end, inaction or 'alternative' action (for example, moving house) is just as likely to result from the situation. One significant element in these modes of political mobilization is that there are several steps in the process, and as Henig (1982) has shown, different explanatory factors are at work in the various stages. These models, while not constituting a full-blown theory of participation, clearly have to be incorporated into any integrated, comprehensive approach to the theme, not least because they say something important about both the causes and outcomes of political demand-making.

POLITICAL ECONOMY/NEO-MARXIST THEORY

While the approaches outlined thus far take the overall political economy as given, those who subscribe to the validity of neo-Marxist analysis see the links between any empirical theme such as political participation (or housing, crime, racism, the built environment, social/spatial inequality) and the economic structure/mode of production of a society as crucial. Not only are the mechanisms and concepts to be fully understood but the emphasis is firmly on how the economic system, in a country like Britain, sets the parameters for political life. Just as it would be difficult to imagine an analysis of the major dimensions of political

participation in a state socialist society like the Soviet
Union without reference to its mode of production and the
dominant role of the Communist Party (see Oliver, 1968), so
it is argued it is necessary to see the form and function of
political activity in Britain in terms of advanced capitalism.
Following Pahl (1977), the focus is not on who does what, or
who decides who does or gets what, but rather on what
determines (who decides) who does and gets what from
political participation. The emphasis is, thus, not on
individual/organisational/spatial aspects but on the broad
economic structures in the context of which political
activities or alienation occurs.

The basic tenets of this approach include the central
role of accumulation of capital, reproduction of social
relations, and class conflict. In a bourgeois
(parliamentary/liberal) democracy like Britain, the class
interests of capital are secured and legitimised. In urban
areas local authorities (the local state) 'serve' the
interests of private capital accumulation and regulate its
social relations. The size of the local public sector, the
mix of public expenditure and services, and the level and
scope of political participation are 'constrained'. The
autonomy of municipal decision-makers is limited. Citizen-
ship is defined and political participation is channelled by
suppression and fragmentation into forms which rarely
threaten the status quo. Concessions are occasionally made
to working class demands when they are able to be articulated
(as social movements) but, for the most part, it is the needs
of capital and the control which is exerted by a business
elite which holds sway in the local political arena. Socio-
economic inequality and ideological control serve to ensure
that the pluralist model of local politics is an 'unrealistic'
version of reality. For example, in chapter five,
Ossenbrügge has characterised local forms of participation as
part of the legitimation system in which the local state
serves as an active organisation of class compromise.

Clearly, there are variants in emphasis and interpretation within this political economy approach, but neo-
Marxist writers agree about certain assumptions concerning
the nature of British society, the role of 'urban' public
authorities, and the function of local participation both at
and between elections. It is beyond the scope of this
chapter to outline, let alone attempt a critique, of this
holistic approach. What needs to be elucidated in greater
detail, however, is the Marxist view of political participation in a given city. How is local voting, contacting, and
protesting to be interpreted? Why do these activities take
the form they do? How are working class demands diffused or
managed in the interests of those who own, control and
benefit from the accumulation of capital? There is a varied
and uneven body of the sometimes opaque theoretical writing

and a limited range of empirical research on which to draw out some research hypotheses.

Harvey has written several papers which analyse the mechanics of capital accumulation and what he calls displaced class struggle over the built environment, the swelling place and social consumption. He points to the crucial role of residential segregation in diffusing working class consciousness and role of the state in investing capital in the built environment and shaping the city to match the needs of private capital accumulation.

Castells has elucidated the significance of social movements in relation to issues of collective consumption. He postulates that state oppression through local media, the educational system, planning authority and housing departments will stimulate the mobilization of protest (the development of urban social movements) and, when this does not occur, then some kind of false consciousness must exist.

Cockburn, whose formulation of the term 'the local state' appears to have triggered off its universal use (though with varying interpretation of the concept), studies a London Borough facing economic decline and urban decay. Lambeth attempted to alleviate the inner city crisis by a strategy of managerial innovation. Corporate management involved centralising and de-politicizing decision-making.

> The remoteness of the officers and councillors ...
> from the working class meant that despite their
> sophisticated managerial structures they could not
> manage once forced to adopt new strategy of
> neighbourhood councils which would channel the
> struggles of the working class over housing and
> community services in the direction desired by the
> local state (Cockburn, 1977:46).

Dearlove (1979) interprets the institutional changes in local government in the 1970s in the same way - they removed power from working class control by giving power of the 'shire' counties in many areas. William Bunge (1977:64) has written a somewhat polemical treatise on working class struggles and further central government control in American cities:

> Part of life is spent at home, in urban
> neighbourhoods ... Capital encourages profligacy
> and indebtedness at home and in contrast
> dedication and restraint at the workplace ...
> Working class consciousness is diluted by this
> separation. Working class interests are cemented
> in the crucible of daily production ... and
> unravelled just as fast ... at the point of
> reproduction!

Dear (1981) argues that the local state co-opts and controls
the population through its expenditure on social consumption
(as opposed to social investment). It will accede to some
working class demands and develop citizen participation
channels to legitimise local state decisions. Political
action is directed at the 'visible' agencies of the local
state which have little autonomy (for example, they have to
pay huge repayment-of-interest charges).

Dunleavy points to the ways by which the local
government is influenced by capital in formulating and
implementing its policies. This is partly achieved by a
'professional' conspiracy by senior officials and
representatives of private companies. Companies, in
persuading local authorities and the public bodies to produce
high-rise prefabricated public housing, motorways and large
hospitals, have ensured their own profitability and the
dependence of their clients for future contracts. For
example, building companies made handsome profits from the
construction of high-rise blocks of flats and have been
subsequently awarded lucrative contracts to maintain and
renovate them. In the meantime, working class tenants and
residents were forced to move from their inner city Victorian
dwellings to high density and/or peripheral housing estates.
Dunleavy indicates how the protests of those whose interests
were adversely affected were ignored or manipulated.

Ruth Fincher (1980) has also provided a theoretical
account of the local state's dependence on 'economic
realities'. Many cities, she argues, are in crisis because
a decline in revenue is matched by increasing demands for
services. Footloose companies indulge in 'fiscal blackmail'
and cities are forced to spend massively on capital
improvements, encourage private investment and prevent
disinvestment. When there is a threat that such large scale
infrastructural investment or spatially uneven targeting of
public spending may be opposed by residents, then a strategy
of encouraging the proliferation of community protest groups,
a 'divide and rule' tactic, is employed to ensure that the
policies to which the local state is committed will be
implemented without undue delay or major modification.
Neighbourhood interest groups are ignored, or acknowledged as
representative, depending on the nature of their demands.

Rich (1982) also postulates that the process of capital
accumulation will influence and constrain the size and
composition of the public sector. He believes that, despite
greater working class mobilization in Western Europe (than in
the United States), capital investment and its attendant debt
service costs, will be favoured in budgetary allocations over
collective consumption expenditures. He suggests that:

> while city council decisions that commit huge
> quantities of tax dollars to debt service and

> maintenance of capital investments often go
> largely unnoticed by citizens, the daily decisions
> of public agencies and personnel ... can become
> the focus of intense political attention
> (Rich, 1982:12).

Class interests will be served in that those who own and
control capital will benefit while poor, service-dependent,
groups will be at a disadvantage. Thus, while political
participation involving demands for improvements in the
quality of public services may make a marginal difference in
distributive decisions and service delivery, it will have
little impact on the major budgetary and allocative policies
which constrain them. Thus, capital will

> succeed in reducing the costs of the state's social
> control and reproductive activities while
> preserving as much of the state's accumulation and
> production supporting function as possible
> (Rich, 1982:19).

Cutbacks in social services, health, and housing are achieved
despite protests because those activities supporting
accumulation ... are more often performed through insulated,
politically invisible government agencies and special
authorities (Friedland, Piven and Ashford, 1977).
    Thus, although Marxist theory sees the social relations
of production based on the work place as central to
capitalist society, nonetheless, class conflict is evident in
the politics of urban neighbourhoods. Participation is
'managed' by a local state which ultimately operates in the
interests of capital. Managers who are faced by working class
and consumer protests and demands will be unable to accede to
demands which are in opposition to those of local business
and/or major companies. Community groups will be manipulated
in such a way that they will only succeed in making minor
concessions related to, for example, service delivery and
land-use. While major economic decisions are 'outside' the
local and even national political agenda, political
participation at the scale of everyday experience giving a
semblance of democratic involvement, legitimizes the system.

MISCELLANEOUS THEORIES

The theories and approaches discussed thus far are
significant ones in providing concepts and insights relating
to political participation. Of course, there are others
which ought not to be totally excluded even if their
relevance is more peripherical.
    Recent developments in <u>organisation theory</u> clearly have

relevance to understanding how neighbourhood organisations and public agencies actually behave. Salamon (1979) has identified some key elements in this approach and its relevance to urban politics. Organisations involved in making or converting political demands, he suggests, will attempt to defend and enhance their territorial, functional and resource domains, and 'manage' their dependency on the organisations by co-opting, or otherwise influencing, their activities. It is likely, therefore, that urban bureaucracies will be more sympathetic to demands which are seen to add to their staff, revenues, powers and status than to those which are likely to diminish them. Williams (1982) has recently identified a number of ways that the study of organisations is important in urban politics. He states that 'the actions of agencies cannot be simply deduced ... they can only really be uncovered by an examination of practice' (Williams, 1982:98). Organisations have their own external relations, structure and dynamics and these crucially influence the behaviour of individuals within them.

In its various forms and interpretations <u>systems theory</u>, based on the pioneering work of David Easton, represents another analytical framework to gain insights into the 'confused reality' of a case study. From the empirical research which explicitly or implicitly employed a systems approach, for example, Kasperson, 1969, Whitney, 1969 and, from a number of theoretical papers, (Munns, 1975), the benefits of employing the systems framework are:

1. It helps to chart the complex interactions between individuals and organisations – these can then be recorded and classified and their contents analysed in terms of the significance of the political information contained.
2. One of the outstanding features of the policy-making process and, as has been seen, political participation, is its dynamic character. It involves a series of stages and decisions over a period of time. A systems framework helps to structure this process in terms of inputs, conversion, outputs and feedback. It shows how the outcomes of one decision may operate renewed demands.
3. It provides a rich code of concepts including 'demands', 'withinputs', 'stress', etc. and, more important, at least in its dynamic form (see Munns, 1975), it elucidates the relationship between environment, demands, the conversion process, and policies.

It may not be able to fully explain why some environmental changes are the subject of political demands or why some demands are positively received and others shunned or denied, but it at least offers some useful signposts.

TOWARDS A SYNTHESIS

As a result of casting the net wide, a whole series of paradigms have been identified as being of relevance to the study of neighbourhood political participation. The intrinsic adequacy, or otherwise, of each theory has not been discussed in detail. Rather, salient and significant features have been pinpointed. This broad scanning strategy has its potential dangers in that contested and alternative perspectives can confuse rather than illuminate. However, as has already been noted at the outset, all too many theoretical publications are content to try to vindicate a particular philosophical position and there are points of convergence between them and scope for integration. It is assumed that integration is a desirable goal mainly because it is believed that to depict paradigms as vying for theoretical supremacy is wrong, since they are concentrating on different slices of the same reality.

Goldsmith (1980:46) puts it as follows:

- each model alone fails to provide a complete explanation of the city's political process ... and therefore to adopt any single perspective is to close one's eyes to the possible virtues and contribution of other theoretical perspectives ... models need to be fused together if we are to approach an adequate understanding of the complexities of urban politics!

Likewise, Henig (1982:225) reinforces the point as follows:

The various theoretical positions mapped ... have contributed something to the understanding of collective mobilization, and it is conceivable that these contributions would have been smaller if theorists had removed their blinkers, opening themselves to the uncertainty and complications that faithful adherence to key assumptions allowed them to avoid. Thus the rational choice theorists tell much about the potentials for mobilisation of rational, self-interested individuals, although people do not always adhere to the model of rational self interest that those theorists take as their starting point ... And the radical analysts clarify the role of consciousness among neighbourhoods of the same class. While there is undoubtedly even more that can be learned

from those who continue to work within the
confines of each of these alternative paradigms,
it is time to bridge the gaps between them.

The problem is how to bridge the gap and by what means. One
method is to conceive of an explanation of political life and
participation in terms of several levels. A multilayered
approach has been advocated by Herbert (1979), amongst others.
Thus, a political economy represents the highest level (or
scale) of explanation. In a median position comes the
managerialist paradigm and its focus on organisations and
interests/rules that they persue. At the 'lower' level,
individual participant's activities are explained in terms,
for example, from public goods and behavioural perspectives.
This framework would seem to be logical and coherent, even if
linking the three levels is not always easy.

As a means to help in the formulation of research
hypotheses, however, a second strategy can be proposed. This
is one which fuses perspectives by applying them each to
different stages and aspects of the process of political
participation (Figure 3.1). The model juxtaposes selected
theories and aspects of political participation. The arrows
indicate the relevance of a particular theory to a specific
aspect, and the labels show the key explanatory variables and
indicate the sort of hypotheses that may be formulated.

CONCLUSION

It is not being argued in this paper either that political
geography should become exclusively theoretical or that any
one paradigm is suited to guide all political research
currently being undertaken by geographers or, indeed, that
all empirical studies must be theoretically based. Clearly,
there are detailed and competent case studies which stand by
themselves regardless of any theoretical considerations.
Model building and methodology may be furthered, and
significant findings outlined, in a non-theoretical way. For
example, there are several such pieces of research in the
theme of neighbourhood and political activism (Davidson, 1979;
Burnett and Hill, 1981).

The basic proposition being made in this paper is that,
given the range of competing paradigms which are available to
provide frameworks, concepts and hypotheses for empirical
research, it is surely short-sighted for political
geographers to ignore them? Which theories will be helpful
will depend on the sort of topic being pursued. Whether an
eclectic or single theoretical stance is taken, will depend
on the preferences of the individual researcher. In relation
to neighbourhood participation, it has been shown that no one
theoretical approach has a monopoly of wisdom, and insights

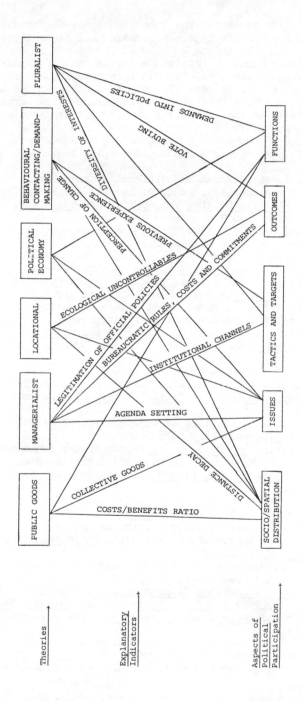

Figure 3.1: Links between theories and neighbourhood political participation

45

can be gained from several. The same is undoubtedly true for
the topics such as public facility location and regional
separation.

It certainly cannot be claimed that the task of understanding contrasted theories, let alone integrating and
applying them, is an easy one. But perseverance and
sensitivity in theorisation can be rewarding, both in terms
of greater understanding of specific topics and as a guide to
empirical research.

REFERENCES

Agnew, J. (1981) 'Structural and dialectical theories of
    political regionalism', in A. D. Burnett and P. J. Taylor
    (eds.), Political Studies from Spatial Perspectives,
    Wiley, Chichester, U.K.
Bassett, K. and Short J. (1980) Housing and Residential
    Structure, Routledge and Kegan Paul, London
Brown, S. D. (1982) 'The explanation of particularised
    contacting', Urban Affairs Quarterly, 18, 217-234
Burnett, A. D. and Taylor, P. J. (1981) Political Studies
    from Spatial Perspectives, Wiley, Chichester, U.K.
Burnett, A. D. and Hill, D. M. (1981) 'Neighbourhood
    organisations and distribution of public service outputs
    in Britain', in R. Rich (ed.), Causes and Effects of
    Inequality in Urban Services, D. C. Heath, Lexington,
    Ma.
Burnett, A. D., Cole, K. and Moon, G. (1983) 'Political
    participation and resource allocation', in M. A. Bustein
    (ed.), Developments in Political Geography, Academic
    Press, New York
Bunge, W. (1977) 'The politics of reproduction: a second
    front', Antipode, 9(1), 66-76
Cockburn, C. (1977) The Local State, Pluto Press, London
Cornelius, W. A. (1974) 'Urbanisation and political demand
    making', American Political Science Review, 68,
    1125-1146
Cox, K. R. and McCarthy, J. (1980) 'Neighbourhood activism in
    the American city', Urban Geography, 1, 22-38
Cox, K. R. (1983) 'Residential mobility, neighbourhood
    activism and neighbourhood problems', Political Geography
    Quarterly, 2, 99-117
Couclelis, H. and Golledge, R. (1983) 'Analytic research
    positivism and behavioural geography', Annals,
    Association of American Geographers, 73, 331-339
Davidson, J. L. (1979) Political Partnerships, Neighbourhood
    Residents and their Communal Members, Sage, Beverly
    Hills, Ca.
Dear, M. (1981) 'A theory of the local state', in
    A. D. Burnett and P. J. Taylor (eds.), Political Studies
    from Spatial Perspectives, Wiley, Chichester,U.K.183-200

Dear, M. and Clark, G. (1978) 'The state and geographic process: a critical review', Environment and Planning, A9, 137-147

Dearlove, P. (1979) The Reorganisation of British Local Local Government, Cambridge University Press, Cambridge, U.K.

Dunleavy, P. (1977) 'Protest and quiescence in urban politics: a critique of some pluralist and structural myths', International Journal of Urban and Regional Research, 1, 192-218

Dunleavy, P. (1981) Urban Political Analysis, Macmillan, London

Elkin, T. (1974) 'Comparative Urban Politics and Inter-governmental Behaviour', Policy and Politics, 2, 289-308

Eyles, J. and Lee, R. (1982) 'Human Geography in Explanation', Transactions of Institute of British Geographers, NS 7, 117-122

Fincher, R. (1980) 'Local implementation strategies in the built environment', Environment and Planning, A13, 1233-1252

Fincher, R. (1983) 'The inconsistency of eclecticism', Environment and Planning, A15, 607-622

Friedland, R., Piven, F. and Ashford, R. (1977) 'Political Conflict, urban structure and the fiscal crisis', International Journal of Urban and Regional Research, 1, 170-191

Goldsmith, M. (1980) Politics, Planning and the City, Hutchinson, London

Harvey, D. (1978) 'Labour, capital and the class struggle around the built environment in advanced capitalist societies', in K. R. Cox (ed.), Urbanisation and Conflict in Market Societies, Maaroufa, Chicago

Hain, P. (1981) Neighbourhood Participation, Temple Smith, London

Henig, J. (1982) Neighbourhood Mobilisation, Rutgers University Press, New Brunswick, N.J.

Herbert, D. (1979) 'Geographical perspectives and urban problems', in D. Herbert and D. Smith (eds.), Social Problems and the City, Oxford University Press, London, 2-25

Jones, B., Greenburg, S., Kaufman, C. and Drew, J. (1977) 'Bureaucratic response to citizen-initiated contacts: Environmental enforcement in Detroit', American Political Science Review, 72, 148-165

Kasperson, R. (1969) 'Environmental stress and the municipal political system', in R. Kasperson and J. Minghi (eds.), The Structure of Political Geography, Aldine, Chicago, 481-96

Kirby, A. M. (1983) The Politics of Location, Methuen, London

Knox, P. and Cullen, J. (1981) 'Town planning and the
    internal survival of mechanisms of urbanised capitalism',
    Area, 13, 183-188
Lee, R. (1979) 'The economic basis of social problems in the
    city', in D. Herbert and D. Smith (eds.), Social
    Problems and the City, chapter 4, Oxford University
    Press, London, 87-101
Manley, J. F. (1983) 'Neo-pluralism: a class analysis of
    pluralism I and pluralism II', American Political Science
    Review, 78, 111-27
Munns, J. M. (1975) 'The environment, politics and policy
    literature: a critique and reformulation', Western
    Political Quarterly, 28, 646-667
Nelson, B. J. (1980) 'Help-seeking from public authorities:
    who arrives at the agency door?', Policy Sciences, 12,
    175-192
Nivola, P. (1978) 'Distributing a municipal service: a case
    study of housing inspection', Journal of Politics, 40,
    59-81
O'Brien, D. J. (1976) Neighbourhood Organisation and Interest
    Group Processes, Princetown University Press, Princetown,
    N.J.
Oliver, J. H. (1968) 'Citizen demands and the Soviet
    political system', American Political Science Review,
    63, 465-475
Rich, R. (1980) 'The political economy approach to the study
    of neighbourhood organisations', American Journal of
    Political Science, 24, 559-592
Rich, R. (1982) 'Urban Development and the Political Economy
    of Public Production of Services', paper given at
    Annual Conference, Institute of British Geographers,
    University of Southampton.
Salamon, L. (1979) 'Urban politics, policy, case studies and
    political theory', Public Administration Review, 37,
    418-428
Saunders, P. (1979) Urban Politics: a Sociological
    Interpretation, Hutchinson, London
Sharp, E. B. (1982) 'Citizen-initiated contacting of
    Government officials and socio-economic status:
    Determining the relationship and accounting for it,
    American Political Science Review, 76, 109-115
Short, J. R. (1982) An Introduction to Political Geography,
    Routledge and Kegan Paul, London
Thrift, N. (1982) 'Editorial. Towards a human geography',
    Environment and Planning, A14, 1283-1305
Vedlitz, A., Dyer, J. and Durrand, R. (1980) 'Citizen
    contacts with local governments: a comparative view',
    American Political Science Review, 24, 50-67

Whitney, J. (1969) <u>China - Administration and Nation
    Building</u>, Department of Geography, University of Chicago,
    Research paper <u>123</u>
Williams, C. (1981) 'Identity through autonomy: ethnic
    separation in Quebec, in A. D. Burnett and P. J. Taylor
    (eds.), <u>Political Studies from Spatial Perspectives</u>,
    Wiley, Chichester, U.K., 389-418
Williams, P. (1982) 'Restructuring Urban Managerialism:
    towards a political economy of urban allocation',
    <u>Environment and Planning</u>, <u>A14</u>, 95-105

Chapter Four

SPATIAL STRUCTURE OF THE STATE: THE LOCAL STATE

Bryan H. Massam

PREFACE

The purpose of this paper is to present comments on the study
of the local state which may help political geographers
define a focus for their work on this important phenomenon.
Following Dear and Clark (1981:1278) the local state can be
defined "as any government entity having a political and
spatial jurisdiction at less than the national scale, and
having the authority to raise revenue from, and make
expenditure on behalf of its constituents".   Fincher
(1981:1233) provided brief comments on the term 'local state'.
She suggests that it is a theoretical-empirical hybrid, with
the state being "the Marxian theoretical category, that set of
institutions which acts to reproduce the interests of capital
in general".
     The introductory section will indicate the breadth of
studies of the local state and provide suggestions which
could guide the activities of a Working Group or Commission in
Political Geography.   Specifically, the two key topics we
suggest are: (1) the provision of public goods and services,
and (2) collective decision-making.
     These topics should be viewed within the broader context
of the organization of a state.   This section will be
followed by a discussion on a systemic view of the provision
of public goods and services, noting it is within the context
of local states that many of these are provided.   It will be
argued that a systems view potentially accommodates a variety
of traditional approaches of geographers, regional
scientists, and political scientists, among others, who seek
to understand how and why public goods are produced,
delivered and consumed.   The third section will briefly
consider some recent work on public choice and collective
decision-making models especially as they relate to voting
and the provision of public goods.   The context within which
we can examine both the provision of public goods and
problems of public choice and collective decision-making is

the local state, and this raises broader questions of relationships among local states, between local states and the state, and the position of a local state in the international context. While it is clear that a number of political geographers are interested in the local state, Kirby (1982a:309) notes that: "The development of theory with respect to the local state is still nascent ..."

To quote another of Kirby's (1982b) points "It can be argued that 'there is no ready-made theory of local government' (Cockburn, 1977:41). Indeed, many empirical studies have emphasised the wide diversity within local affairs, and even the uniquenesses of each local authority. Nonetheless, attempts have recently been made to develop a theoretical understanding of 'the local state' (Broadbent, 1977; Cockburn, 1977; Saunders, 1980). This body of multi-disciplinary research emphasises that the local state complements its national counterpart, and that both possess similar aims, albeit with different responsibilities. In simple terms, these aims involve the maintenance of social relations, which is achieved via economic intervention at the national scale, and the provision of public goods at the local scale (Dear, 1981a).

It would appear that the time is ripe for political geographers to tackle the problem of trying to develop a theory of the local state.

INTRODUCTION

Short (1983) suggests that the spectrum of contemporary studies on the state lies between the innocence of some empirically competent but politically naive work (typified according to him by Bennett's (1980) work on public finance), and the conspiratorial approach in which the state appears as an aid to the capitalist mode of production, with no limits to its finances or legitimation. The work of Dear and Scott (1981) is cited by Short as falling into this category. A key to integrating this range of work is perhaps provided by a study of the decision-making processes involved, and the related institutions. We need to know more about the relationships among the actors and the links between the outcomes of the decisions and the accountability of those who make the decisions.

If we accept that the study of authoritative decision-making is a critical element in the study of the functioning of local states then we can identify three distinct approaches. First, the study of judgements of individuals when faced with hypothetical choice problems. This work has largely been undertaken by social psychologists, management specialists and those interested in welfare and utility maximizing models. The work of Hammond and McLelland (1981)

and their colleagues at the Center for Research on Judgement
and Policy in Colorado falls into this category. Second, the
study of the results of decisions contained, for example, in
legal pronouncements, public policy statements, bills, white
papers, committee minutes, etc. There is a rich growing body
of literature in political geography which is of this genre.
And in the third category we could include the investigative
approach which seeks to find out who influenced whom, and
precisely how a particular decision was arrived at. Bordessa
and Cameron (1980, 1982) offer very useful examples of this.
However, we would submit that these approaches, important as
each one is, must be related to higher level statements about
human behaviour and institutional organisation, in order to
move towards a general theory of the local state. We concur
with Dear (1981b:1793) that, "... a key research task in the
eighties (in political geography) is to provide a systematic
analysis of the ... state beyond simply cataloging its
involvements in specific instances (although this issue has
continuing significance)".

To determine the validity of a particular approach
raises fundamental research questions of knowledge and
understanding. How much time should be spent on such a
discussion? Should this be our pre-occupation? We submit
that some attention be focussed on this issue. Let us not
rush off and collect data, study archives and interview
politicians without first standing back and reflecting on the
nature of the exercises we are pursuing.

The breadth of current work on the local state and its
place in political geography is considerable (Cockburn,1977;
Boddy and Fudge, 1980, Dear, 1981a; Dear and Clark, 1981;
Kliot, 1981; Flowerdew, 1982, Kirby, 1982c; Short, 1982;
Lea, 1983; and Paddison, 1983) and in the absence of any
agreed-upon agenda we suggest that we try to accommodate a
range of perspectives that allow us to pursue a variety of
empirical, theoretical and practical studies. We should seek
to take advantage of comparative studies afforded by working
under the aegis of the I.G.U. Narrowly focussed studies, for
example, on the spatial configuration of administrative units
in country X, or regional differences among the quantity and
quality of public goods in townships in country Y, must be
placed within the larger context of states, especially their
organisation, development and functions.

Is it sufficient at this time to identify the study of
local-states as a worthy topic within political geography or
should we go further and suggest that within this topic a
series of sub-topics or approaches be identified? We suggest
that a major focus of attention be on the local state, with
the specific purpose of seeking to use empirical and
theoretical work to provide a coherent theory of the local
state.

With this in mind we would further suggest that

attention be focussed upon the following two major topics:
(1) public goods and services; (2) public choice and
collective decision-making.

The framework within which both of these topics should
be placed could be either the state or some larger international context. In the following section, after brief
comments on public goods and services, a systems approach is
developed to indicate the types of linkages among major
components of the local state. For the purposes of this
exercise seven components are identified. Details are
provided on the key to Figure 4.1 together with summary
statements about the linkages among the components.

An elaboration of the theoretical relationships among
the major components of the system with respect to the
provision of public goods in rural areas is provided in
Massam and Askew (1984). The second section draws on this
work.

PUBLIC GOODS AND SERVICES

The provision of public goods and services is of interest to
government officials, analysts and planners.

Government officials are concerned with the direct and
opportunity costs of the services, the determination of
priorities among services and the amount of each service
offered, the impact of the investments on the local and
national economies, the consequences on regional development
policies, as well as the impacts on voting patterns and
political stability. The complexity of the issues regarding
the involvement of governments in the provision of public
services is summarised in a White Paper by the British
Government Development and Compensation: Putting People First
(Department of the Environment 1972) which clearly indicates
that the heart of contemporary political debate (in most
mixed economies) is to strike a balance between,

... the overriding duty of the state to ensure that
essential developments are undertaken for the
benefit of the whole community and no less
compelling need to protect the interests of those
whose personal rights or private property may be
injured in the process.

At a higher level of generalisation Russell (1950)
suggests that:

The fundamental problem of ethics and politics is
that of finding some way of reconciling the needs
of social life with the urgency of individual
desires.

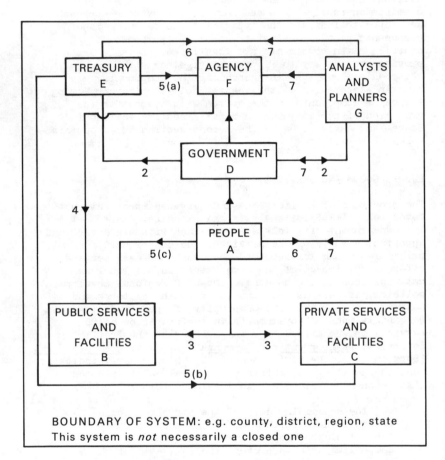

BOUNDARY OF SYSTEM: e.g. county, district, region, state
This system is *not* necessarily a closed one

Figure: 4.1: A systems view: the provision of public goods
and services

It has been noted by Smith (1982) and Agnew (1982) that
in many parts of the world we are caught between rising costs
for services, and stable or declining revenues. Government
responses tend to be pre-occupied with short-term expenditure
and revenue policies. Recent articles in Transatlantic
Perspectives on the role of governments in catering to
contemporary social needs include the following comments:

> Partly they (governments) are slashing programs
> and benefits; partly, as these cuts wound affected
> groups, they are restoring programs and benefits;
> and raising some taxes. But this approach
> represents a stop-gap course of action ...
> ... a basic reshaping of the traditional model,
> which postulates a governmental agency financed
> by appropriations derived from taxes, providing
> services uniformly available and accessible without
> charge, with professionals accountable to elected
> officials and elected offials accountable to the
> voters (Kolderie, 1982:6).

The uniformity of availability and accessibility, and
the zero price assumption clearly do not stand up to empirical
verification, and we can ask, what kind of basic reshaping of
the system is possible? From the monetarists we note that
privatisation has been suggested (Frazier 1981), whereas
decentralisation with increased participation of individuals
forms part of the creed of some political parties (see
Williams, 1981). Other suggestions which are being made to
accommodate massive structural employment patterns of
advanced industrialised countries, and to provide decent
lives to individuals, include alternate versions to the
market economy for distributing income and for providing
services (Roberts 1982; Clarke 1982). The state of tension
between the means of providing public services and the
increasing demands for social services has been widely
documented (The Economist, 1982). No simple solutions
appear to be acceptable to a majority.

Analysts of the quantitative persuasion attempt to
structure relationships among components of the political
economic system, parsing using the terminology of Huggett
(1980) to try to understand what impacts emerge from
alternate policies. Not infrequently analysts and planners
attempt to suggest ideal patterns which have maximum
efficiency or equity. For narrowly defined location-choice
problems McAllister (1976), Hodgart (1978) Hansen and Thisse
(1981) and Massam (1983) have shown that different 'best'
locations exist depending upon whether the definition of best
considers equity, efficiency or is derived from a voting
procedure. We should note that there is a large body of
theoretical work which focuses on the problem of identifying

a procedure to provide a consensus from individual
preferences. While much of this work does appear to consider
questions of reasonableness and fairness, it is difficult to
apply any single numerical procedure to a public service
provision problem, to accommodate accessibility, and to allow
trade-offs among criteria. There are also severe
difficulties associated with accounting for time and
differential effects on groups and individuals (Schaffer and
Lamb, 1981). A complete operational definition of a numerical
social welfare function remains to be provided.

It is obvious that formal practical policy analysis must
involve the measurement of impacts, and we are reminded by
Taaffe (Introduction to Smith, 1973:1) that, "We really have
no way of knowing if things are getting better or worse in
view of the bewildering diversity of standards of measurement
attached to most social problems", and Teitz (1968:48) notes
that, "rules of thumb (for comparing alternate policies) have
been developed but for the most part without ways to evaluate
the results or to stimulate investigation of new systems".
He argues for a solid theoretical base to help determine the
optimum size and location of public facilities. In a more
practical vein Hatry (1972) offer a comprehensive table of
workload measures and quality factors (often called measures
of effectiveness of evaluation criteria) for a wide range of
public services. A recent example of the application of
formal measures of effectiveness and efficiency for public
services is provided by Allen (1982). He quotes the empirical
studies currently underway to improve public service
provision in the City of Thunder Bay, Ontario, Canada. With
the increasing use of social indicators Taaffe's criticisms
have to some extent been answered.

Hatry (1972:777) comment that:

> Many new productivity improvement approaches need
> to be tried out in local governments if productivity
> is to be improved ... However, without adequate
> measurement, so-called evaluations are likely to be
> little more than public relations stories by the
> sponsors and of minimal practical use.

Measurement is clearly one of the keys to the
improvement of planning the provision of services. Bracken
(1981:21) emphasises the important role of evaluation in
planning and policy-making:

> Evaluation can be regarded as the corner stone of
> attempting to improve the quality of planning
> activity and policies, and will involve making
> explicit value judgements about the worth of
> particular policies.

Without ways of evaluating or measuring alternate policies
rational policy making will not emerge.
   Within the framework of the system for providing public
goods and services we can identify five structural features.
They have been the focus of theoretical work (Teitz, 1968)
and are usually referred to as: (1) N - the number of
facilities; (2) S - the size of each facility; (3) L - the
location of each facility; (4) B - the location of the
boundary enclosing consumers who are eligible to use or be
supplied by a particular facility. (May be de facto or
de jure boundary); (5) NW - the network through which
services are delivered.
   It is combinations of these features which gives rise to
a system which in turn provides benefits and causes costs to
be incurred. Clearly alternate configurations have
differential distributional effects of benefits and costs.
The crux of the policy analysis question or prescription is
then to evaluate the alternatives in terms of the
distribution of impacts, and with reference to some defined
objectives in order to identify the most satisfactory
alternative. From a positive standpoint we should seek to
understand why a particular configuration occurs. This can
perhaps be undertaken by considering hypotheses on the
purpose of states. For example, Dear and Clark (1981:1277)
assert that:

   the local state is a purposely-constituted branch
   of the central state; the local state functions
   largely to facilitate central state actions of
   crises management and control.

We might also refer to the summary of O'Connor's work
provided by Paddison (1983:148):

   O'Connor (1973) argues from a Marxist perspective
   that the capitalist state needs to fulfil two
   different and often contradictory functions -
   ensuring the profitability of the economy and
   maintaining social cohesion and legitimacy.

Are these testable hypotheses? How can be undertake
rigorous analyses of such statements? What kinds of
analytical tools are required? What sorts of data are
needed?
   In the following sub-section we move to a consideration
of the system which exists within a local state.

The Public Facility System
In Figure 4.1 only the major components and essential
linkages of the system for providing services to citizens are

presented. It is the interaction between people, as
potential consumers and actual taxpayers, and government as
service providers which gives rise to the system of public
facilities. The pattern which is manifest as a combination
of N, S, L, and B and the utility networks develops over time
in response to the nature of the interactions involving flows
of information, money, people, and decisions among the
components. Without flows the system will atrophy; a system
is a creature of evolution and development. The type of
system shown in Figure 4.1 can manifest itself in an
enormous variety of specific styles depending upon, at the
very least, the local physical conditions, and the social and
economic history of the region. Empirical studies attest to
the variation of patterns of public facilities we find in
different parts of the world, under different political
systems, and in regions which enjoy different levels of
technology and suffer varying types and amounts of hardships.
The apparent unique qualities of each state should not
automatically lead us to believe that completely different
systems operate in each one. The nature of the information
flowing among the components may vary, but in essence the
provision of public goods demands that a system exist.

Components. The seven components in Figure 4.1 are:

- A People. Location, Purchasing power,
  information on alternatives, perceptions
  of need for and quality of supply, preferences
  among competing demands on their resources.
- B Public goods and facilities. Quantity and
  quality of services provided. N, S, L, B
  (de facto and de jure) and networks.
- C Private goods and facilities. Quantity and
  quality of services provided. N, S, L, B
  (de facto) and networks.
- D Government. Style of bureaucracy and
  organisation, degree of centralisation/
  decentralisation in decision-making, and
  ordering of priorities.
- E Treasury. Methods of taxation and distribution of finances, methods of incentives.
- F Agency. Operational authority for a
  particular service.
- G Analysts and Planners. Serves government,
  treasury, people, and agencies by analysing,
  designing, and evaluating provision system.

<u>Linkages</u>. The components are linked together as follows:

1. Procedures for the selection of decision-making body.
2. Delegation of responsibility and authority to specialised governmental bodies.
3. Consumption of services by public either by delivery of services or by movements of consumers to supply points.
4. Provision of services by governmental agencies, either to facilities or to consumers.
5a. Financing of agency for services provision
5b. Subsidies and incentives to private sector
5c. User charges for public services to consumers
6. Data concerning demand and supply characteristics for services
7. Advisory information about the organisation and performance of the system.

The public facility component of the system model can be analysed in terms of the features N, S, L, B, and the networks, and more importantly, in terms of their relationships. Although these features are of interest in themselves, for the agency, funding body, and consumer it is the relationships among the features which have important implications for service provision and utilisation.

In simple terms we can consider that components B and C represent the <u>output</u> of the system. Paddison (1983:150) provides a good review of the problems of measuring the output of public services.

The use of a systems approach is suggested as a frame of reference in which to accommodate comparative studies. Possibly the most critical aspect of the system relates to the ways in which preferences of individuals can be transmitted to those who make the decisions regarding the provision of goods and services. For this reason it is appropriate to look at collective decision-making. In the following section brief comments on this are offered.

PUBLIC CHOICE AND COLLECTIVE DECISION MAKING

Shelley and Goodchild (1982:1) have suggested that:
"Recently, political geographers have initiated research applying the public choice perspective, which focuses on rational economic behaviour in collective decision context, to the analysis of locational conflicts". In this section we would like to draw attention to three bodies of literature which attempts to deal with collective decision-making.
First, those theoretical studies of voting procedures

which tackle the problem of seeking a consensus from individual preferences (Blair and Pollock, 1983). A number of these studies have tackled location problems for public goods (Massam 1983, Massam and Askew, 1982, Shelley and Goodchild, 1982, Hansen and Thisse, 1981, Rushton et al. 1981. Stewart, 1979, Cook and Seiford, 1978). Second, those studies, for example by Shelley and Goodchild (1982) and Archer and Reynolds (1976), that move from abstract theory towards practical conflict resolution by studying the fairness of the procedures for reaching collective decisions for practical issues. A review of the literature by Shelley and Goodchild (1982:11) concludes that: "... the naive and uncritical acceptance of the public choice paradigm is misleading and perilous: careful scrutiny of the implications of public choice analysis is necessary if it is to be successful in providing new insights into political-geographic processes". One particularly troublesome aspect is that emphasis on allocative efficiency without reference to distributional questions does not allow, or at least encourage, analysis of inequalities and the processes which generate and maintain them. This point has been noted by Dear and Clark (1978). The work of Reynolds (1982) on school enrollment decline and fiscal entrenchment for education in U.S.A. is a good example of the way in which empirical studies can be placed within a broader context of public choice statements. The third body of literature extends this empirical work to consider how the redefinition or evolution of the form and organisation of local states influence the distribution of public goods to citizens. Questions of inequality are addressed as are questions of public acceptance and acceptability of spatial changes to local states. Frisken's (1981) work on the factors contributing to public service equalisation in a restructured metropolitan region (Toronto) illustrates this approach. Atkinson's (1980) work provides a good example of the use of a public survey for evaluating the acceptability of changes to a public service system. However, we should note that the context within which the metropolis (as made of a set of local states) is defined and studies is limited. Reality demands that we relate the local state to the larger state, and to the international scene. A simple example will suffice. Consider the availability of housing. Provision of housing in a metro jurisdiction, for example, Toronto is linked to Canadian Federal housing subsidy policies, and not least of all to the flow of capital from outside the state specifically towards local real estate markets. This larger context has recently been brought to public attention by the collapse of certain financial institutions in Canada due to external flows of capital and unclear managerial policy and government control. The point about international linkages to local states has been made by Taylor (1982) in

Kirby (1982c:6).

The study of collective decision-making procedures and practices should be linked to the larger system. An attempt to provide a view of this larger system has been offered earlier. While we would support case studies of either the abstract theoretical kind or empirical variety, probably one of the major activities of an international group is to deal with larger questions taking advantage of the comparative approach. For this reason we suggest that a systems framework provides a possible mechanism for integrating collective decision-making with the basic components of the local state.

EPILOGUE

In this paper we have tried to suggest that the study of local states is an appropriate one for political geographers to be engaged in. While the ultimate purpose of such an exercise is probably to seek a theory for the local state we recognise that there is no clearly defined path to this goal. Within the context of two themes, first, the provision of public goods and second, public and collective decision-making, we suggest that empirical and theoretical studies could be undertaken. Further we argue that a systemic approach might provide a suitable framework for linking the various components and for encouraging comparative studies to be undertaken. Such an approach might also allow relationships among local states to be studied at different scales. In conclusion we would suggest that if in ten years time we are able to look back on our activities and conclude that we have moved beyond the stage of case studies then we can conclude that we have progressed intellectually. Now is the time to gear ourselves for the challenge of seeking ways of integrating our rich empirical heritage on local states into meaningful theoretical statements.

REFERENCES

Allen, J. R. (1982) 'Step One: measure municipal productivity', mimeo, Ministry of Municipal Affairs and Housing, Government of Ontario, Toronto

Agnew, J. (1982) 'Federal policy and the possibility of urban triage', Paper, AAG Annual Conference, San Antonio

Archer, J. C. and Reynolds, D. R. (1976) 'Locational Logrolling and Citizen Support of Municipal Bond Proposals: the example of St. Louis', Public Choice, 27, 22-40

Atkinson, T. (1980) 'Evaluations of neighbourhood conditions and municipal services in Metropolitan Toronto and its boroughs', Report 3, Institute for Behavioural Research, York University, Canada

Bennett, R. (1980) The Geography of Public Finance, Methuen, London

Boddy, M. and Fudge, F. (1980) The Local State, Theory and Practices, Working Paper 20, School for Advanced Urban Studies, University of Bristol

Bordessa, R. and Cameron, J. (1980) 'The investigative Genre: problems and prospects', Professional Geographer, 32, 164-172

Bordessa, R. and Cameron, J. (1982) 'Growth management conflicts in the Toronto-centred region', in K. R. Cox and R. J. Johnston, (eds.) Conflict, Politics and the Urban Scene, Longmans, London

Bracken, I. (1981) Urban Planning Methods, Research and Policy Analysis, Methuen, London

Broadbent, T. A. (1977) Planning and Profit in the Urban Economy, Methuen, London

Clarke, R. (1982) Work in Crises, St. Andrews Press, Edinburgh

Cockburn, C. (1977) The Local State, Pluto Press, London

Cook, W. D. and Seiford, L. M. (1978) 'Priority Ranking and Consensus Formation', Management Science, Vol. 24, 1721-1732

Dear, M. (1981a) 'A Theory of the Local State', in A. D. Burnett and P. J. Taylor (eds.), Political Studies from Spatial Perspectives, Wiley, Chichester, U.K. 183-200

Dear, M. (1981b) 'The State: A research agenda', Environment and Planning A, 13, 1791-1796

Dear, M. and Clark, G. L. (1978) 'The State and Geographic Process: A critical review', Environment and Planning A, 10, 173-183

Dear, M. and Clark, G. L. (1981) 'Dimensions of Local State and Autonomy', Environment and Planning A, 13, 1277-2194

Dear, M. and Scott, A. J. (1981) 'Towards a Framework for Analysis', in M. Dear and A. J. Scott (eds.), Urbanisation and Urban Planning in Capitalist Society, Methuen, London

Department of the Environment (1972) Development and Compensation: Putting People First, H.M.S.O. London cmnd. 5124

Fincher, R. (1981) 'Local Implementation Strategies in the Urban Built Environment', Environment and Planning A, 13, 1233-1252

Flowerdew, R. (1981) Institutions and Geographical Patterns, St. Martins, New York

Frazier, M. (1981) 'Private Alternatives to Public Services', Transatlantic Perspectives, 5, 2-7

Frisken, F. (1981) 'Factors Contributing to Public Service
    Equalisation in a Restructural Metropolis: The case of
    Toronto', Paper, Annual Meeting of Canadian Political
    Science Association, Halifax
Hammond, K. R. and McClelland, G. H. (1981) Integration of
    Theory and Research in Judgement and Decision-making:
    Final Report, Center for Research on Judgement and
    Policy, University of Colorado, Boulder
Hansen, P. and Thisse, J. F. (1981) 'Outcomes of Voting and
    Planning: Condorcet, Weber and Rawls Locations',
    Journal of Public Economics, 16, 1-15
Hatry, H. P. (1972) 'Issues in Productivity Measurement for
    Local Governments', Public Administration Review, 32,
    776-784
Hodgart, R. L. (1978) 'Optimizing Access to Public Services:
    a review of problems, models and methods of locating
    central facilities', Progress in Human Geography, 2,
    17-48
Huggett, R. (1980) Systems Analysis in Geography, Oxford
    University Press, London
Kirby, A. (1982a) 'Education and the Local State', in
    R. Flowerdew (ed.), Institutions and Geographical
    Patterns, St. Martins, New York, 309-17
Kirby, A. (1982b) 'The External Relations of the Local State
    in Britain: some empirical examples', in K. R. Cox and
    R. J. Johnston (eds.), Conflict, Politics and the Urban
    Scene, Longmans, London
Kirby, A. (1982c) The Politics of Location: an Introduction,
    Methuen, London
Kliot, N. (1982) 'Recent Themes in Political Geography - A
    Review', Tijdschrift voor Economische en Sociale
    Geografie, 73, 270-9
Kolderie, T. (1982) 'Government in the Eighties: Shifting
    Roles and Responsibilities', Transatlantic Perspectives,
    6, 6-9
Lea, A. C. (1983) 'The Efficient Location, Size and Tax
    Distribution of a System of Facilities Providing a
    Delivered, Impure Public Good', Paper, AAG Annual
    Conference, Denver
Massam, B. H. (1983) A Note on Voting and the Location of
    Public Facilities, Working Paper 7, Urban Studies, York
    University, Canada
Massam, B. H. and Askew, I. D. (1982) 'Methods for Comparing
    Policies Using Multiple Criteria: An Urban Example',
    OMEGA, The International Journal of Management Science,
    10, 195-204
Massam, B. H. and Askew, I. D. (1984) 'Theoretical
    Perspectives on Rural Service Provision', in G. Enyedi
    and R. E. Lonsdale (eds.), Rural Public Services:
    International Comparisons, Westview Press, Boulder,
    Colorado

McAllister, D. M. (1976) 'Equity and Efficiency in Public
    Facility Location', Geographical Analysis, 8, 47-63
O'Connor, J. (1973) The Fiscal Crisis of the State,
    St. Martin's Press, New York
Paddison, R. (1983) The Fragmented State: The Political
    Geography of Power, Blackwell, Oxford
Reynolds, D. R. (1982) 'School Retrenchment and Locational
    Conflict: Crises in Local Democracy', paper presented at
    Symposium on Public Provision and Urban Politics,
    Virginia
Roberts, K. (1982) Administration, Unemployment and the
    Distribution of Income, European Centre for Work and
    Society, Maastricht
Russell, B. (1950) Unpopular Essays, Allen and Unwin, London
Rushton, G. et al. (1981) 'Optimum Locations for Public
    Services: individual preference and social choice',
    Geographical Analysis, 13, 196-202
Saunders, P. (1980) Urban Politics, Penguin, London
Schaffer, B. and Lamb, G. (1981) Can Equity be Organized?
    U.N.E.S.C.O., Paris
Shelley, F. M. and Goodchild, M. F. (1982) 'Equilibrium in
    Majority Voting on Salutary Facility Location', Mimeo,
    Oklahoma
Short, J. R. (1982) An Introduction to Political Geography,
    Routledge and Kegan Paul, London
Short, J. R. (1983) 'Political Geography', in Progress in
    Human Geography, 7, 122-125
Smith, C. J. (1982) 'The Urban Services Paradox: Shrinking
    supply in times of rising demand', Paper, AAG Annual
    Conference, San Antonio
Smith, D. M. (1973) The Geography of Social Well Being,
    McGraw Hill, New York
Stewart, T. J. (1979) 'A descriptive approach to multiple
    criteria decision making', TWISK 128, National Research
    Institute for Math Sciences, Pretoria
Taylor, P. J. (1982) 'A materialist framework for political
    geography', Transactions, Institute of British
    Geographers, NS7, 15-34
Teitz, N. B. (1968) 'Towards a Theory of Urban Public
    Facility Location', Papers, Regional Science Association,
    21. 35-51
The Economist (1982) 'The Withering of Europe's Welfare
    State', October 16-22, 67-71
Williams, S. (1981) Politics is for People, Penguin, London

Chapter Five

SOCIO-SPATIAL RELATIONS BETWEEN LOCAL STATE, COLLECTIVE
IDENTITY AND CONFLICT BEHAVIOUR

Jürgen Ossenbrugge

The role of the local state as a more or less independent
institutional part of the spatial organisation of western
societies has gained a significant meaning in recent
developments of political geography. The discussion about
this topic has often been connected with explanatory efforts
on the increasing conflicts around the natural and built
environment. In reviewing theories of the local state by
emphasising the ways local conflicts are analysed, this essay
tries to work out unsolved problems and deficits in two
theoretical approaches: the 'public choice paradigm'
and 'marxist structuralism'. Although both approaches of
political economy provide complex and consistent abstractions
of those functions which constitute the local state as a
spatial unit, they are not sufficient to explain the
relationship between political systems and conflicts on
local level. Therefore the final argument tries to elaborate
a theoretical research agenda combining a structural approach
with a theory of action[1].

THE CONFLICT SOLVING CAPACITY OF THE LOCAL STATE AND
RATIONAL BEHAVIOUR OF INDIVIDUALS

In a recent review on research agendas the editors of
Political Geography Quarterly optimistically evaluated one
approach, which has been derived from 'New Political
Economy':

> The most comprehensive theoretical departure of
> this type, however, comes with the application
> of the public choice paradigm to political
> geography. This provides a rigorous framework
> based upon individual choice for assessing
> existing institutions and suggesting improve-
> ments. This is undoubtedly one of the major
> theoretical developments which we can expect to

influence political geography in the 1980s
(Editorial Board, 1982:11).

In fact, the public choice paradigm in political geography
fills a gap. Certain imperfections in the market mechanism,
like uneven regional developments and locational conflicts
and inadequacies in scientific research, e.g. locational
analysis and regional science, have resulted in a renaissance
of old concepts of political economy connected with new
theories concerning the pluralistic organisation of society.
The discussion about this approach should give two answers
about the nature of the local state and his mechanism and
capacities to regulate conflicts.

Following the concept of social choice elaborated by
Reynolds (1981), one of the main arguments is that the
spatial organisation of political systems in democratic
market societies depends on individual preferences for
specific types and amounts of public goods and services.
Because of the conflicting implications of allocational
decisions, any society is forced to find ways which keep
political externality costs as low as possible. According to
Reynolds, there are two different ways to achieve this aim:
One way is built around the fiscal federalism thesis which is
based on the assumption that a spatial decentralisation of
decision making processes should be organised according to the
resources of the local state. This technology of power
distribution leads to a spatial segregation of preferences and
solves the problem of free and forced riders. Finally, local
elections will reveal preferences in respect to the quantity
and quality of public goods provided on a local level. In
reviewing empirical studies, Archer (1981:81) declares that
"... the logic of the connection between preference
revelation by voting and by moving suggests that a public
choice theory of the political-space-economy is highly
plausible". Furthermore Reynolds introduces the
constitutional choice approach based on the norm of
procedural justice. Here, allocational decisions affecting
the spatial distribution of public goods on local level are
legitimised by specific procedures, like elections of
representatives, participation etc. This, however, has no
significance for the spatial structure of the local state
because every political system on local as well as on
national level can be built on principles of constitutional
choice. That means that Reynolds' approach should be viewed
as a rational pleading for a representative and pluralistic
organisation of the state and management of regional
development where political outputs affecting the spatial
structure are legitimised by the decision making process.

An application of the public choice paradigm to the
political organisation of space, especially the local state,
produces a framework for defining the size of jurisdictions

(e.g. internalisation of external effects versus preference homogeneity) or offers principles for decision-making processes affecting the spatial allocation of public goods and services (e.g. constitutional choice). Therefore, it has to be evaluated as a theoretical perspective for political and spatial organisation of society. The activities of the local state are a function of aggregated individual preferences and of procedures transforming these into political outputs. This perspective helps to interpret the political system as a conflict solving mechanism. Competitive individual preferences for social welfare are considered as an input and collective choices about the quality of welfare as a legitimised output.

Two critical questions to this mode of explanation will help to illustrate the importance for analysing the underlying assumptions of individual behaviour, especially in conflict situations. First, the public choice paradigm is based on a methodological individualism, the ego acts in a self-orientated manner which is utility maximising similar to a capitalistic enterprise. This hypothesis assumes the same legal rights and equal access to political power for everyone. Conflicts in urban systems seem like natural situations of individualistic competition to improve the personal relative location in society (e.g. Cox, 1979:3). The question is whether every subject has got equal possibilities to participate in locational decisions or, referring to a scientific discussion, whether the pluralistic version of community power research is accurate[2]. In public choice paradigm individual motives for becoming involved in a political conflict are of a rational character. They are structured by the economic system. The historical evolution of this way of acting is described by Cox (1981:437):

> Hence at both neighbourhood and municipal levels labour forms coalitions to protect, from the depredations of capital, a commodity yielding a stream of utility and to which it has purchased rights of access. Labour joins with others to protect an individual interest rather than the interest of some community with which it might once have identified ... For while labour enters conflicts as guardian of a common resource, it is willing to bargain with capital for compensation, environmental improvements in the development scheme at issue, land for public housing, etc. The posture is rational, utility-maximising and in its assumptions of arbitration by the money system, remarkably analogous to market place relations.

Individuals act as entrepreneurs and in doing so they constitute a political market, which is structured in analogy to the market economy. In fact, there is no problem to apply theorems and methods of neoclassical economics in the examination of political processes affecting the spatial distribution of public goods and services. Individual choices for residential quality and private income (Cox, 1979), vote buying activities of local governments (Johnston, 1979) etc. are based on a similar motivation, analogous to the rationality of free market conditions. Consequently, the spatial and political structure of the local state is a function of individual preferences for market regulations. The same could be said by examining marxist theories of the state (e.g. the derivation argument, see Short, 1982), if the specificity of social relations derived from the capitalist mode of production is ignored. In doing so, the advocates of the public choice paradigm artificially divide between political and economic power. They presuppose an egalitarian democracy, without giving proofs of its existence and they neglect the effects of non-decision-making (Bachrach and Baratz, 1970). Without emphasising the ideological context of this abridged method here, a second critical point stresses the poorly developed theory of group behaviour.

In his derivation of the social choice argument Reynolds (1981) evaluates the meaning of political procedures and spatial organisations in line with the methodological individualism. Allocational problems of public goods and services have to be solved deductively by regarding subjective interests of economic man as a constant factor in variable spatial settings or empirically by revealing the preferences by voting or other forms of individual action[3]. He thereby neglects the historical process, which has led to a selective evolution of the political system. A dualism appears: Are the processes to regulate locational choices a result of utility maximising individuals or a derivation from a historical process structured by the capitalistic mode of production? Although this question needs a theoretical comparison of both modes of explanation, a major weakness of the social choice argument should be noted: Society and social groups are always a pure aggregate of individuals, whereas place-based communities, class-interests and social movements within their specific historical conditions are without any effect or nonexistent.

In a recent critique of modern theory of democracy and neoclassical theory of the spatial organisation of government, Clark (1981) refers to two main theoretical deficiencies in this approach: At first, he mentions the missing recognition of the socialisation process, in other words, the missing concept of territoriality as a collective identity of individuals and groups. The second argument is that it is inadequate to equate political processes with the economic system: Local conflicts just appear as situations of competition among utility maximising individuals, who strive for locational advantages:

> The abstraction and negation of ideology, class, and economic inequality as vital and inherent mechanisms of political decision-making enforces a rigid and very narrow view of human nature and political institutions (Clark, 1981:119).

Both critical questions which have been mentioned earlier strongly support this point of view. Although the restrained explanatory quality of collective choice arguments is emphasised in this way, its normative implications remain attractive for evaluating further developments on a local level. Because of the recent neoliberalist political practice in western democracies, the cutting back of the welfare state and the propaganda about individual responsibility to survive with free market conditions, the public choice paradigm may evolve into a scientific sub-structure of capitalist society (Lepage, 1979). On the one hand there are many proofs of the loss of independence of the local state as a part of the institutionalised political system[4]. Those proofs have changed the lines of inquiry from community power to local or urban politics in political science. At the same time, theories of pluralism have been replaced by descriptive theories of political corporatism. Although a growing awareness of the complex structure concerning the political and social organisation of space can be considered, the public choice approach - on the other hand - ignores the dependencies between world system, nation-state and local state. Its proposers are posing questions about economically rational modelling of political processes within isolated local systems and about the efficiency of the state to regulate individual conflicts. A socio-spatial scenario becomes visible, in which even claims for a pluralistic democracy seem to be nonrealistic: When a minimal state exists, as Reynolds assumes (1981:97) and as it is postulated by the neoliberalist political parties, and when the political market is reduced to control externality effects, to compensate market failures and to maintain some unspecified collective security, the society of the 'one-dimensional man' is reality[5]. Within this political development collective choice arguments predict spatial equilibrium and political stability. Social conflicts remain unavoidable, but they are not dangerous for the political and economic status-quo or for a formal democracy within capitalistic development.

SOCIO-SPATIAL RELATIONS OF THE LOCAL STATE IN CAPITALIST WORLD ECONOMY

Arguments against the individualistic public choice approach have recently been derived from marxist perspectives on world economy and on the nature of capitalistic state (e.g. Taylor, 1982, Dear, 1981). Two aspects of materialist theory of society are of importance.

First, according to the German derivation debate (Offe, 1972, Habermas, 1973) an explanation of the capitalist state has to be related to the logic of capitalist development. As a dependent system, although relative autonomous, the institutions and functions of the state can be divided into a field of accumulation and of legitimation. Activities of the state as an agent of accumulation are directed in order to harmonise the logical irrationalities of capitalist market economies, which are a result of competition and striving for profit. Interventions in economic exchange processes and in regional developments should provide conditions which guarantee an optimal circulation and accumulation of capital.

Another main function of the state can be characterised as an 'active organisation of class compromise' (Offe, 1972: 22), capitalist state must produce mass loyalty which is organised by a system of formal democratic institutions[6]. After World War II the development towards a welfare state became a significant manifestation within this structural constraint in western societies, whereas today strategies of conflict avoidance, conflict isolation and conflict delegation have become more important to guarantee political legitimation. Examples of this development are decisions towards formal decentralisation, whereas a functional central-isation takes place, or the application of complex and complicated institutional procedures. Illustrative examples are location decisions concerning nuclear power plants, chemical industries and other high technological enterprises. Whereas the constitution gives the local level a high degree of independence in respect of the spatial development in West Germany, 'relevant' decisions are not affected by local interests. Modern tendencies to decentralise the political system should therefore be confronted with the context of austerity policy, which stands for reduced expenditures for the peripheries on local, regional and national level and tries to legitimate this with an ideology of decentral-isation. Finally, this process becomes obvious in activities, where public attention is diverted from questions of power by establishing middle- and long-term constraints, Consequently, the political system is developing in a way in which 'the state is legitimised through its own actions and diversity' (Clark, 1981:123).

It becomes obvious that the state in a capitalist democracy fulfills an ideological function by separating the

'level of experience' from the 'level of reality' of
capitalistic world economy: Taylor (1982) describes a
materialist framework for political geography in these
categories. His approach offers an explanation of the fact
that objective interests of the working class do not form a
collective identity or class consciousness. The capitalist
nation-state as a whole, but especially the modern local
state mystifies class relations.

Ideological functions of the political organisation of
space have been analysed in several ways, for example in the
field of integration or decentralisation. In the case of the
latter, the local state receives the political responsibility
and obtains administrative management for those conflicts
which derive from the crisis of the welfare state and modern
contraditions of capitalistic development. Therefore,
conflict phenomena are not only sectorally divided (e.g.
class struggle in the field of production versus environmental
pollution in the field of reproduction). A major component
to keep struggles latent and isolated lies in vertical and
horizontal divisions of space. The local level vertically
absorbs conflicts of the whole political system which is an
important effect of the hierarchical political organisation
of space. In a horizontal direction conflicts are isolated
because of the areal divisions in a pattern of different
local political systems.

Moreover, ideological functions of the local state
become obvious in institutionalised procedures of
participation which allow an early revelation of a critical
potential within local populations. Up to now this has not
been integrated into the existing political system by
enlarging and obscuring procedures - called participation -
or by withdrawal from political processes. In summary,
institutionalised participation is powerless. This situation
is intensified by a growing anticipation of potential
individual preferences within the planning system and its
transformation to a defined public preference 'from above'.

If this theoretical approach is applied, concepts like
public choice paradigm in political geography are to be
evaluated as a production of spatial ideologies for
stabilising the political and economic status-quo. In a
materialist perspective, as it is outlined by Taylor (1982)
and Dear (1981), the local state and its function for social
reproduction within the legitimation system is structured by
capitalist accumulation on a world scale and the nature of
the nation-state within this process. An explanation of
local conflicts and of individual behaviour has to be related
to this structure. This view is emphasised in a recent
introduction to urban political geography:

> What appears as a conflict over turf is actually
> generated by the much deeper social forces of

> capital-labour antagonism. What appears as
> separate, independent, and thing-like, is only
> made possible and meaningful by the social
> tensions inherent in a dynamic yet conflict-
> ridden social system. Thus our case studies are
> illustrations of the many ways in which basic
> conflict in a capitalist society are realised as
> local conflicts (Cox and Johnston, 1982:15).

This orientation may serve as a holistic theoretical
departure for explaining socio-spatial conflicts in the
urban scene. Social action in local conflicts is analysed as
a dependent element of capital-labour antagonism. The
continuation of private accumulation and the status-quo of
its political and institutional preconditions is endangered
by a spatially displaced class-struggle. If this interpretation is evaluated as an accurate one, a relevant
question to use the marxian class concept necessarily
remains[7]: What are motives for entering a conflict and what
are basic experiences for forming a collective identity?
Here we are confronted with a similar problem which has been
outlined by Agnew (1981) concerning political regionalism.
If his critique towards structuralist theories is transferred
to the approach taken by Cox and Johnston, analogous
theoretical inadequacies become obvious. On the one hand
local conflicts are evaluated as a specific type of displaced
class-struggle, whereas on the other hand the structure of
urban development in late capitalism is separated from the
field of human experience and action within this process.
This proceeding is justified, because "... at any one time,
degrees of freedom are available which may result in
particular bureaucratic decisions, in the success of
particular pressure groups, or in the electoral success of
a particular faction within society" (Johnston, 1982:109).
Consequently, basic assumptions of materialist structuralism
are connected with an ahistorical theory of political
pluralism in a separated form[8]. That means, a dialectical
unity of structure and action or subject and object is
denied and therefore the 'level of experience' is not linked
to the development of the economic and political system. The
difficult but most important question within marxist
structuralism remains unanswered: What are the dynamic
relations between diverse subjective class interests and the
concept of objective class? (Harvey, 1974:161). The underlying theory of human action is still based on the assumption
of purposeful rationality or of an instrumental and
functional mode of thinking as in public choice paradigm.

THE IMPERIALISM OF THE ECONOMIC AND POLITICAL SYSTEM IN WESTERN DEMOCRACIES: RATIONAL TRANSFORMATION OF SOCIAL SPACE

A dialectical relationship between the logic of capitalist accumulation on a world scale and social-spatial processes on local and regional level exists, for example, around the ecological problematic, urban deprivation and gentrification. Many protesting groups and alternative movements are expressing the many ways in which the self-denying tendencies of this mode of production become manifest phenomena. In spite of that objective finding within a structuralist theory, individual and collective motives for acting are not derived from objective interests, which are defined by the specificity of the historical situation in late capitalism. Furthermore, the common political perspective of these groups is not orientated towards a functional restructuring of society, e.g. from capitalism to socialism. By using terms of Friedmann (1978) the orientations of these groups are 'territorial' and 'reciprocal' against the 'functional' and 'effective' organisation of space and society in the western world of capitalism as well as in the states of the 'real existing socialism'.

A far reaching explanation of this observation offers the theory of action by Habermas (1981). He criticises different directions of social theory, because they use a model of man, who is solely directed by an instrumental rationality and by an orientation towards a successful self-assertion.

A similar weakness is noticeable in the axiomatic foundation of action theory within the (marxian, J.O.) theory of value as we have been able to recognise as well in the work of Weber as in both lines of his reception in western marxism and Parsons: the model of purposeful rationality is taken as a fundamental of social action too (Habermas, 1981, volume 2:503)[9].

As it has been emphasised in different approaches of urban research, a theory of conflicts has to take into account interdependencies between objective structure and subjective intention (e.g. Pickvance, 1977, Ley, 1979, Mollenkopf, 1981). This means that an emergence of spatial and environmental conflicts are not only a result of traditional capital-labour antagonism, but also an effect of a rational transformation of the communicative structured lifeworld into functional organised space. The latter category is developed in the phenomenological approach in geography as the place concept: common symbolic meanings of landscapes and places, place-bound social integration and personal socialisation within specific environments are main components of the urban conflict scene (Ley, 1979).

Habermas does not argue within the phenomenological approach, but connects his conception of lifeworld with communication theory. The difference between both approaches is that in Habermas' theoretical approach the concept of lifeworld is based on a philosophy of languages: Lifeworld is a result of communication processes, which reflect collective experiences, cultural values and social norms. Therefore, a communicative structured lifeworld is always a category, which describes a collective identity[10]. In the context presented here it is more important that the lifeworld and the economic and political subsystems are dialectically intertwined. Historically, lifeworld is penetrated and transformed by the development of both subsystems, e.g. the penetration of instrumental and functional competitive behaviour into social life (as it is assumed in public choice paradigm) as well as the expansion of bureaucratic institutions to administer and promote social uniformity. A result of Habermas' theoretical analysis is that people become involved in conflicts for defending their lifeworld against demands of economy and politics, because of the shrinking variability of components of the lifeworld and losing possibilities to use their environment as a social resource. Conflicts on local level become manifest as a subjective reaction against objective imperatives of those systems which transform political and economic issues of power to social constraints. In doing so they legitimate a spatial and social change in order to preserve system stability. This restorative or conservative element of conflict behaviour is obvious in activities to protect urban neighbourhoods, to restore the ecological system or to preserve its status-quo. Those phenomena cannot be explained within a theory of displaced class-struggle, likewise localism and regionalism.

The theory of Habermas combines objective structure and subjective action in a dialectical interrelationship by using the categories 'system' and 'lifeworld'. While being regarded as a system the historical evolution of capitalist world-economy and welfare state transform the reproduction process of lifeworld. As a result, new crisis phenomena become manifest on a local level which reflects a technocratical functionalism in modern urban development.

A theoretical approach concentrating on local conflicts and urban political geography should not only be concerned with space as a scarce and valuable resource in terms of political economy, but also with social space as a part of the materialistic and symbolic reproduction of lifeworld. Functional uniformity of the environment and analogous tendencies in capitalist and socialist countries indicate manifestations, which seem to be independent of the mode of production. But empirical analyses and comparative urban conflict studies which try to confirm or to differentiate these general arguments are rare. An example is Ley's (1980) case study concerning urban development in Vancouver. He analyses a ruling liberal party which tries to perform policies towards environmental preservation and reconstruction, using an ideology of aesthetic viability within capitalist economy. The failure of this political practice at a time when the economy slows down has to be evaluated as a logical consequence of capitalist system rationality. It is because of the dependency of liberal politics on the economic system that its political perspective is too limited, being only orientated to relieve the alienation of man from his cultural and natural lifeworld while the generating causes are not changed or affected. But this kind of policy is not only short-termed but also producing new inequalities, as Ley notes himself: "In free market conditions an urban strategy favouring a high level of consumption with style will only serve to attract the wealthy and penalise social groups with limited market power" (Ley, 1980:257). The same could be said about those parts of the green movement, who are arguing that nothing more than a strong ecological orientation within the existing political practice is needed. A political grass root movement, observable in some cities in West Germany, seems to be more progressive, because of a combination of restorative demands for a liveable cultural and natural lifeworld with socialist challenges. Radical decentralisation and social control of the political and economic system are basic topics of radical local politics and an alternative approach to the present local state[11].

Beside this practical reasoning, the consideration of both theories - structural theory of the economic and political system and action theory of the social lifeworld - may lead to a consistent and far-reaching theoretical approach of local state and urban conflict. In this context a political geographical perspective should recognise not only horizontal, regional inequalities (division by area) and vertical, spatial dependencies (division by scale). It is also important to integrate the explanation of local conflicts as a result of the rational transformation of social space into functional space of the political and economic system.

CONCLUDING REMARKS

It is hardly possible to derive some generalisations about the spatial structure of the local state from the context presented here. While the combination of 'welfare economics' and 'new political economy' allows a lot of abstractions about size, provision with public goods and electoral systems, this approach to political geography and explanation of the local state is speculative. The social or public choice argument is too strongly related towards an utilitarian penetration of social life in its underlying behavioural assumptions which functions as an ideological support for capitalist development in an era of economic descent and finance crisis of the state. Theoretical inadequacies are due to an ahistorical modelling of political processes and an assumed independency of the political from the economic system. Therefore, the call for a decentralised local state and procedural justice in decision-making processes have to be considered in relation to a scientific practice which is stabilising the status-quo. Existing spatial and social inequalities are converted into quasi-natural results of individual competition in order to maximise its wellbeing.

A stronger explanation of the role of the local state in capitalist societies is provided by the historical and dialectical materialism which relates the function of this political institution to the historical development of class antagonism and a derivated theory of the state. Spatial allocation of public goods and services as well as elections and other forms of participation are part of the legitimation system, in which the local state functions as an active organisation of class-compromise. Beside activities in the field of accumulation, this function is directly confronted with conflicts around the natural and built environment. The identity of the local state in late capitalism has to be described as a suppression or a canalisation of displaced class struggles which derive from socio-spatial dialectics (Soja, 1980).

In so far as it is reasonable to link local conflicts to the structure of social relations which are a result of capitalist mode of production, this leads to a comprehensive critique of the normative assumption of 'welfare economics' and 'new political economy'. But the recent progress in urban political geography is hitherto indicating that a nondialectical acceptance of marxist structuralism is unable to explain the motivational structure of subjective behaviour in conflicts. As it has been shown within conflicts concerning regionalism, the level of experience cannot completely be described in a frame of the theory of value: As a matter of fact local conflicts exist between groups and classes, which act strategically because of opposite or antagonistic interests for one's own purposes and utilities. But conflicts are also initiated by reciprocal-acting subjects and territorial-based groups as a defending reaction against a functional transformation of social space and natural areas.

The increase of an ecological problematic, the emergence of a local and regional economic crisis and the loss of political legitimation in the field of planning and regional policy generate latent and manifest conflicts which are not removable within the present economic and political practice, but are a result of it. Beside a scientific explanation of these phenomena, urban political geography should fulfil an enlightened function in order to become aware of consequences of this practice and elaborate concepts for alternative local politics.

ACKNOWLEDGEMENT

I would like to thank Carolin Meder and Uwe Herrmann for their suggestions concerning the translation of this text, and the participants of the conference of Political Geographers in Oxford 1983 for their comments and criticism on an earlier draft of this paper.

NOTES

1. The main ideas of this paper are fully developed in a doctoral dissertation, dealing with theoretical approaches to political geography (Ossenbrugge 1983).
2. An introduction to community power research is provided by Dunleavy (1980). Developments of locational conflict studies are described in Janelle (1977), Dear and Long (1978), Cox and Johnston (1982).
3. Compare the strategies of individual or group actions in locational conflicts noted by Dear and Long (1978).
4. This development has been analysed in West Germany in respect of the legal system by Roters (1975), of political economy by Evers and Lehmann (1973), of regional planning and decision-making on local level by Ossenbrugge (1982).
5. Compare Marcuse (1967). The adoption of system theory within this approach is indicating that modern liberal political theory is converting into a social technology of a functional rationality. This development in human geography is analysed by Gregory (1980).
6. Compare the politics of legitimation within the geography of elections, see chapter 8 below.
7. In the scheme of Marx, there is a distinction between the concept of subjective and objective class. The term objective class describes a basic division within capitalism between a class of producers (labour) and a class of appropriators of surplus value (capital). The concept of subjective class describes the consciousness which different groups have of their position within a social structure. If objective and subjective interests become an identity, we may theoretically speak of a 'right' consciousness. Furthermore, there is empirical evidence for 'false' and 'lacking' consciousness (Harvey, 1974:161; Balbus, 1970/71). The ignorance of traditional left parties and groups of the increasing gap between objective and subjective interests of

labour is one factor for the development of political groups and movements in the left scene, which are not based in the working class.

8. Johnston (1982:109) legitimates his interpretation by quoting empirical results of Ley (1980), which illustrate the dialectical effects of urban development in late capitalism. They will be discussed later on.

9. Translated by the author. A similar critique of western marxism (Althusser) is outlined in Sloeterdijk (1983:184-197).

10. For example: A neighbourhood is a collective identity because neighbours are talking about themselves and the environment they share and realise that they have similar attitudes towards the area they live in. If this is not the case, a usage of categories like 'territorial interests' (Friedmann) or 'community' (Mollenkopf) make almost no sense.

11. As a part of the new party 'Die Grunen', the Green-Alternative List (GAL) is represented in the local parliament of Hamburg, where it forms like the CDU (Christian-Democratic Party) an opposition to the ruling SPD (Social-Democratic Party).

REFERENCES

Agnew, J. A. (1981) 'Structural and dialectical theories of political regionalism', in A. D. Burnett and P. J. Taylor (eds.) Political Studies from Spatial Perspectives, Wiley, Chichester, U.K., 275-290

Archer, J. C. (1981) 'Public choice paradigms in political geography, in A. D. Burnett and P. J. Taylor (eds.) Political Studies from Spatial Perspectives, Wiley, Chichester, U.K., 73-90

Bachrach, P. and Baratz, M. S. (1970) Power and Poverty. Theory and Practice, New York

Balbus, I. D. (1970/71) 'The Concept of Interest in Pluralist and Marxian Analysis', Politics and Society, 1, 151-177.

Clark, G. L. (1981) 'Democracy and the capitalist state: towards a critique of the Tiebout hypothesis', in A. D. Burnett and P. J. Taylor (eds.) Political Studies from Spatial Perspectives, Wiley, Chichester, U.K., 111-130

Cox, K. R. (1979) Location and Public Problems. A Political Geography of the Contemporary World, Maaroufa, Chicago.

Cox, K. R. (1981) 'Capitalism and Conflict around the Communal Living Space', in M. J. Dear and A. J. Scott (eds.), Urbanisation and Urban Planning in Capitalist Society, Methuen, London, 431-455

Cox, K. R. and Johnston, R. J. (1982) 'Conflict, Politics and the Urban Scene: a Conceptual Framework', in K. R. Cox and R. J. Johnston (eds.), Conflict, Politics and the Urban Scene, Longman, London, 1-19

Local State, Collective Identity and Conflict Behaviour

Dear, M. J. (1981) 'A theory of local state', in A. D. Burnett
    and P. J. Taylor (eds.), Political Studies from Spatial
    Perspectives, Wiley, Chichester, U.K., 183-200
Dear, M. J. and Long, J. (1978) 'Community Strategies in
    Locational Conflict', in K. R. Cox (ed.), Urbanization
    and Conflict in Market Societies, Maaroufa, Chicago,
    113-127
Dunleavy, P. (1980) Urban Political Analysis: The Politics of
    Collective Consumption, Macmillan, London
Editorial Board (1982) 'Editorial Essay : Political Geography-
    Research Agendas for the Nineteen Eighties', Political
    Geography Quarterly, 1, 1-18
Evers, A. and Lehmann, M. (1973) Politisch-ökonomische
    Determinanten für Planung und Politik in den Kommunen
    der BRD, Offenbach
Friedmann, J. (1978) 'On the Contradiction between City and
    Countryside', Comparative Urban Studies, 6, 5-41
Gregory, D. (1980) 'The Ideology of Control : Systems Theory
    and Geography', Tijdschrift voor Economische en Sociale,
    71, 327-342
Habermas, J. (1973) Legitimationsprobleme im Spätkapitalismus,
    Frankfurt, Suhrkamp. Translated into English (1976) as
    Legitimation Crisis, Heinneman, London
Habermas, J. (1981) Theorie des kommunikativen Handelns,
    Vol. 1: Handlungsrationalitat und gesellschaftliche
    Rationalisierung. Vol. 2: Zur Kritik der funktional-
    istischen Vernunft, Frankfurt, Suhrkamp.
Harvey,D. (1974) 'Class-Monopoly Rent, Finance Capital and
    the Urban Revolution', in S. Gale and E. G. Moore (eds.),
    The Manipulated City. Perspectives on Spatial Structure
    and Social Issues in Urban America, Maaroufa, Chicago,
    145-167
Johnston, R. J. (1979) Political, Electoral and Spatial
    Systems, Oxford University Press, London
Johnston, R. J. (1982) 'Institutional Context and Conflict
    over Location: Editor's Introduction', in K. R. Cox and
    R. J. Johnston (eds.), Conflict, Politics and the Urban
    Scene, Longman, London, 107-110
Lepage, H. (1979) Der Kapitalismus von morgen, Campus,
    Frankfurt
Ley, D. (1979) 'Social Geography and the'Taken For-Granted
    World', in S. Gale and G. Olsson (eds.), Philosophy in
    Geography, Reidel, Dordrecht, 215-236
Ley, D. (1980) 'Liberal Ideology and the Postindustrial City',
    Annals, Association of American Geographers, 70, 238-258
Marcuse, L. (1967) Der eindimensionale Mensch, Neuwied,
    Luchterhand. Translated into English 1972 as
    One-Dimensional Man, Abacus, London
Mollenkopf, J. (1981) 'Community and Accumulation', in M. Dear
    and A. J. Scott (eds.), Urbanization and Urban Planning
    in Capitalist Society, Methuen, London, 319-337

Offe, C. (1972) <u>Strukturprobleme des kapitalistischen Staates</u>, Suhrkamp, Frankfurt

Ossenbrugge, J. (1982) Industrieannsiedlung und Flächennutzungsplanung in Stade-Bützfleth und Drochtersen. Lokale Interessen end Politikverflechtung im kommunalen Entscheidungsprozess, in H. Nunn and J. Ossenbrügge (eds.), <u>Wirtschafts- und sozialgeographische Beiträge zur Analyse der Regionalentwicklung und Planungsproblemutik im Unterelberaum</u>, Hirt, Hamburg, 33-88

Ossenbrügge, J. (1983) <u>Politische Geographie als räumliche Konfliktforschung. Konzepte zur Analyse der politischen und sozialen Organisation des Raumes auf der Grundlage anglo-amerikanischer Forschungsansätze</u>, Hamburger Geographische Studien 40, Hamburg

Pickvance, C. G. (1977) 'From 'Social Base' to 'Social Force': Some Analytical Issues in the Study of Urban Protest', in M. Harloe (ed.), <u>Captive Cities</u>, Wiley, Chichester, U.K., 175-186

Reynolds, D. R. (1981) 'The geography of social choice', in A. D. Burnett and P. J. Taylor (eds.), <u>Political Studies from Spatial Perspectives</u>, Wiley, Chichester, U.K. 91-110

Roters, W. (1975) <u>Kommunale Mitwirkung an höherstufigen Entscheidungsprozessen</u>, Kohlhammer, Köln

Short, J. R. (1982) <u>An Introduction to Political Geography</u>, Routledge and Kegan Paul, London

Sloterdijk, P. (1983) <u>Kritik der zynischen Vernunft,</u> Vol. 1 Suhrkamp, Frankfurt

Soja, E. W. (1980) 'The Socio-Spatial Dialetic', <u>Annals, Association of American Geographers</u>, <u>70</u>, 207-225

Taylor, P. J. (1982) 'A materialist framework for political geography', <u>Transactions, Institute of British Geographers</u>, <u>7</u>, 15-34

Chapter Six

THE STATE CRISIS AND THE REGION - PRELIMINARY THOUGHTS FROM
A THIRD WORLD PERSPECTIVE

Bertha K. Becker

As the twentieth century draws towards its close, the
national question is becoming acute. Given the economic and
political crisis of the state, its nature and its fate pose a
basic question for the future.

From a Third World perspective based on studies carried
out in Brazil, the state crisis is an expression of the
global crisis, which has not only an economic dimension, but
also - and fundamentally - a political and a spatial one
manifested in different spatial scales. Alongside the
fundamental contradiction between the dominators and the
dominated from 1970 onwards, the contradition in the power
bloc between global social interests and private interests,
i.e., between the state and the corporations, is taking on
significance. The conflict between national and international interests is associated with the state and the
regional crisis, and at the local level is related to the
organisation of social movements acting against the central
power.

It is therefore important to develop studies that will
try to articulate crisis manifestations on different scales,
since neither macro-level economic generalisations nor
analysis of the crisis in a single scale or area are able to
do it.

Alternatives which are being proposed to bypass the
state crisis focus on the issue of power centralisation or
decentralisation and use the mediation of space referring to
specific scales. Liberal tendency proposals favour local
communities or the small region (Friedmann and Douglass,
1970; Stöhr, 1980 and 1982; Friedmann, 1982a and b).
Authors of a Marxist tendency, on the other hand, feel
either that the region is being destroyed by capital
internationalisation (Damette, 1980), or propose the
strengthening of state power through locational control of
private and public corporations (Holland, 1976), and the
strengthening of the region to make it suitable for the
demands of the new industrial age (Aydalot, 1981).

A relationship is beginning to be delineated, though
not explicitly, <u>between the crisis/legitimisation of the
nation-state</u> and the <u>regional scale</u>. It is this relationship
that this paper will try to analyse on an exploratory basis.
Focusing on the contemporary crisis, it seeks to offer a
helpful basis for the discussion of political alternatives to
the social question of the so-called Third World.
    In the first section, there is a short discussion of
some current contributions to this relationship. The second
section tries to analyse the contemporary situation and in
the third section some conclusions are proposed for further
reflection.

SOME BASIC ELEMENTS FOR, AND LIMITATIONS TO, THE ANALYSIS OF
THE STATE AND THE REGIONAL CRISIS IN CURRENT CONTRIBUTIONS

The crisis of the state and the region can be recognised via
two distinct lines of approach: (1) that of the theory and
policy of regional development; and (2) that of Marxist
structural analysis.

The Theory and Policy of Regional Development
In regional development theory and policy the crisis of the
state and the region are only implicit. They spring from
what this approach considers the failure, or at the least the
problems, of the industrialisation model and the growing
functional integration linked with it, which have been
having profoundly negative effects upon the population at
local level.
    Four limitations can be pointed out in this
contribution:

1. Dealing with regional development policy, the
    role of the determinants of the economic structure
    in the crisis is minimised. The regional crisis
    may be identified in the depressed or downward
    transitional region (Friedmann, 1965); it may be
    derived from the structure of spatial relations,
    which form an autonomous determinant of social
    relations.
2. The role of the state in the failure of the model
    and in the regional crisis is not made explicit;
    it is only implicit, underlying the centre-
    periphery relation. Regional policy conciliates
    the conflicts between regions and therefore the
    state is implicitly seen as a conciliatory
    element of society. The crisis, in its turn, is
    understood as a policy crisis, not as a state
    crisis.

3. With the aim of achieving the differentiated and complementary organisation of production over the whole of the national territory, spatial policy has identified the subnational region as the optimum scale for the purpose. And, consistent with the failure of the regional policy and the proposal for decentralisation, spatial policy has chosen a new spatial scale: the 'small region' of the local community. In this conception, the community is the territorial basis for social mobilisation (Friedmann, 1982a) and the population is considered homogeneous, free from conflicts. Again the state is seen as the conciliatory element of society, planning as a process of solving conflicts, and the region as an interface between the state and the local population.

4. The basic argument of this approach, considering industrialisation and regional policies as a failure is an oversimplification. On the contrary, they may be seen as successful in helping the expansion of international enterprises and modernisation in national territories. The real problem lies, on the one hand, in the contradictions generated by this model and, on the other, in the fact that regional policies have become obsolete and powerless to overcome such contradictions manifested in the contemporary crisis.

It must therefore be asked: what is the effect of the proposed alternative policy on the state? Is this policy able to find a language that can speak for the nation? Is it sufficiently representative to legitimate the state?

Marxist Structural Analysis

In Marxist structural analysis, state and regional crises are explicit. There are, however, other kinds of limitation to understand them:

1. The political dimension is minimised: the crisis is understood as a product of the determination of the economic structure. Under global capitalism and the pressure of international competition, hypermobile monopoly capital is driven to discover new locational strategies which will permit surplus profit to be realised. A new interregional division of labour is brought about, together with a regional

crisis: some regions decline while others grow,
and problems also arise in the growing regions
as a result of the disruption of prevailing
social condition. The search for cheap labour
leading to the industrialisation of regional
labour reserves is stressed by some authors as
one of the basic mechanisms of regional crisis
(Carney, Hudson, Lewis, 1980). Unequal
geographical development and the geographical
transfer of value are other fundamental issues
to be related to regional crisis (Lipietz, 1980;
Soja, 1981).

2. The state crisis and its relation with the
   regional crisis is made explicit; however, the
   state is reduced to a mere instrument of monopoly
   capital. Its main role is to co-ordinate the new
   interregional division of labour required by
   accumulation imperatives. Therefore, its crisis
   derives from the fact that it is no longer
   capable of performing this role. There is an
   aggregate irrationality of relationships between
   accumulation imperatives and the state; "State
   monopoly capitalism has begun to lose control, a
   process which is most clearly expressed at a
   regional level" (Carney, Hudson, Lewis, 1980).
   Although limits to state power and control are
   recognised, again it is a crisis not of the state,
   but of its co-ordinating role.

3. The role of space is also minimised. It is not
   known what type of regional scale the problems
   refer to; nor does the region possess a social
   content - it is simply an object for capital
   manipulation while regional problems derive
   increasingly from state interventions. It is,
   however, recognised that unsolved regional
   problems can give rise to social crisis.

4. The political alternative for the state is not
   clear.

The Need for Political Geography

It can be seen from the above that the two lines of approach
mentioned have similar limitations:

1. Both minimise the political dimension: the
   state is regarded as a unit without the actors
   and their conflicts being specified, and as
   having only one function, that of dominating or
   conciliating;

2. Both minimise space, draining it of its social
   content and giving to it either excessive

        autonomy or none at all. They make it into a
        mere object to be manipulated by a single actor;
3. Both deal with policy or economic regionalisation,
        in which the region is seen as a conceived and
        imposed spatial division; the region as an active
        historical product - that is to say, considering
        population's rights to its territory - is not
        taken into account, thus making it difficult to
        examine its relationship with the state.

A place has therefore been opened up for a fundamental contribution from political geography, as long as it is able to overcome its own limitations: the apparent apolitical nature of its unidimensional and totalitarian conception of the nation-state as the only source of power. This conception is harmful to scientific analysis because it considers only one scale of spatial analysis, namely that delimited by the political boundaries of states, and because it denies the existence of conflicts inside the state. Today in view of the state crisis, it is no longer possible to deny that power is multidimensional. This implies the recognition of social agents with different and frequently conflicting strategies that are to be found on different intra-national spatial scales. This recognition would necessarily change the conception of the state usually held in political geography, rewinning this field of geography for the social sciences (Becker, 1982a).

THE CONFLICT BETWEEN THE STATE AND THE CORPORATIONS

The state crisis is an expression of the politico-economic contradiction that has emerged in the power bloc at this end of the twentieth century; the contradiction between the state and the corporation, due to the growing power of the latter parallel to state fragmentation.

The state crisis is a facet of the present global economic and political crisis originating in the new system of accumulation - monetary accumulation - developed in core countries. The international crisis has two faces: the accumulation crisis of core countries where the rate of profits and accumulation decreases and the growing debt of peripheral countries where financing and investments were made by core countries with extraordinary high rates of interest. The growing debt creates a new type of dependence that reduces state political autonomy in foreign affairs and destroys its credibility within the nation.

This process has a spatial expression: corporation strategy no longer favours the existing regions, thus reducing at the same time the role of the state and of the region.

Accumulation imperatives: the strategy of the enterprise in favour of the country and the locality.

After World War II, between 1950-70, the reconstruction of the economic order brought out the significance of the region and the strengthening of the state apparatus. The subnational regional scale appears to have been the optimum spatial scale for the politico-economic strategy which aims at unifying markets and political power in national territories. It is the optimum territorial basis for operations leading to accumulation on a productive basis, concentrating economic and political power and organising a monopoly through a process of destroying or co-opting the economic and political hegemonies that control the whole of the subnational space. At such a time the interests of private enterprise and the government coincide completely, thus strengthening the state apparatus; regional policy becomes one with nation-building.

In Brazil, production of consumer durables and capital goods by foreign capital became the dynamic core of the economy, with the state participating as an entrepreneur and creating preconditions and incentives. The industrial growth of São Paulo and Rio de Janeiro was based on the geographical extension of the markets and mobilisation of labour and resources. Mobile capital seeks to penetrate all sectors of the economy and all spaces. Incentives and subsidies for capitalisation were institutionalised in sectoral and regional agencies in order to favour the transfer of capital. Concentration of enterprises gave rise to a centre-periphery spatial structure, helped by regional development bodies for macro-regions, established in the country in the 1960s.

The main reaction to the "unifying" movement took place in the regional power bloc of the Northeast region. Co-optation of regional hegemonies and the partial modernising homogenisation of the region made possible both the economic growth of enterprises and corporations and the rearticulation of power in a centralised form. Provincial governments lost their decision-making power since the resolution of conflicts was transferred to national scales. Labour force and peasant reactions were repressed by the new national bloc in power, which included the corporations and the co-opted elites.

The contradictions between the state and the corporation in the world economy has its roots in the reorganisation of the capitalist system at the beginning of the 1970s on the basis of the large corporation. Technological development of production and transportation make the large organisations independent of their immediate environment (Aydalot, 1981). Capital becomes hypermobile. This independence is a trump-card which allows them to take advantage of the diversity of space and seek lower-cost resources for operations split up among different countries.

This therefore renders obsolete the conventional

principles governing the location of firms which aim at
ensuring external economies, since the corporations
internalises the greater part of their technical and
industrial relations. National economies cease to be
isolated states (Holland, 1976); large enterprises select
less developed countries for their location, and within
these countries, the most appropriate localities. At the
same time, there is a tendency towards reducing accumulation
on a productive basis and increasing monetary accumulation.

In peripheral countries such as Brazil, financial
capital investments parallel capital productive ones and land
speculation becomes an alternative for investment, during the
1970s. Intense labour mobility was induced by state
policies to meet the needs of the new investment poles in the
metropolitan region and on the frontier (Becker and Machado,
1980; Becker, 1981, 1982b). In view of the world-wide scale
of its activity and of its movement towards monetary
accumulation, as far as the corporation is concerned, the
existing subnational region loses its significance as a basis
of operations, its place being taken by the country as a
whole; within the country corporations begin a new economic
regionalisation through the allocation of huge production
units in selected places, isolated from their environment but
with close connections with the other units of the
corporation located in different countries.

World diffusion of a model based on intensive technology
and consumerism is not carried out without structural
tensions taking place. There is ever sharper competition for
space as a source of raw materials, as a labour reserve, as a
market and as a reserve of value, competition which also takes
place within the peripheral countries which are becoming
industrialised. The growing functional integration, with a
withdrawal of the decision-making nucleus from the socio-
spatial basis, means a loss of information which makes itself
felt as a drop in creativity and innovation, particularly in
connection with ways of meeting the new social needs and
problems brought about by the technology itself. Highly
concentrated as it is in certain sectors, technology is
unable to diffuse itself into the other sectors of society
essential for answering their social requirements.

Within this framework, the small local "region"
possesses positive features for overcoming problems of the
corporations. It makes it possible (Becker, 1982a): (1) to
use new labour reserves on site, reducing migration to the
big cities and lessening social costs and tensions; (2) to
save scarce resources, undertake more effective exploration
and discover new local raw materials, especially in the
primary energy and foodstuffs sectors; (3) to transfer the
cost of development to the community itself; (4) to obtain
vital information for control and innovation; (5) to expand
the market for the new industrial products of the age of

electronics and telecommunications. It also makes it possible to maintain patterns of regionally differentiated preference, since there are decreasing marginal returns for innovation once it has spread to a certain extent and, in addition to this point, non-innovation may again be an economic advantage (Stöhr, 1980).

The strongest roots of the crisis lie, however, in the political and social fields, owing to the reduction that has been taking place in the efficiency of the decision-making systems of nation-states.

The strategy of the state, the region and the limits of government power in peripheral countries

The penetration of meso-power (Holland, 1976) into the peripheral countries has been made possible by the state. By socialising losses by means of subsidies and investing directly in the sectors where investments are greater and capital returns are slower, the state has continued the process of modernisation. Once they have reached a certain size, state enterprises acquire growing autonomy; thanks to the financial power they accumulate, they ally themselves to international groups which control the technology they need (Furtado, 1980).

Between 1950 and 1970 the policy of regional development via investment in infrastructure and incentives or disincentives was basic for the expansion of the core's services and industries into the periphery. In the 1970s the emergence of the transnational corporation, while becoming independent of the subnational scale and attaching greater importance to countries and localities, weakens the nation-state: government intervention loses its influence on the locational decisions taken by the large enterprises which because of their high degree of sectoral and spatial mobility, do not depend on price competition or on transport (although in peripheral countries transport is still vital for the opening up of regions). At the end of the decade, the external debt reinforces the peripheral countries dependence on global capital.

In this process the contradiction between the global social interests and the private interests of capital becomes stronger, manifesting itself in many contradictions between and within national societies:

1. As regional policy becomes inoperative, and as debts grow, competition sharpens between countries whose incentives now no longer have the problem-region in view, but aim instead to attract capital to the country, so as not to halt economic growth. Problems linked to regional interests cease to have priority for the state,

and the regional development bodies set up in
previous years are depleted.

In Brazil, spatial policy begins to be
undertaken for the country as a whole and for
selected localities producing territorial
integration around urban and regional development poles. Incentives facilitate the spatial
adaption of firms and favour exports and the
appropriation of lands as reserves of value,
compensating for the burden of inflation on
productive investments. As a result there is
an extraordinary extension of land appropriation in the Amazonian frontier area. In the
last few years, central government agencies or
state-run enterprises, financed by foreign
capital, have developed giant projects in
selected localities which are run directly by
them, thus appropriating segments of various
provincial territories. As a result a new
regionalisation emerges, induced by the state.

2. A situation emerges of a state capitalism with
   liberal measures for the enterprise, the
   situation of an authoritarian state with a
   government fragmented into powerful state-run
   and private enterprises. This, then, gives rise
   in the alliance between private enterprises and
   the state to a contradiction between measures to
   safeguard national interests and the need to
   liberalise the policy of commercial exchange and
   investments. The integration of nation-states
   into the world economic system dominated by
   meso-power implies the loss of economic
   sovereignty, and of sovereignty in regional
   policy which becomes inoperative. Nation-states
   reduce their power of co-ordination since their
   economic and social activities can no longer
   always be kept compatible with national aims.
   This happens as a result of the fact that part of
   the productive resources are inserted into
   subsystems which extend into other national
   economies and possess a logic of their own which
   is to some extent autonomous (Furtado, 1980).

3. The corporation/state contradiction, i.e. between
   the economic and the political levels, generates
   a new contradiction: the need of maintaining the
   state and the limits of national territories to
   sustain the spatial differentiation vital for
   the corporations, while at the same time,
   national states reduce their decision-making
   power.

4. Within the nation, the state's spatial strategy
   brings about many conflicts. One of them is
   between central and provincial governments. The
   new regionalisation undertaken by the state
   overlaps provincial boundaries; keeping the
   decision-making power over the new territory,
   the state by-passes provincial governments which
   lose power over part of their own territories.
5. The location of transnational units ignoring the
   problem-regions also brings a growing divergence
   between private costs and social costs: the
   inadequate use made of basic social capital in
   the problem regions and the high cost of
   congestion for the government in the developed
   centres (Holland, 1976) expressed in metro-
   polisation. These costs, transferred to wage
   demands, represent higher production costs. At
   the same time, there are social movements
   against the inability of the state to provide
   all the infrastructure needed.
6. The result is that at the same time as economic
   growth is proceeding rapidly, the effectiveness
   of national decision-making systems is being
   reduced, and there is a decline in the ability
   of national governments to interpret the social
   aspirations of their respective countries or to
   make them compatible with the economic objectives.
   The disparity between the economic and the
   social accumulates structural problems,
   generating economic crisis and social tensions
   at local level.

In Brazil, underlying these movements is the intense
spatial mobility of the labour force, which is led to move
from one area to another in order to answer the needs of the
various investment poles generated by the growing mobility
of financial capital. Such mobility signifies the
disruption of a population with its territory. In the rural
areas the breaking of the ties with the land transforms
peasants into wage-earners; the conflict is one of loss of
territory and reveals itself in the struggle for access to
the land. In towns and cities, where the labour force piles
up on the periphery, the conflict is one of trying to create
a new territory for itself revealed in demands for access to
work and housing (Becker, 1982a).

It is the population at local level who suffer the
impact of the continuous spatial reorganisation; and as a
result they resist the manipulation of their territories.
And since, owing to this same process of integration and
centralisation, they are denied any channels of expression,
they manifest their opposition to the state directly from the

territorial base in which they live, outside the institution-al framework (Becker, 1982a).

Centralisation made possible with the co-optation of regional hegemonies broke the links of communication with the base, making the summit incapable of turning into and registering social grievances. The elimination or incorporation of regional hegemonies suppressed a whole range of negotiations which had enabled the government to control the region; there is an extension of the front on which conflicts are taking place. Government thus no longer keeps the movements under control. In order to maintain its control of space, it tries to co-opt the movements or to institutionalise power at the local level, which would be capable of negotiating and articulating with it. Hence the interest also by the state in the strategy of decentralising the decision-making power (Becker, 1982a).

CONCLUDING REMARKS

It is possible to come to some conclusions about the situation just analysed, taking Brazilian reality in 1983 as a basis.

The state
As a politico-bureaucratic institutional whole made up of groups of various political leanings, ideologies and interests, the state is neither a neutral mediator nor a mere instrument of capital. It is not a neutral mediator as it acts in favour of the interests of the dominant groups, and it is thanks to its mediation that the transnational corporations expansion into the peripheral countries has been made possible. Nor is it a new instrument of capital: by appropriating part of the surplus, this state becomes a decisive force in productive investments and in labour force reproduction through social legislation. As a result of the amplification and growing complexity of its duties and the adoption of modern technology in connection with them, the state gains autonomy; it circumscribes the modernisation process and develops reform programmes in strategic areas.

The two opposing positions - neutral mediator or instrument - forget that as a unity of the political and civil society, the state ensures the material and ideal conditions for the hegemonic role of bourgeoisie. It is a mediator of class interests which on a consensus basis, reproduces the necessary conditions for the functioning of the compromise between social classes; that is, the state does not interfere in the economic sphere only: through ideologic institutions it reproduces its own legitimisation (Altavater and Maya, 1981).

The State Crisis and the Region

Furthermore, the state is at the same time subject and
instrument and to each new historic subject corresponds a
new organ of direction of allied social groups and of
domination of antagonic social groups, a situation that seems
to be emerging at the end of the twentieth century.

The state crisis
The state is being transformed through a crisis/restructur-
ation process. There is a growing contradiction between the
main interests of the large economic groups on the one hand,
and the overall social interests of the nation on the other,
a contradiction which is at the root of the present state
crisis. In favouring the corporations, the state has
created a situation in which it is gradually losing decision
power. Moreover, owing to the extraordinary political
centralisation of the last few decades, the state has become
incapable of controlling all activities and providing all
means to attend its commitments, a situation that is being
aggravated by the present shortage of resources. Social
movements at local level question the state's managerial
capacity as do the corporations.
Crises however are double-faced: contradictions become
more acute at the same time that restructuration takes place.
In this late twentieth-century crisis, tendencies towards
restructuration are awakening with a new correlation of
forces.
The new imperatives of monetary accumulation are
extending in Brazil corporation action to sectors and spaces
that were formerly "reserved" for state dominion, either
direct state dominion or that of state enterprises. In this
process, the corporations are seeking to act directly,
relegating the state to a secondary position, substituting or
reducing its role as a mediator and taking over direct
financing of state government programmes, government research
institutions, etc., with a bitter struggle going on in the
technological sector - especially in the field of information
control and data processing - and in the banking sector.
Tensions are emerging from this competition between the state
and the corporations; the corporations advance as far as they
can, but they cannot (must not) destroy the state.
The state crisis is not, therefore, a crisis of
managerial capacity, that is only the given appearance; it is
in fact a political crisis, a crisis of legitimisation,
related to the conflict within the power bloc.

State, corporations and social movement
New forms of state legitimisation are thus necessary,
concerning both the corporations and the state itself. In
Brazil, the discourse of popular participation and

decentralisation of decision-making seems to be the new mode
which, paradoxically, serves the interests of very different
segments with distinct ideologies and motivations: To begin
with the opposing interests of the corporations and the
social movements. Rural and urban community organisation
has been the keystone of Catholic Church action with social
justice as its aim; it is also the policy followed by the
World Bank in order to release financing, as well as the
regional development policy alternative, a selective tactic
which allows the use of local factors, makes accumulation
possible in the peripheral regions with a minimum of
investment, and prevents the mobility of the population from
overflowing on to the national level where it causes
tensions which the state can no longer control.

The social movements, authentic and fundamental as a
process of creating popular political awareness, are
extremely fragmented, and their action is localised. They do
not yet represent an organising force capable of supporting
the state in the direction of overall social interests, for
they are vulnerable to co-optation by various actors and by
state institutionalisation.

Thus the corporations appear to be dominant in the
political movement towards state fragmentation, character-
ising this crisis not as a revolutionary one, but as a
rearrangement of forces within the power bloc, in which the
nation-state seems to have a smaller role to play compared
with the direct action of the corporations. This also means
that the only possible force capable of resisting the growing
domination of global capitalism is being weakened.

Within this complex and contradictory configuration,
it is becoming very difficult to discern what, socially
speaking, has priority, and this difficulty shows itself in
some of the antagonic political positions in the country.
For example: (1) one of them sees the state as the only
possible force capable of looking after overall social
interests and considers that the maintenance of the state in
its centralised character - although not so strongly, has
priority at any price, even at the cost of institutionalising
the social movements, a position sustained by part of the left
and by some national financial groups; (2) another position,
held by another part of the left, part of the Church and the
local states, believes that the strengthening of the social
movements is a viable possibility and considers decentralisation a priority matter even if it runs the risk of the
co-optation or repression of the movements; (3) to a third
position, supported by transnational groups and part of the
technocrats, decentralisation is the solution for the
continuance of modernisation and the technological process,
even at the cost of the autonomy of the nation-state

It seems that together with neoliberalism a new
conception emerges whose declared objective consists in

"disorganisation" of organised capitalism and "de-statisation"
of state capitalism, placing the brutal sectoral market
forces against the interests of large sectors of the
population. That is, the disorganising trends of the market
economy themselves become conservative movements strengthening
the bourgeoisie domination (Altavater and Maya, 1981).

All these arguments point out to a position in favour
of the maintenance of the state with a certain degree of
centralisation at least for the moment.

State, space and power

The state's legitimisation crisis implies the restructuration
of "state" space and of the region.

As a constituent of social reality, space is power and
the new correlation of forces in the power bloc will
necessarily be expressed in the production of a new space.

After World War II the growing co-ordination action of
the state was done using space as its main instrument. The
state tended to control flows and stocks and to ensure their
co-ordination by integrating previous space and producing its
own space, a political, logistical space with general and
strategic interests which is set against the local space of
private interests and objectives. In this way the state
generated a specific product, a two-faced global/fragmented
abstract space where there is a minimum of consensus which is
a condition for general economic, social and political -
reproduction (Lefebvre, 1978).

Today, corporations extend their action to the abstract
"state" space which tends to be restructured. Once their
action must be developed in concrete space, on a territorial
basis, they also provoke a territorial reorganisation.

In this context there is a process of dissolution/
reproduction of regions acting at the same time in two
opposite directions:

1. Economic and political integration of national
   territory involving the partial economic
   homogenisation and regional productive process
   and co-optation of its hegemonies as well as
   the territorial disruption of the regional
   populations, a process tending to destroy
   regional identities.
2. New economic-political regionalisation promoted
   by corporations in association with the state,
   immense regions profiting from selected local
   conditions and rapidly implanting a complete
   co-ordinated system of exploitation, a process
   tending to be independent from regional historic
   roots and even not respecting provincial state
   boundaries. At the same time "local regions"

through community organisation are induced.

State, region and legitimation

The state crisis seems to be related to the process of
homogenisation of existing regions and formation of new ones
linked to the new correlation of political forces. It is
acting through the regions that state's legitimisation is
achieved. Spatial and political restructuring may bring
regionalisms against the state. However, the cultural
identity of the region as a nucleus of nationality, is
essential for the state. Regional coalitions are also
essential because, operating on an intermediate level, they
are more capable of promoting and controlling transformation
than alliances at national level, and because the existence
of various regional blocs gives the state a wide margin for
negotiation.

Through this negotiation the state performs a certain
social role, being able to attend different segments of the
population of different regions. And, as an ideologic
instrument, the region is a basis for state's legitimisation:
national integration is seen as a process for equal regional
development.

Thus the region, the spatial expression of the
differentiation in the mode of production and contradictory
relations of power, emerges from this analysis as an
expression of a contradiction in the expansion of the mode
of production and social reproduction and inside the state
in a given social formation. It represents the resistence to
homogenisation and, as such, it needs to be dissolved, but it
is also functional because regional differentiation ensures
the state's survival and therefore needs to be reproduced.
At different moments of overcoming the divisions spatial
scales become privileged.

If regional "crisis" may be a consequence of state's
action, state's crisis may be seen associated to the process
of regional homogenisation/differentiation. Present subnational regions and blocs are losing their role as a result
of the fragmentation of the state brought about by the
growing autonomy of the corporations and their locational
strategies, which are creating new regions. And in this
process the state is becoming more vulnerable to fragmentation by the corporations and is going through a crisis of
legitimisation.

Finally, two points should be stressed for further
reflection. The first one refers to the issue of scale.

It seems that in huge countries like Brazil, regional
scale could be the optimum spatial scale for the strategy
of unifying and legitimising the nation-state, not for power
centralisation, but on the contrary, for decentralising
decision-making power and resources to provincial governments

and activating the regions representation as basic nuclei of
nationality.
The second refers to the issue of culture. Throughout
the process of homogenisation/differentiation of the
historical region a cultural identity is left, the relic of
a former age, which remains not only in loco but also in the
population whom modernisation has made to suffer territorial
disruption. Thus the social movements would seem to
reproduce regional identity, keeping alive popular-based
regionalism in a fragmented form which yet reveals the
potential importance of culture as a social force.

REFERENCES

Altavater, E. and Carlos, M. (1981) 'Capitalismo monopolista
    de Estado', Cuadernos Politicos, 29, Ediciones Era,
    Mexico
Aydalot, P. (1981) 'The Regional Policy and Spatial Strategy
    of Large Organisations', in A. Kuklinski (ed.),
    Polarized Development and Regional Policies, Mouton
    Publishers, The Hague
Becker, K. and Machado, O. (1980) 'Labour Mobility in
    Amazonia: a Geographical Contribution', in International
    Geographical Union, Brazilian Geographical Studies,
    IGU's National Commission of Brazil, Rio de Janeiro
Becker, K. (1981) The state and the land question in the
    frontier: a geographical contribution, IGU's National
    Commission of Brazil, Rio de Janeiro. (English
    translation, 1982)
Becker, K. (1982a) 'The Political Use of Territory',
    paper presented IGU's Latin America Regional Conference,
    Rio de Janeiro
Becker, K. (1982b) 'Strategies for social differentiation
    and labour mobility in Amazonia: a neglected field in
    regional development theory and policy', paper
    presented at Seminar on regional development
    alternatives in the Third World, Commission on Regional
    Systems and Policies (IGU), Belo Horizonte
Carney, J., Hudson, R. and Lewis, G. (1980) Regions in crisis
    Croom Helm, London
Carney, J. (1980) 'Regions in Crisis: Accumulation, Regional
    Problems and Crisis Formation', in J. Carney et al.,
    (eds.), Regions in Crisis, Croom Helm, London, 28-49
Damette, F. (1980) 'The Regional Framework of Monopoly
    Exploitation: New Problems and Trends', in J. Carney
    et al., (eds.), Regions in Crisis, Croom Helm, London
    76-92
Duarte, A. C. (1980) 'Regionalização - Consideraçoes
    Metodológicas', Boletim. Geogradia Teoretica, 10, (2)
    AGETEC, Rio Claro

Friedmann, J. and Douglass, M. (1978) 'Agropolitan
    Development: Towards a New Strategy for Regional Planning
    in Asia', in Fu-Cheu Lo and K. Salih (eds.), Growth Pole
    Strategy and Regional Development Policy, Pergamon Press,
    Oxford
Friedmann, J. (1982) 'Regional Planning for Rural
    Mobilization in Africa', paper presented at Symposium on
    Regional Development Alternatives, Commission on
    Regional Systems and Policies, (IGU), Belo Horizonte
Friedmann, J. (1982) 'Political and Technical Moments in
    Development: Agropolitan Development Revisited', Mimeo
Furtado, C. (1980) Pequena Introdução ao Desenvolvimento -
    Enfoque Interdisciplinar, Cia. Ed. Nacional,
    Rio de Janeiro
Holland, S. (1976) The Regional Problem, McMillan, London
Lacoste, Y. (1976) La Géographie, Ça Sert a Faire la Guèrre,
    Masrepo, Paris
Lipietz, A. (1977) Le Capital et son espace, Maspero, Paris
Lefebvre, H. (1973) La Survie du Capitalism, Ed. Anthropos,
    Paris
Lefebvre, H. (1978) De l'Etet. 4: Les Contradictions de l'Etat
    Moderne, Union Génerale d'Editions, Paris
Massey, D. (1978) 'Regionalism: Some Current Issues',
    Capital and Class, 6, 106-25
Markusen, A. R. (1981) 'Region and Regionalism: a Marxist
    Approach', Mimeo
Soja, E. W. (1980) 'The Socio-Spatial Dialectic', Annals,
    Association of American Geographers, 70, 226-37
Soja, E. W. (1981) 'A materialist interpretation of
    Spatiality', paper presented at Colloquium on
    Geographical Transfer of Value, Canberra
Stöhr, W.B.(1980) 'Development from Below: the Bottom-Up and
    Periphery Inward Development Paradigm', Diskussion, 6,
    IIR, Wien
Stöhr, W.B.(1982) 'The World Economic System and the
    Development Alternatives', paper presented at Seminar
    of the Commission on Regional Systems and Policies,
    Latin American Regional Conference, (IGU), Belo
    Horizonte and Rio de Janeiro

Chapter Seven

PARTITION - A PROBLEM IN POLITICAL GEOGRAPHY

Stanley Waterman

INTRODUCTION

Partition is a term, commonly used in the context of sovereign
states, in which an existing political geographical entity is
divided into two or more separate parts. Is it simply a
general term to describe several different phenomena or
processes or is it something sharper which can be described,
explained and modelled? Is it simply another word to explain
such processes as independence, boundary development,
secession and separation (see Smith, 1982)? Some preliminary
thoughts on the topic of partition are presented here, and by
asking tentative questions and using examples, I provide some
food for thought and future action. Two short case studies
are presented in which the problem of partition is encountered
and is central.

With only a small number of exceptions (Spate 1947, 1948;
Pounds, 1964; Mayfield, 1955; Ahmad, 1953; Jones, 1960)
precious little exists in the literature of geography
specifically relating to partition in its political-
geographical sense. As Pounds (1964) pointed out some two
decades ago, even an adequate dictionary definition for the
word is lacking.

The Oxford English Dictionary offers several definitions
for the word 'partition', none of them in the sense that we,
as political geographers, might use it. It is defined as
follows:

1. The action of parting or dividing into parts, or
   division into shares or portions.
2. The action of parting or separating two or more
   persons or things
3. Something that separates
4. Each of the parts into which any whole is
   divided, as by boundaries or lines - a portion -
   part - division or section
5. In a legal sense - a division of real property,
   especially lands between joint tenants or

> tenants in common, a judicial decree or
> private act of parliament by which contenancy
> or co-ownership is abolished and their
> individual interests are separated; a division
> into severalty.

The fourth and fifth definitions come closest to what we
want. As geographers, we have to alter the scale of the
definition from real property - the estate, the farm, the
house - to that of the state.

A more adequate definition has been provided in a
dictionary devoted to Political Science (Plano et al., 1974,
274) in which it is stated that partition is:

> The division of territory between two or more
> sovereign entities. Partition can involve an
> entire state, a portion thereof, or an area that
> does not have the status of statehood. Partition
> may be imposed by a powerful state upon a weaker
> one by war or by threat of war. It might also
> occur as a result of mutual agreement or as a
> method of peaceful settlement offered by a third
> state or international organisation, as in
> mediation or arbitration. Partition may be
> determined by political elites or by plebiscites
> or other forms of self-determination.

Muir (1975) refers to partitioned states as 'politico-
territorial anomalies', ranging from the temporary to the
permanent. The essential feature of this is that the parts
of the partitioned state function as two separate states,
thus exhibiting at least de facto sovereignty, and represent
a geographic realignment of political forces.

In essence, partition is a process resulting from a
situation in which two or more groups differentiated on the
basis of ethnicity, nationality or ideology find conditions
more comfortable to govern separate, more uniform areas than
to live in partnership with one another. Thus, partition
usually results when a specific combination of political
and geographical forces are sufficiently strong to permit it.
The smaller and weaker a group, or the less one of its
powerful political supporters pushes for it, the less likely
is that group to win independence through partition, some
other solution, such as autonomy, provincial or cantonal
status, or incorporation as a separate unit into a federal
state, being sought to answer its grievances. Partition is
associated with more extreme forms of political instability
or lack of political viability (Hartshorne, 1960), but such
conditions do not always lead to partition.

Perhaps the word "partition" appears in the geographic
literature less frequently than might be expected because it

has taken on a more general and abstract meaning, such as the division of any geographical space into two or more constituent and smaller parts (Haggett, Cliff and Frey, 1977, 454-456). Even in the field of political geography, the term is being increasingly used to describe the internal division of the state. Short (1981:130) notes that "most states are divided into a number of separate and distinct units ... (This) partitioning may reflect administrative convenience, political differences or historical accident." Short also notes that partitioning leads to different policies being exerted in different areas, leading in the longer term to marked spatial differentiation, he is thus using the term in the sense of a redesigning of the political geography of administrative areas (Adejuyigbe, 1983).

Partition is related to plural states, plural societies and their changing interrelationships and intrarelationships such as war, boundary changes, peace treaties, compromise, occurring either when the contending sides reach the conclusion or have it forced upon them that it is preferable to live apart under separate sovereignty than to live together under one roof. If federalism is sometimes referred to as the 'ideal geographical' solution to the problems of ethnic minorities within states (de Blij and Glassner, 1980, 112), then because of the way in which it brings about boundary changes, partition is the 'un-ideal' solution, the solution of 'last resort'. At the same time, it might be thought of as the 'best worst solution' - preferable to war. Partition is a 'parting of the ways', perhaps temporary, in which a single state metamorphoses into two new states, each of which often sees itself as the legitimate heir to the raison d'etre of the unit which existed prior to partition. So, in addition to the creation of more than one state where only one had previously existed or the transfer of territory from one state to another, new state, partition also involves a change or loss of identity (Pounds, 1964: 162).

The creation of new states through the geographical and political partition of older ones is not novel to the twentieth century (Hachey, 1972, xi). The division of Poland in the eighteenth century amongst the major European empires is usually referred to as the 'Partition of Poland'. The term is sometimes used also when dealing with the collapse of the great empires - Austria-Hungary, Turkey, Russia, Spain and France. However, these examples are not entirely relevant to partition as a modern twentieth century politico-geographical process and the term usually used to describe the changes following the collapse of empires is "break-up" or "collapse".

In the twentieth century, several examples spring to mind. Many have already forgotten the partition of Sweden into the separate kingdoms of Sweden and Norway in 1905

(a dynastic split) - mainly because the Swedes and
Norwegians have permitted us to forget it. Ireland in the
1920s provided a legacy which lives on to the present day;
Palestine of the 1940s has almost turned a full circle;
India's partition has since undergone a further stage - and it
was never a simple partition scheme in the first place;
Vietnam was partitioned and then unified; both Koreas talk of
reunification in some form or another; German reunification,
it would appear, remains the dream of one side mainly. Cyprus
finally underwent de facto partition in 1974 following the
invasion of the island by Turkish forces and the population
exchanges that took place in the wake of the occupation, a
process extended further in late 1983. Rwanda and Burundi are
now separate states having been administered together as
Ruanda-Urundi by the Belgians. In addition, Denmark is
currently undergoing partition, as Greenland seeks independence. This represents a peculiar form of partition, as it
does not involve a land border. South Africa is administering
its own peculiar form of partition as it grants 'independence'
to the Bantustans, and Canada and Lebanon are often seen as
prime candidates for partition among those states with ethnic
problems the solution of which might prove otherwise difficult
(Knight, 1983a; Kliot, 1983).

BASIC QUESTIONS

Is partition simply a general catch-all for several different
processes which bear only superficial resemblance to one
another? Are there any common threads that run through the
cases outlined above? Can we construct a model through which
we can determine when partition will occur and when another,
less drastic, solution will work to solve the problems of
conflict within a state?

Several questions concerning partition should be
addressed first before examining two short case studies.
These questions are neither all-encompassing nor exhaustive
and they include:

1. Is partition planned and/or perceived as a
    temporary or permanent solution to a set of
    problems? Partition leads to separate
    statehood although perception of the time
    factor is variable. Thus what appears to be
    permanent in the short term may well be
    perceived as temporary given a more extensive
    view of time. Thus, partition and its spatial
    and behavioural consequences should be seen in
    the overall light of integration and formation
    of states on the one hand, and their
    disintegration and partition on the other.

2. Is it a voluntary or imposed solution? Are the
   origins of partition from within the state
   itself or are they imposed by external forces?
3. What kind of political and economic consequences
   arise as a result of partition?
4. What spatial forms are associated with partition?
5. Can we predict the type of state in which
   partition is more likely to be proposed as a
   solution to an existing problem?

PERMANENCY AND IMPOSITION

Whether a partition is perceived and designed as a final
solution to a set of problems is related to the more complex
question of whether all partitions are, in fact, identical or
at least, similar. Henderson and Lebow (1974) make a sharp
distinction between <u>divided nations</u> and <u>partitioned countries</u>.
In both cases, single states have been divided into two or
more separate sovereign states, but for radically different
reasons.

Amongst the divided nations, they give the examples of
Germany, Korea, Mongolia, China, Vietnam, Laos and Cambodia
(note the year of writing - 1974). Among the partitioned
countries, they include Austria-Hungary, India, Indochina,
Palestine, Cyprus, Ireland and even Holland and Belgium.

They note that at the time of separation each dyad of
the <u>divided nation</u> was to a considerable degree identical
culturally, ethnically and linguistically. In this case, we
are definitely dealing with a one-nation concept in which
leaders on both sides have been reluctant to relinquish the
idea of common nationality. If we accept this basic
dichotomy among states which have undergone such a
fundamental transformation, East Germany stands out possibly
as a major exception, claiming national uniqueness on the
basis of its socialist system - a rare instance of nationality
being determined on the basis of an economic system.
Certainly, the one-nation theme is expounded primarily by the
Federal Republic (Mellor, 1978 : 180-81).

In these cases, ideology is the main instrument for
structuring separate identities and justifying a separate
existence. The further apart the ideologies remain from one
another, the more permanent the partition would appear to be.
However, if the ideologies appear close or if tensions relax
between the individual states or between their major
supporters, then the partition often appears less permanent.
Henderson and Lebow (1974:438-439) note that relations among
divided states are a function of (1) the degree of stability
and legitimacy of each divided state, (2) the relations
between the divided state and its superpower and (3) the
current superpower relationships. It is worth noting,

however, that the political and economic viability of a divided state might also be a considerable factor here.

If the divided nations see themselves as the sole legitimate successors of a prior state or nation and have asserted a legal identity with the forerunner, unification is more likely to remain an ultimate aim. Thus, North Vietnam saw itself as the sole legal successor of the Vietnamese nation - in its eyes, the existence of two separate states bearing the name Vietnam was an impossible situation. In South Vietnam, where interests lay in containing the Communist insurgence within the state and in maintaining the existence of a non-Communist state in South Vietnam, the partition was viewed as permanent and unification of the Vietnamese nation was not a major goal. Until recently, a similar situation existed in the German case, though with the roles reversed, the Federal Republic acting the role of legitimate successor to the German state defeated in World War II.

So, in the case of divided nations, unification often remains as an ultimate aim and can be brought about either by war or through a political settlement. However, in the absence of sufficient military power to bring about the first solution or of sufficient political and/or ideological flexibility to permit the second, a third solution, peaceful coexistence, acceptance of the status quo, might result. In this case, the temporary nature of the division appears to become more permanent.

Henderson and Lebow (1974) suggest yet another possibility - a hazily-defined zone in which there is increasing co-operation between the states, as in the situation which exists among the Nordic states or between Belgium and Luxembourg - but where each state maintains its own independence. The eventual aim of reunification remains in the background, even in a situation such as this. The de facto acceptance by West Germany of the status quo in its relations with East Germany is perhaps an example of something approaching this among divided nations.

In the case of partitioned countries, partition was nevertheless intended to resolve conflict by separating hostile ethnic communities and allowing each to satisfy its demands for nationhood in separate political units, thus acting as an additional conflict-regulating practice to those outlined by Nordlinger (1977) - coalitions, proportionality, mutual veto, purposive depoliticisation, compromise and concessions. However, as we are all too well aware, this form of partition brings with it the problems of ethnic minorities "trapped" in enclaves or mixed with the majority group. The hostility between the ethnic groups that caused the partition in the first instance usually remains even after the partition and often leads to civil strife and even to outright war. Because of the intermingling of the various

ethnic groups, location of the border between them is
problematic and hardly ever satisfactory. Irredentist groups
often remain on both sides of the border and territorial
disputes tend to continue. This contrasts with the situation
in the divided nation category where, although open hostility
might exist between the rival sections of the nation, the line
of division is generally sharp and tensions are mitigated
within the state itself.

It can be hypothesised that in such partitioned countries
the partition will be perceived as permanent; in many cases,
it was indeed planned as such. The permanence becomes
apparent if irregularities and gross minority problems can be
rectified. Such solutions have been on occasion brought about
by population transfers, as in Northern India between India
and Pakistan, in Ireland and in Palestine.

Where the distinction between divided nation and
partitioned country is nebulous, as in the case of Ireland,
where the two-nation hypothesis is not generally accepted by
the Republic or the Catholics (Boal, 1980; Pringle, 1980),
the trend is to recognise the border as ephemeral.

Thus, in the case of the partitioned country, we can
point to a partition brought about, as a last resort, by the
inhabitants of the prior state, sometimes with heavy
prompting from outside forces. In the case of India, the
Muslims pressed for a state of their own, even if it did not
include all the Muslim population of British India. The
British complied with this wish - the Muslim pressure for the
creation of Pakistan eventually bringing the Hindu leaders to
the reluctant conclusion that this was the solution least
likely to bring bloodshed. The partition of Ireland was a
British solution to meet the demands of the Ulster
Protestants for protection from a Catholic-dominated Free
State. The case of Palestine involved the wider forum of
the United Nations, but essentially met the demands of the
Jews for a state of their own in Palestine.

In the cases of divided nations, in almost every case,
with the exception of China, the causal factor was
imposition by outside forces as a result of war or revolution.
It is doubtful that had not the major powers been situated in
Germany in the years immediately following World War II that
Germany would have become a divided nation. Border changes
would probably have occurred, but nothing as substantial as
the externally enforced partition. Even the Chinese case
involved the results of the Communist Revolution in China.

POLITICAL AND ECONOMIC CONSEQUENCES

Henderson and Lebow (1974) provide a paradigm of division into
four stages for understanding the relationships between states
that have undergone either partition or division. In the

Initial Stage, the states exhibit intense mutual hostility.
With time, this passes into a second, Middle Term Stage with
its de facto acceptance of one another. Rapprochement
represents the third stage, in which the separate states
attempt to carry on normal relations with one another, and
this leads to the final, Unification Stage.

One of the characteristic features of partition is that
in the period immediately following the division or partition,
the newly created states tend to be inward-looking and
mutually hostile. Only at later stages in relations between
the states does this mutual hostility relax and normal
interstate relations begin to develop. A partial explanation
might be offered by stating that their raison d'etre is as yet
poorly defined.

As a result, economic co-operation between the two
sections remains inadequately developed, it is worth noting
that because Germany was already one of the most industrially
advanced states there was greater inertia towards maintaining
some of the interregional flows that had existed prior to the
division and to encourage co-operation. Nevertheless, the
emergence of Brandt's Ostpolitik and the subsequent reaction
of East Germany occurred some twenty years after the division.
Similar examples can be given, such as in India/Pakistan, the
two parts of Cyprus and, of course, Palestine, where the
sealing off of the two sectors of Jerusalem, which symbolised
the wider sealing off of the partitioned country, was almost
total up to the Six Day War in 1967.

One of the less-well documented consequences of
partition is what might be called the "petty consequences".
Areas which prior to the imposition of the boundary had been
geographically part of a single political unit and a single
geographical region find themselves after partition in
separate states. Thus, in addition to the macroconsequences
such as arrest of economic development, which can burden the
region as a whole and, as a result, its inhabitants, there
are also the direct consequences on the residents of the
border areas in particular, such as in the splitting of
families and properties, difficulties in mobilising the
labour force and restrictions in movement and transportation
(Brawer, 1983).

There are many other spatially manifested features
associated with partition. Some of these, such as changes in
the landscape - the emergence of fortifications and boundary
fences, may result directly from a partition. Others, such
as the development of separate communal infrastructural
systems as road networks and settlements prior to the formal
division, can be thought of as catalysts in the creation of
partition, as was the case in Palestine during the British
Mandate and as might be the case in a future Lebanon.

CASE STUDY 1 : IRELAND

Ireland was partitioned effectively in 1920 as a result of
intense political activities evident from 1916 onwards.
Intense political activities were a major factor of the
Hiberno-British problem for a century or more before this,
but the Easter Rising of 1916 brought the conflict to a head
and the period around the end of World War I and immediately
following it found Britain willing to talk seriously about
the future of Ireland. It also found some Irish politicians
willing to talk to the British and make some form of
compromise from strictly - held principles.

Ireland in recent history had either been a unitary
state or part of a unitary state. Essentially, the major
cleavage in Ireland was between the "true" Irish and the
Anglo-Irish, and later between the Protestants and Catholics.
Only with the massive colonisation of Ulster in the
seventeenth century was there a clear geographical element
added to this cleavage and even then the cleavage was not
clearcut, for Presbyterians as well as Catholics were without
full rights for many years (Fitzgerald, 1972:8). However,
the differences between Ulstermen and other Irish began to
become noticeable, partly, perhaps because of the cultural
affinities of northeastern Ireland with Scotland (Buchanan,
1982; Lyons, 1979:25).

From about 1800 onwards the seeds of partition had been
sown. In the predominantly Protestant northeastern Ireland,
an industrial nucleus developed based on linen and ship-
building. This led to an area in which free trade was
important as compared to an area in the south best served by
forms of economic protection and which differed also in forms
of landholding.

The partition of the island after World War I had both
religious and economic prompting. Until relatively late in
the nineteenth century, both Home Rulers and Unionists hoped
to maintain the geographical unity of the island, the former
as a self-governing entity in association with Great Britain,
the latter as an integral part of the United Kingdom. Only
with the vivid dramatisation of events in 1916, the intense
politicisation of the religious divide and the tenacity of the
Ulster Unionists did the reality of partition strike home and
the myth of the ability to maintain unity fade away
(O'Brien, 1972 : 85-102).

There was a belief that the partition was only a
temporary device. A basic unity was being broken, marked by
an unwillingness (at least until 1979) to bring about a
divergence in the currencies or structures of the trades
unions, in customs regulations, immigration or mutual voting
rights. Ireland's joining the EEC alongside the United
Kingdom, may have served to heighten Ireland's sovereignty and
self-confidence as a state (vis-a-vis Britain) in the short

run. In the longer term, however, the differences ought to be
ironed out if one of the aims of the Common Market <u>actually is</u>
the political integration of Western Europe.

The question of how to effect partition was set out in
the Government of Ireland Act of 1920 by the British
government. Partition brought little satisfaction. The
Ulster Unionists were attracted to a nine-county Ulster but
this would have resulted in a Catholic minority of nearly
44 per cent and too many areas in which there were Protestant
minorities. In any event, county boundaries were retained
even though the 1921 Anglo-Irish Treaty recognised the "wishes
of the inhabitants" (Douglas, 1982:107-116) and an attempt was
made to alter the partition scheme in 1924 (Andrews, 1960).
The partition that resulted left many enclaves and exclaves of
both Catholics and Protestants and exhibited most of the
problems of partitioned countries in this respect.

How is partition seen in Ireland sixty years on? Have
the Irish become used to the idea of two Irelands? Are there
two Irelands? (Boal, 1980; Pringle, 1980). It would appear
that Sinn Fein is on the upswing in both parts of Ireland,
even though its absolute numbers remain small. Thus, among a
small but vociferous minority of Catholics, the partition of
Ireland is definitely seen as a temporary expedient. The
unification of Ireland and the eventual withdrawal of British
forces is the ultimate aim of this group and probably the
ultimate hope of many more Irishmen. In this sense, there may
be two or more Irish cultures but only one Irish state (see
Lyons, 1979).

On the other hand, the Unionists, too, see themselves as
part of a unitary state. They see themselves as citizens of
the United Kingdom, either as British or as Ulstermen, or in
external environments, as an exotic type of Irishman.

In the long run, the answer to whether partition is
temporary or permanent depends on the British as well as the
Irish. Partition was an agreed compromise in order to
protect the interests of the Protestant minority in Ireland by
creating a Protestant majority in part of Ulster within a
nominally Protestant United Kingdom. Objectively, several
things have changed and Great Britain may look one day on the
Northern Ireland Protestants as more of a liability than an
asset. In particular, this might be true as Ulster no
longer provides the Conservative party with automatic all-out
support at Westminster; the province has been an economic
liability for over fifty years and as the Catholic minority
could possibly become the majority (Compton, 1974:446-47).

CASE STUDY 2 : PALESTINE

If one ignores the division of the Ottoman Empire into
independent states and mandated territories that occurred

after World War I and concentrates on events in the areas administered by the French and the British under League of Nations mandates, then it was a relatively short time before proposals were made to divide these territories into more manageable entities (Biger, 1981:158-59).

In British Palestine, partition was first effected in 1922 when the eastern part, Transjordan was detached from the original mandated territory of Palestine. This partition was mainly to mollify the Hashemite family who received kingdoms in Iraq and Transjordan as compensation for non-receipt of Damascus and Syria (Kleiman, 1970:68).

The territory retaining the name Palestine, emerged as a source of contention between the Zionists, whose numbers were growing rapidly by immigration through the 1920s and 1930s and the Arabs, whose nationalism was developing slowly but significantly. The British at first encouraged Jewish immigration, when they agreed to establish a Jewish National Home in Palestine. Changes in British policies, already in evidence in the 1920s and more acute in the following two decades, brought about a favouring of the Arab cause. The seeds of a Jewish state had been sown by the 1930s with a prototype of almost every future government department evident in the Jewish Agency. By the time the British authorities realised that they were dealing with two virulent nationalisms competing for the right to sovereignty over the same territory, it was too late (Rodinson, 1968:22-40). In an effort to retard and later halt further immigration of Jews, the 1939 White Paper was published limiting the number of immigrants drastically and strictly curtailing those parts of the country which could be purchased by and sold to Jews. Nevertheless, the Jews continued to migrate and set up new settlements; the Arabs continued to resist Jewish settlement (Sykes, 1965; Segre, 1969).

Already by 1937, thought had turned to partition as a solution to the "Palestine Problem". The Royal Commission headed by Lord Peel, investigating the disturbances of 1936 approached Weizmann, as the Zionist leader most amenable to and friendly towards the British, and talks were held in which the idea of establishing a Jewish state along the coastal plain and in Galilee were broached. Although Weizmann and several other Zionists regarded the British offer as fair and accepted the idea of partitioning Palestine so as to create a Jewish state, pressure came from other members of the Zionist executive to reject the offer. More extreme Arab nationalism also won through in this regard.

Notwithstanding this opposition, plans for partition of Palestine occurred at regular intervals - the Woodhead Commission of 1938, the White Paper of 1939, the Anglo-American proposals of 1946, the U.N. Plan approved in 1947 and the Armistice Lines, which served as de facto boundaries of Palestine for the eighteen years between 1949 and 1967.

The Arab states were quite clear in statements and actions that partition was an unacceptable solution to the problems of Palestine. Their objection was of a more fundamental nature. Over the years, it would appear that some Arab states such as Egypt, and perhaps Sudan and Saudi Arabia, and even Lebanon, have come to terms with the existence of Israel and tacitly, with partition. This tacit acceptance is independent of a final solution or lack of solution to the Palestine problem. Thus, with time, one side of the equation has come to terms with it even though the sovereignty of the Arab state in the equation is not agreed by the interested parties themselves.

The other side of the coin is that partition was seen by many Israelis as a temporary expedient. Although throughout the eighteen years between 1949 and 1967 the Jewish state flourished and developed right up to the frontier in many cases, without any formal claim on territory outside the borders of the state except for the right of freedom of access to the Holy Places, several elements within Israeli society refused to recognise the legitimacy of partition. In fact, it was generally recognised that the transformation of the Armistice Lines into "permanent", legally recognised international borders would involve some alterations. Nevertheless, in the 1950s and 1960s, there were no predetermined demands for outright amalgamation of the two parts of (western) Palestine.

This changed with the Six-Day War in 1967. De facto, Mandate Palestine was reunited. There had been no de jure change over the years, but de facto, two states had existed. Both of those in Israel who had tacitly accepted partition and to those who rejected it for a variety of reasons, a new set of circumstances had been created. In practice, there remains a distinction between the "West Bank" (of the Jordan) and Israel proper. But as the present Israeli government's West Bank settlement policy continues, the pressures for outright annexation of the West Bank (or Judaea and Samaria) will grow. Moreover, the sixteen years since 1967 have seen the emergence of a whole generation of Israelis for whom the "Green Line" (the Armistice Lines) of 1949-1967 is just another set of lines on another set of historical maps (Waterman, 1979).

The current situation has now existed for almost as long as the Armistice Lines! The clear distinction between Israel and the "occupied" or "liberated" parts of the Land of Israel has become more indistinct. There is direct contact between Israel and the West Bank for all activities, and as Jewish settlement spreads through the West Bank (Rowley, 1983), the inability to distinguish between the two separate territories, already apparent in many younger Israelis, will fade even more. And, although the status of the West Bank Arabs is not well-defined, the ultimate hope of most of them must also be the emergence of a single state in the region.

IRELAND AND PALESTINE

What general lessons can be learnt from this cursory glance
at two of the best-known cases of partition?

For the majority, in both cases, partition is regarded as
a temporary expedient until a more suitable, permanent
solution can be found. The nature of the permanent solution,
however, tends to appear as a return to the status quo ante
or to its mirror image. Only in the case of the Ulster
Unionists would partition appear to be seen as a lasting and
successful solution to a political problem.

Although in the Irish case the partition might appear to
have come about as a result of voluntary acceptance by both
sides and thus to have been an internally motivated (if not
internally generated) solution, closer examination reveals
that the role of British governments was all-important in the
decision to partition Ireland. In the Palestinian case,
external forces were, and continue to be, the instigators of
most of the partition schemes presented. It might be noted
that whereas the principal actors see partition as a
temporary solution, the external actors often regard it as
permanent.

In both cases, partition led to the creation of negative
and opposing forces which caused the newly created entities
to seek closer ties with foreign forces rather than with one
another. Thus, the Republic of Ireland, after a long period
of introspective gestation and isolationism, began to develop
its ties with western Europe; Northern Ireland turned more
closely towards Britain. Israel looked to the West, in
particular to the United States, while the Palestinian cause
is the perpetual rallying cry of the Arab world. Perhaps as
a result of these heightened external contacts, the future
may hold a restoration of contacts between the partitioned
territories/states.

In both cases too, the imposition of a boundary, without
sufficient consideration to the geography of the area
concerned brought about hardships to the population living in
the areas most directly affected by the partition. This is
true even though the nature of the boundary in either case
was different. In the Irish case, the border followed the
historical county boundaries whereas in Palestine, the cease-
fire lines between the combatants became the de facto
boundary. Attempts to rectify the lack of foresight in the
creation of this "temporary" expedient met in both cases with
mutually negative reactions.

A CONCEPTUAL FRAMEWORK FOR PARTITION AND QUESTIONS FOR RESEARCH

Henderson and Lebow's (1974) division into partitioned countries and divided nations provides us with one conceptual framework for studying partition.

Another way of looking at partition is to see it as part of a continuum ranging from the unitary state on one side to those states that have undergone partition on the other (Paddison, 1983:27-33). The states in which centripetal forces outweigh the centrifugal are administered as unitary states. Those in which regional differences reach a sufficiently high level may take on a federal form. Whether this will take place is often related to size, population and form of political ideology in addition to ethnic pluralism. In states in which the contending political ideologies are equally strong and are too far apart to reach a compromise or where the extremities of the plural spectrum are too distant to be accommodated even within a loose federal structure, then partition becomes an alternative possible solution. Should there be a rapprochement between the partitioned states, then a loose refederated structure remains a possibility, akin to Henderson and Lebow's "zone of de facto acceptance", with retention of sovereign powers but with considerable co-operation between the states.

Pluralism also serves as a framework for examining partition, especially in cases where strong socio-cultural cleavages such as ethnicity, religion or language exist. This framework has already proven useful in individual studies such as India/Pakistan (Spate, 1947; 1948), Ireland (Heslinga, 1962) and Cyprus (Drury, 1979).

Whereas pluralism and the political-ideological continuum provide internally-based frameworks for study, the roles of colonialism and imperialism can provide us with a framework for examining the role of external forces in bringing about partition. Whereas pluralism and the unitary-partition continuum allow us to study centrifugal, internally generated forces, an examination of the role of colonial and imperial powers in the affairs of a state or region permits us to examine the role of external forces involved in bringing about partition. In this way, we can examine, say, the influence of the French government in the partition of Indochina or North Africa, the British Mandate government's attitude to the eventual partition of Palestine, the British role in the partition of India or great power competition in the partition of Germany.

Likewise, the role of colonial power competition in the nineteenth century and the continuing influence of former colonial powers can serve as a basis for understanding current political partitions in Africa, where the political map of the 1980s is in most cases a direct descendant of

European power competition in the last century. How might the political map of Africa have developed had the Europeans been less successful overall or had the individual European powers been more or less successful each at the expense of the other? Might current tensions such as those in Chad, Sudan, Nigeria or Zimbabwe have already ended in partition as a result of different cultures and nationalisms were it not for the "holiness" of the "European" borders inherited by Africa? (see Knight, 1983b:149-50).

Many other valid research questions concerning the political geography of partition can be isolated and it might be useful to outline some of these:

1. What influence does level of economic development at the time of partition have on the partitioned state? Are more developed states, such as Germany, more likely to withstand the separation than states with less developed economies, or vice-versa?

2. Does uneven division of resources hinder the separate development of partitioned states? Does it encourage their eventual unification? Or does it prompt the stronger state to continue separate development?

3. How long does it take for partitioned states to develop separate identities and when these identities develop do the individual states still resemble one another more than they do any other state? This is particularly true of divided nations where the real differences in character between say, the two Koreas or the two Germanies are difficult to determine and are veiled by different formal political ideologies. To what extent do the two states develop separate raisons d'etre?

4. What effect does the partitioning of a state have on the flows of people, goods and ideas? How have forced migrations and displacements been influenced by partition and what are the effects in the opposite direction? How long does it take and under what circumstances do cultural differences begin to be observed between the different parts of the divided nation?

5. Is there any essential difference between most partitions (which are land-based and result in contiguous neighbours) and partitions such as those of Denmark (the parts separated by sea), Pakistan (the parts separated by another state) or South Africa (where the partition is piecemeal and internally generated by the

government as part of the national social policy of apartheid?

6. In what way do variables such as area, total population, population density or length of time the prior state existed influence the propensity to partition? How does the development of separate, communally-based infrastructures prior to partition catalyse the political decision to partition, and how does isolation and the consequent separate development of spatial and economic systems help crystallise the status quo?

7. Under what circumstances do amalgamation of states, such as Tanganyika and Zanzibar, Gambia and Senegal, Egypt and Syria, and reunification take place? Both these processes represent the reverse of partition and division.

CONCLUSION

The question of partition in political geography raises several interesting points concerning approach. Although the specific causes and effects of individual partition solutions might be local, the apparent role of external forces in partition seems to demand that greater attention be paid to historical and global approaches than has been fashionable recently in geographic research (Taylor, 1982). As the consequences of partition have important bearing on the nature and functioning of the states concerned and thus on decisions taken by the states regarding the territories involved, due attention should be paid to this.

Partition is related both to attempts at national self-determination (internal forces) and to international rivalries (external forces). Recognition of this begs the questions of who takes part in exercises of national self-determination, what alternatives to partition exist in any given situation, the power that can be exerted by national groups within the state and how the boiler-rooms of nationalism are fuelled, and how national stereotypes and prejudices can influence political standpoints regarding partition.

Partition appears to be a process more prevalent in non-Socialist states and in the Third World than in the Soviet Bloc. Is this because the eastern bloc countries have developed more successful social systems for dealing with minority regulation within plural societies or is it the result of crudely repressive policies in this regard?

What is needed at this stage, in addition to looking at some of the topics shortlisted above, in order to expand our understanding of partition, is to attempt to close the gap between our abilities to develop theories of society and international relations on the one hand and to develop appropriate methodologies for the study of specific cases on the other.

ACKNOWLEDGEMENT

Once again, many thanks are due to my colleague, Nurit Kliot, who read this preliminary foray in several versions and has offered me much in the way of ideas, criticism and advice. The responsibility for what actually lies here is, of course, mine.

REFERENCES

Adejuyigbe, O. (1983) 'Political geography of administrative areas', paper presented at the Political Geography Conference, University of Oxford

Ahmad, N. (1953) 'The Indo-Pakistan boundary dispute tribunal 1949-1950', Geographical Review, 43, 329-338

Andrews, J. H. (1960) 'The 'Morning Post' Line', Irish Geography, 4, 99-106

Biger, G. (1981) 'Where was Palestine? Pre-World War I perception', Area, 13, 153-60

Boal, F. W. (1980) 'Two nations in Ireland', Antipode, 12 (1), 38-44

Brawer, M. (1983) 'Dissimilarities in the evolution of frontier characteristics along boundaries of differing political and cultural regions', in N. Kliot and S. Waterman (eds.), Pluralism and Political Geography, Croom Helm, London, 159-172

Buchanan, R. H. (1982) 'The planter and the Gael: Cultural dimensions of the Northern Ireland problem', in F. W. Boal and J. N. H. Douglas (eds.), Integration and Division, Academic Press, London, 149-173

Buckland, P. (1972) Irish Unionism 1, Gill and Macmillan, Dublin

Compton, P. (1974) 'Religious affiliation and demographic variability in Northern Ireland', Transactions, Institute of British Geographers, NS4, 433-52

Douglas, J. N. H. (1982) 'Northern Ireland: spatial frameworks and community relations', in F. W. Boal and J. N. H. Douglas (eds.), Integration and Division, Academic Press, London, 75-104

Drury, M. P. (1981) 'The political geography of Cyprus', in J. I. Clarke and W. B. Fisher (eds.), Change and Development in the Middle East, Methuen, London, 289-304

Fitzgerald, G. (1972) Towards a New Ireland, Charles Knight, Rochester

Hachey, T. E. (1972) The Problem of Partition: Peril to World Peace, Rand McNally, Chicago

Haggett, P., Cliff, A. and Frey, A. (1977) <u>Locational Analysis in Human Geography</u>, Edward Arnold, London

Hartshorne, R. (1960) 'Political Geography in the modern world', <u>Journal of Conflict Resolution</u>, 4, 52-66

Henderson, G. and Lebow, R. N. (1974) 'Conclusions', in G. Henderson, R. N. Lebow and J. G. Stoessinger (eds.), <u>Divided Nations in a Divided World</u>, David McKay, New York, 433-456

Heslinga, M. (1962) <u>The Irish Border as a Cultural Divide</u>, Van Gorcum, Assen

Jones, E. (1960) 'Problems of partition and segregation in Northern Ireland', <u>Journal of Conflict Resolution</u>, 4, 96-106

Kleiman, A. S. (1970) <u>Foundations of British Policy in the Arab World</u>, Johns Hopkins University Press, Baltimore

Kliot, N. (1983) 'Geography of hostages - the case of Lebanon', in A. Shachar (ed.), <u>Yearbook of the Israel Geographical Association, 1983</u>, (in Hebrew)

Knight, D. B. (1983a) 'The dilema of nations in a rigid state structured world', in N. Kliot and S. Waterman (eds.), <u>Pluralism and Political Geography</u>, Croom Helm, London, 114-37

Knight, D. B. (1983b) 'Self-determination as a geographical force', <u>Journal of Geography</u>, 82, 148-52

Lyons, F. S. L. (1979) <u>Culture and Anarchy in Ireland 1890-1939</u>, Clarendon Press, Oxford

Mayfield, R. (1955) 'A geographical study of the Kashmir issue', <u>Geographical Review</u>, 45, 181-197

Mellor, R. E. H. (1978) <u>The Two Germanies</u>, Harper and Row, London

Muir, R. (1975) <u>Modern Political Geography</u>, Macmillan, London

Nordlinger, E. A. (1977) <u>Conflict Regulation in Divided Societies</u>, Harvard U.P., Cambridge

O'Brien, C. C. (1972) <u>States of Ireland</u>, Pantheon, New York

Paddison, R. (1983) <u>The Fragmented State</u>, Basil Blackwell, Oxford

Plano, J. C., Greenberg, M., Olton, R. and Riggs, R. E. (1973) <u>Political Science Dictionary</u>, Dryden Press, Hinsdale, Illinois

Pounds, N. J. G. (1964) 'History and geography: a perspective on partition', <u>Journal of International Relations</u>, 18, 161-172

Pringle, G. D. (1980) 'The Northern Ireland conflict: a framework for discussion', <u>Antipode</u>, 12 (1), 28-38

Rodinson, M. (1968) <u>Israel and the Arabs</u>, Pelican, London

Rowley, G. (1983) 'Space, territory and competition - Israel and the West Bank', in N. Kliot and S. Waterman (eds.), <u>Pluralism and Political Geography</u>, Croom Helm, London 187-200

Segre, D. A. (1969) <u>Israel - A Society in Transition</u>, Oxford U.P., London

Short, J. (1982) _An Introduction to Political Geography_,
    Routledge and Kegan Paul, London
Smith, A. D. (1982) 'Nationalism, ethnic separation and the
    intelligentsia', in C. H. Williams (ed.), _National
    Separatism_, University of Wales Press, Cardiff, 17-41
Spate, O. H. K. (1947) 'Partition of Punjab and Bengal',
    Geographical Journal, _110_, 201-222
Spate, O. H. K. (1948) 'The partition of India and the
    prospects of Pakistan', _Geographical Review_, _38_, 5-30
Sykes, C. (1965) _Crossroads to Israel_, Collins, London
Taylor, P. J. (1982) 'A materialist framework for Political
    Geography', _Transactions, Institute of British
    Geographers_, _NS7_, 15-34
Waterman, S. (1979) 'Ideology and events in Israeli human
    landscapes', _Geography_, _64_, 171-181

Chapter Eight

ACCUMULATION, LEGITIMATION AND THE ELECTORAL GEOGRAPHIES
WITHIN LIBERAL DEMOCRACY

Peter J. Taylor

Consider the following two electoral geographies. In the
years leading up to the civil war, America had a very
competitive party system. It was unique among American party
systems because it did not have a regional basis. The north-
south conflict may have produced a civil war but for more
than a generation before it was not reflected in the
electoral geography. In 1910 a British election pitted
protectionism against free trade. In the north, where much
of the industry would have benefited from protection, the free
trade party won overwhelmingly. In the commercial south the
protectionist party was equally victorious. The purpose of
this chapter is to explain how we can unravel these and other
electoral paradoxes. In the process we derive a new
explanatory basis for electoral geography. The argument
proceeds in four stages. First recent attempts to integrate
electoral geography into political geography are criticised
as merely describing liberal democracy at its own face value.
Electoral geography is then located as part of a political
geography that centres on a theory of the state set within
the world-economy. From this vantage point we are able to
suggest a dialectical study of electoral geography based upon
the opposing politics of power and support.
Finally the two electoral paradoxes described above and
further similar paradoxes are examined and resolved in terms
of these electoral geography dialectics.

ELECTORAL GEOGRAPHY AT THE LEVEL OF APPEARANCES

It was perhaps inevitable that after the 'boom' in
quantitative electoral geography of the 1970s attempts would
be made to integrate political geography's fastest growing
'subfield' into political geography. Various forms of
'systems analysis' were being proclaimed and elections were
finally fitted into one of these frameworks. The electoral
system was interpreted as that part of a larger political

117

system where support was marshalled for policies which governments then implemented (Johnston, 1979). A simple linear sequence was envisaged with the input being the geography of votes, the throughput being the geography of representation and the output being the geography of policies with a feedback loop between policies and voters (Taylor, 1978; Johnson, 1980). This framework enabled the study of such favourites as voting maps, gerrymandering and 'pork barrel' politics to be set within the wider political system. At last electoral geography seemed to have found its place within political geography.

This systems model is a very uncritical view of modern liberal democracy. The geography of elections is restricted to those countries that enjoy liberal democracy and no attempt is made to explain this limitation in geographical coverage. Each country is studied as a separate example of the operation of the model so that this 'new' electoral geography promises to be as disjointed as the old one (Taylor and Johnson, 1979). For each of these countries their 'democracy' is accepted as unproblematical, as a natural attribute rather than a relatively recent phenomena. In short elections are treated as a topic for superficial <u>description</u> rather than critical <u>analysis</u>, in Marxist terms the geography of elections does not advance beyond the level of appearances.

There are, no doubt, several routes through this liberal facade to reveal the real nature of elections. In this chapter we concentrate on the role of political parties. Parties appear at the centre of the stage in electoral geography but are, at the same time, curiously neglected. Parties, perhaps more than other political institution, languish at the level of appearances. They appear in two guises. In individual-level models they are treated as active, but unprincipled, vote 'buyers' (Johnston, 1979). In ecological-group level models they are treated as relatively passive and faithful reflectors of cleavages in a particular society (Taylor and Johnston, 1979). Here we will reverse these combinations of attributes and consider parties as active manipulators at the societal level. It is only in this way that the rich tapestry of real politics - the 'U-turns', the policy betrayals, the electoral disasters and landslides - can be incorporated into electoral geography. These are the political parties that appear in Schattschneider's 'realist view' of American democracy. All party systems represent a particular way of presenting choice to voters and as such they reflect victories and defeats for interest-groups <u>before</u> a vote is cast. As Schattschneider (1960:71) so neatly puts it - 'some issues are organised into politics while others are organised out.' Parties, therefore represent a very restricted choice to voters with most issues settled by the nature of the party system rather than by the act of voting itself. With this interpretation we can begin the task of turning electoral geography upside down (Archer and Taylor, 1981).

AN ALTERNATIVE ELECTORAL GEOGRAPHY

To say that political parties are 'manipulators of issues' is not enough. We need to understand in whose interest is the manipulation plus the context in which issues appear or do not appear. Our alternative electoral geography must be set within an alternative political geography. This must be sketched out before the new form of analysis we propose for electoral geography can be understood.

I have described elsewhere a materialist approach to political geography which sets our study in a world-economy framework (Taylor, 1981, 1982a). The important feature of this approach for our argument here is the emphasis on the global scale as the prime level of operation of material forces but with the competitive state system providing an essential part of that operation. The very fact that elections are carried out at the state level means that a wide range of important global issues are organised out of this politics. This represents the triumph of nationalism in the global system and is reflected in the fact that all parties that are contenders for government must be nationalist in nature. This is so pervasive that it is normally overlooked. Nevertheless within their various forms of nationalism parties are able to provide different choices to their national electorates. These choices can be interpreted within a Marxist theory of the state set in the world-economy.

All Marxist theories of the state are based upon a class analysis in which the state is interpreted as the tool of the dominant class or some fragment of it. Hence the state is not the neutral umpire of liberal theory but becomes a springboard for different capitals in their unequal competition in the world-economy. This class analysis is sometimes interpreted as meaning that all conflict including that reflected in elections must be overtly class-based. The fact that a large amount of voting is not along class lines in liberal democracies is sometimes used as evidence for the poverty of a Marxist approach to studying such societies. This is a classic 'straw-man' type argument based upon a very superficial understanding of any critical theory. It treats Marxism as a simple one dimensional sequence of ideas instead of an exercise in the dialectics of opposing forces. The essence of our alternative electoral geography revolves around the relationship between the different social bases of voting and the state in the world-economy as mediated through political parties. Hence empirical evidence of non-class voting in liberal democracies is incorporated into our class-based theory with no problem of contradiction. In fact it stands at the centre of our analysis as described below.

Let us therefore begin the task of fitting electoral geography into a political geography which studies the state set in the world-economy. First electoral geography is concerned with allocation of formal governmental power at the state level or below. Trans-state elections are rare or insignificant (e.g. European Community elections) and trans-state issues are usually not resolved by elections. There is a strong tradition of bi-partisanship in foreign policy in most liberal democracies for example. If elections are primarily about allocation of power in the state arena we need to define what that power is used for. Most Marxist analyses classify state activities into two major functions: (1) the promotion of capital accumulation; and (2) the legitimation of the system. Both accumulation and legitimation are necessary for the survival of the state but they make conflicting demands upon the state. This is the root cause of what O'Conner (1973) terms the fiscal crisis of the state. His theory is about such fiscal crises in western capitalist states and we may generalise it to cover other states. In many parts of the world, of course, legitimacy is a much rarer phenomena. More generally we may consider the requirement for social order which provides the non-economic conditions for accumulation. This social order may be achieved through consensus or coercion. The balance between consensus and coercion varies throughout the world. In the liberal democracies the generation of legitimacy is a prime role of the state to produce a consensual society. In less affluent countries repression becomes a more visible tool for maintaining social order. Both liberal and non-liberal regimes recognise that elections are an important means for legitimising a state.

Following this modification to O'Conner's framework we can identify two related political geographies of state activity: (1) the geography of state support for capital accumulation and (2) the geography of state support for social order. Electoral geography will contribute to both these political geographies when they are concerned with liberal democracies. In the former case the material interests backing political parties are an important aspect of state support for accumulation whereas in the second case elections form a vital aspect of the legitimation of liberal democracies. Moreover, just as in O'Conner's (1973) study of state expenditure, these two state functions provide contradictory demands within the electoral arena. It is around such contradictions that we can build an alternative electoral geography.

THE DIALECTICS OF ELECTORAL GEOGRAPHY

A simple class analysis of elections in the capitalist state
indicates that there are two distinct processes in operation.
First there is the <u>intra-class competition</u> over state
tactics for promoting accumulation which is the concern of
the dominant class. Second all classes are involved in
<u>inter-class conflict</u> over the distribution of the production
generated by the accumulation. Gamble (1974) refers to these
two processes as the <u>politics of power</u> and the <u>politics of
support</u> respectively. Clearly they are the electoral
equivalents of the two political geographies described above.
Political parties, therefore operate through two processes -
they promote material interests in the politics of power and
they mobilise sections of the population in the politics of
support. Figure 8.1 shows a revised model for studying
electoral geography based on this argument.

This model postulates that there are <u>two</u> geographies
underlying elections in liberal democracies. A major task of
this new electoral geography is to investigate the relations
between these two geographies. This can be attempted at
either a concrete or abstract level of analysis. The next
section concentrates on concrete examples; below some
preliminary thoughts on general structural tendencies are
provided. Five such tendencies can be identified:

1. There is no structural need for the two processes
   to provide a single consistent basis for a party's
   actions. The processes occur in two distinct
   political arenas, one elite-based and the other
   popular-based.
2. There is a structural need to mystify the dual
   role of parties. Without this mystification
   the legitimation function of the party becomes
   impossible. This is one of the purposes of
   liberal theories of the state.
3. The balance between action based on one or other
   of the two processes will vary in terms of
   whether a party is in office or opposition.
   Opposition parties operate more in the politics
   of support, for instance 'social democratic'
   parties become notoriously 'socialist' in
   periods of opposition.
4. The prime basis of action in the politics of
   power is class whereas there will be a variety
   of bases for the politics of support. In fact
   the mystification function is facilitated if
   the politics of support is <u>not</u> based upon class.
5. Parties may operate involuntarily to deflect
   attention on contradictions away from the state
   by taking the blame for the situation: A

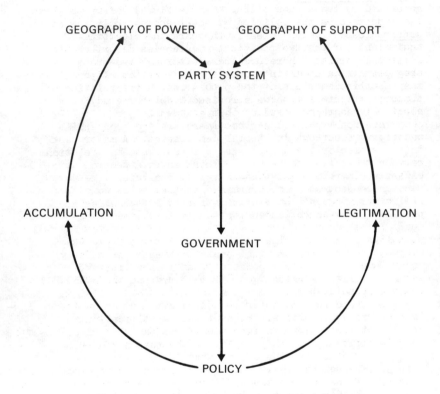

Figure 8.1: A new model of electoral geography

potential crisis of the state becomes a crisis
of the party (e.g. Republican Party in U.S.A.
in 1930s, Labour Party in Britain in 1980s).

These tendencies provide hints on what to look for in
actual electoral situations ... but only hints. The vast
variety in electoral politics among liberal democracies
contrasts sharply with their essentially similar capitalist
social formations. This variety reflects how the needs of
the dominant classes have been satisfied in different ways at
different times and in different places. The particular
tactics of the politics of power and the particular strategy
adopted in politics of support over time and space have
produced a rich mine for electoral studies. But this variety
can only be understood as the result of concrete manifestations of the dialectics of electoral geography as described
here. The remainder of this paper consists of brief cameo
sketches of the unfolding of such dialectics in several
contrasting contexts.

PARADOXES IN ELECTORAL GEOGRAPHY

Figure 9.2 suggests three types of relationship between
politics of power and politics of support. The circles under
'politics of support' represent normal 'cleavage diagrams'
which indicate a division of the electorate; support for
one particular party is indicated by the shading. The circles
under 'politics of power' define 'winners' and 'losers' in
terms of the effects of the policies of one particular party;
those gaining from the action of the party are identified by
the shading. The liberal democratic ideal in this framework
is represented by the case where politics of support is
directly reflected in the politics of power. In Figure 8.2
this is termed congruent politics. In contrast we can
envisage a situation where the cleavage in support is
completely reversed in the politics of power. In such a
situation a party pursues policies directly contrary to the
interests of its popular support. This defines a sort of
'cynical manipulation model' which we term contradictory
politics. These two types of relationship can be viewed as
defining two ends of a spectrum of types. In the middle we
can identify a disconnected politics where support is
unrelated to power. In this case voters are mobilised on one
set of criteria while policy is worked out on another.
    Most studies in electoral geography have assumed we are
dealing with congruent politics as we have seen. The degree
to which parties 'reward' their supporters can be directly
investigated and has been an important research question in
recent years. This literature is not reviewed here because
the new model requires justification by way of identifying

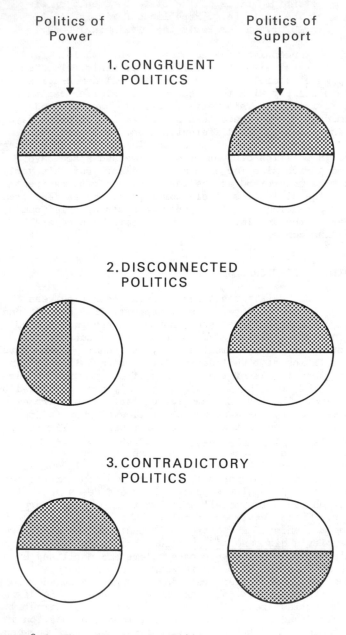

Figure 8.2: Three types of politics

cases of contradictory and disconnected politics. In what
follows eleven examples that do not conform to the liberal
democratic ideal are described with emphasis on the quantity
rather than the detail for the reason just mentioned.

Contradictory Politics

The most extreme violation of the liberal democratic ideal is
found in contradictory politics. Four examples are presented.

Hobson's Paradox in Edwardian England. In a contemporary
study of the geography of the first 1910 election J. A. Hobson
(1968) noted that the country divided between north and south
or what he termed 'Producer's England' and 'Consumer's
England'. The former voted heavily Liberal and the latter
equally strongly for the Conservatives. This geography of
support bears a paradoxical relation to the politics of power
underlying the two parties. The Conservatives were the party
of Protection (Tariff Reform) whereas the Liberals were
maintaining their traditional Free Trade stance. As Hobson
(1968:243) puts it 'why should the great consuming South
uphold Protection, the first effect of which is to raise the
price of consumables?' Hobson's answer is that the election
represents a mobilisation along inter-class grounds which is
separate from the intra-class competition of the tariff
question. The paradox reflects two separate processes
operating together - a politics of power at the top concerned
with tariffs and a politics of support becoming more class-
based.

Power and Support in the South African National Party. The
National Party has ruled South Africa since 1948. The
geography of its support was originally very rural being
based upon the then distribution of the Afrikaner population.
Rural South Africa is still the strongest section of National
Party support despite their inroads into urban areas. Despite
this clear bias in support Nationalist governments have
presided over a massive urban-industrial growth since 1948.
Pirie et al. (1980) have provided evidence for a very
different geography of Nationalist power. The urban-based
Afrikaner secret society, the Broederbond, includes among its
membership the prime minister and 19 of his cabinet and
ministerial colleagues. This is perhaps the most clear-cut
empirical example of a party's geography of power being quite
different from its geography of support.

Sharpe's Labour Party Puzzle. Sharpe (1982:135) asserts that
'as the party of the underdog the Labour Party ought also to

be the party of the periphery and of the localities'. After
describing Britain's geography of inequality Sharpe points
out that the Labour Party, far from tackling this problem is
'surprisingly centralist' in its policies. Hence:

> the Labour Party has been curiously reluctant to
> make (the) elimination (of the geography of
> inequality) a central plank in its programme. This
> is puzzling in itself, but becomes even more
> puzzling when viewed in relation to the growth of
> the party's support in the periphery (Sharpe,
> 1982:139)

In short we have a centralist party based on peripheral
support.

Technocratic Blight in British Cities

Sharpe's puzzle can be transferred to the local government
level. The technocratic politics of the 1960s (Taylor, 1982b)
was often associated with local Labour administrations
pursuing policies at variance with the interests of their
supporters. Cable (1974) reports a classic example for
Glasgow. Here the Labour administration planned the densest
network of motorways for the city with the lowest car
ownership rate in Britain. The main category of 'losers' can
be found in the inner city which would suffer large-scale
demolition and blight whereas the main category of 'winners'
would be car-owning suburbanites who would find commuting and
shopping easier. Of course this geography of power
represents the exact opposite of Labour's geography of
support.

Disconnected Politics

We can suggest that contradictory politics cannot constitute
a long-term phenomenon in liberal democracy. The naked
contrast between support and power is too direct to
facilitate the mystification role in legitimation. Sooner or
later we can expect contradictory politics to be exposed or
to be modified. In Hobson's paradox, for instance, the
contradictory politics represents a transition between two
party systems. Hence we expect disconnected politics to be
more common. Seven examples are presented:

Eliminating Sectionalism in American Elections. From 1828 to
1856 America's second party system of Whigs versus Democrats
operated under white manhood suffrage. Competitive party
politics emerged after 1836 with both parties mobilising
support behind their presidential nominees every four years.

This first liberal democracy illustrates the massive discrepancies that can exist between the politics of power and the politics of support. According to Caesar (1979) the party system was designed as a compromise to maintain the integrity of the new federal state. The state was facing a potentially disintegrating power struggle between southern plantation owners and northern manufacturers. Each fraction of capital had very different interests in terms of state policy towards the world-economy. This competition was kept in check by a very specific politics of support involving highly nationalised parties. Each party was represented in both regions so that the regional conflict could not be reflected in the geography of party support. This most remarkable party system held the U.S.A. together for more than a generation until it was destroyed by the rise of the northern-based Republican Party. In this case, therefore the politics of support is being used to cover over a divisive politics of power (McCormick, 1967; Archer and Taylor, 1981).

The Ethno-cultural Paradox of American Politics. After the civil war a new party system of Republicans versus Democrats emerged. In terms of the politics of power it was very clear where each party stood - the Republicans represented industrial interests and protectionism, the Democrats were the free trade party. At this level, therefore, the distinction between parties is in terms of economic policy. The ethno-cultural paradox is that despite these clear economic differences between the parties the politics of support is not based upon economic interests. Historians have used ecological correlation and regression methods to analyse the bases of support for the two parties and they consistently show no relationship with economic variables but strong relationships with ethnic and religious variables (McCormick, 1974; Kleppner, 1979). While party leaders were debating economic issues in Washington, party workers were mobilising voters along cultural lines in the country. There can be no clearer indication of two distinctive politics each of which has a separate and contrasting geography.

The European P.R. Democracies. The European states that employ proportional representation in elections have allowed a wide variety of cleavages to be represented in their geographies of party support. This party fragmentation has meant a tendency towards coalition governments. Two papers by Lijphart on these democracies clearly show a separation between the politics of power and the politics of support. In the latter case Lijphart (1971) shows that the religious cleavage is by far the most important and class comes a very poor second in most countries. However although these

parties are elected using a religious cleavage, when they
come to form governments the resulting politics of power is
very different. Lijphart (1982) has shown that in terms of
selecting coalition partners the socio-economic dimension is
eight times as important as the religious dimension. The
electorate may be mobilised to vote on religious lines but
the party managers form governments on economic lines.

Liberal Democratic Interludes in Ghana. Liberal democracy
has not normally survived in peripheral states. It has not
been completely abandoned however since it provides a
particularly strong form of legitimation in those cases where
its politics of support can be prevented from conflicting
with the prevailing politics of power. Hence in many
peripheral states military coups and civilian elections have
alternated as different factions of the indigenious dominant
classes compete. Ghana is a particularly good example of
this process. Since the fall of Nkrumah in 1966 there have
been four military coups, two elections and one referendum.
The elections and referendum allow the politics of support to
be mapped and analysed. The bases for this support turn out
to be ethnic with alternative ethnic alliances opposing the
dominant Asante group. These are alternative mobilisations
along a variety of ethnic lines. The politics of power is
much simpler, however. There are two basic strategies for
the dominant class in any peripheral state – an open liberal
policy which favours raw material production or a closed
protectionist policy which builds up the urban-industrial
structure. Nkrumah used the latter strategy employing cocoa-
export revenues for projects such as the Volta Dam. The fall
of Nkrumah and the subsequent alternating politics of power
reflect dominant-class choices between the liberal policy
favoured by the cocoa farming faction and the protectionist
policy favoured by the incipient industrial faction. The
protectionist group in the dominant class have been more
successful because they have been able to develop ethnic
coalitions of support against the Asante cocoa region. A
largely rural ethnic politics of support is used by urban
interests to defeat the economically dominant rural region
(Osei-Kwame and Taylor, 1984).

The 'Catch-all' Nationalist Parties of Ireland. In terms of
the politics of power an analysis similar to that of Ghana
can be applied to post-independence Ireland (Orridge, 1983).
In this case the free-trade-metropolitan interest is
represented by Fine Gael and its predecessor Cumann na
nGaedheal while the protectionist-national interest is
exposed by Fianna Fail. But this politics of power is not
translated into the geographies of support for these parties.

Irish parties have evolved as 'catch-all' nationalist parties thus submerging the metropolitan-national distinction in policies. As Orridge notes (1983:353):

> Throughout the 1920s and early 1930s Cumann na nGaedheal gained some of its highest votes in the counties of northern Connaught, classic 'western' or 'peripheral' areas, and it was not outstandingly strong in some of the prosperous eastern counties.

Geography of power and geography of support are certainly not congruent here.

Nineteenth Century Free Trade Era and British Politics.
Liberal democracy came to Britain much later than U.S.A., but even before the franchise reforms of the late nineteenth century contrasts between geographies of power and support can be identified. The classic example is that of the Peelites in the 1840s. Sir Robert Peel's Conservative administration repealed the Corn laws to usher in the mid-nineteenth century free trade era but in doing so split the Conservative party. After the fall of Peel's government the minority Peelites of the Conservative party worked in parliament to prevent a protectionist (i.e. Conservative) government being formed. The question arises as to how these 'liberal' Conservatives differed from their protectionist colleagues:

> It might in any event have been supposed that through their parliamentary constituencies the Peelites had a close connection with the world of industry, commerce and finance, but if we examine the geographical distribution of their seats we shall find that even this was not the case ... Although progressive in their views on the commercial policy of the newly industrialised Britain, to a curious extent the Peelites represented in their constituencies the old England of the past (Conacher, 1972:67-8).

Once again two geographies are identified, one of power along an agricultural-industrial cleavage and one of support which has no such clear-cut basis.

Modern British Class Politics as a Side-show.
In his recent book Do Parties Make a Difference? Richard Rose (1980) comes to the interesting conclusions that 'yes' there is a difference but it is not between governments of different parties but within the period of office of a single party

government. In short Conservative governments run a 'Stop-Go' economy whereas Labour typically operates in a 'Go-Stop' fashion. What is the politics of power underlying this basic similarity? According to Jessop (1980) the basic politics of power is organised out of British electoral politics. The conflict between finance capital (as represented by the City of London and the Treasury/Bank of England axis in government) and industrial capital (the rest!) has been set aside as a victory for finance capital <u>irrespective</u> of the party in power. At least since 1925 when Britain returned to the gold standard, through ditching the National Plan in 1966, to current de-industrialisation policies the British state has operated in favour of the financial south at the expense of the industrial north (Blank, 1977). In the meantime we have had a politics of support organised along class lines to distribute what is left over (Taylor, 1982b).

CONCLUSION: A NEW RESEARCH AGENDA

Electoral geography has traditionally concentrated on the politics of support and has been only narrowly concerned with the politics of power. The eleven examples above are intended to show that this limitation of electoral geography has meant that, at best, it is only able to tell half the story. There are two geographies in every election and both are essential to the smooth operation of liberal democracy. The geography of support will normally be national in scope as it involves mobilising a large proportion of the population behind an elected government. It is an important modern element of the territorial integration theme that is central to most political geographies of the state. In contrast the geography of power is much less visible and does not require to have any national pretentions. Its geographical scope may be both highly concentrated within a country or be international in range. In the former case power resides in the geographical and economic core of the state so that state policy operates in favour of the dominant class concentrated in that region. Alternatively core powers at the world-economy level may form part of a party's geography of power when that party favours an open policy in line with core power interests. CIA funding of Italian Christian Democrats and their skilful destabilisations in peripheral states indicate such wider geographies of power. For various reasons, both practical and ideological, these geographies of power have been neglected in electoral studies. Arguably we now know enough about geographies of support. Our intellectual resources should be directed at unravelling the power that lies behind the parties we study in electoral geography.

'Catching up' on our research into the geographies of

power is not enough, however. It is a necessary but not
sufficient condition for real progress in our geographical
understanding of elections. The ultimate contribution of
electoral geography to political geography and political
economy will be to specify the conditions under which we can
expect different types of politics to occur. Are contradictory politics transient phenomena as suggested above?
When and where do congruent politics change into disconnected
politics and vice versa? These questions can only be
satisfactorily answered by comparative studies of political
parties set in a world-economy framework. This is the
future agenda of electoral geography and it is an exiting one.

REFERENCES

Archer, J. C. and Taylor, P. J. (1981) Section and Party,
    Wiley, Chichester, U.K.
Blank, S. (1977) 'Britain: the politics of foreign economic
    policy, the domestic economy, and the problem of
    pluralistic stagnation', International Organization, 31,
    673-722
Cable, J. V. (1974) 'Glasgow's motorways: a technocratic
    blight', New Society, September 5th, 605-7
Caeser, J. W. (1979) Presential Selection, Princetown
    University Press, Princeton, N.J.
Conacher, J. B. (1972) The Peelites and the Party System
    1846-52, David and Charles, Newton Abbot, U.K.
Hobson, J. A. (1968) 'Sociological interpretation of a
    general election', in P. Abrams (ed.), The Origins of
    British Sociology 1834-1914, University of Chicago
    Press, 228-49
Jessop, B. (1980) 'The transformation of the state in post-
    war Britain', in R. Scase (ed.), The State in Western
    Europe, Croom Helm, London, 23-93
Johnston, R. J. (1979) Political, Electoral and Spatial
    Systems, Oxford University Press, London
Johnston, R. J. (1980) 'Electoral geography and political
    geography', Australian Geographical Studies, 18, 37-50
Kleppner, P. (1979) The Third Electoral System, 1853-1892,
    University of North Carolina Press, Chapel Hill
Lijphart, A. (1971) 'Class voting and religious voting in
    European democracies', Acta Politica, 6, 158-71
Lijphart, A. (1982) 'The relative salience of socio-economic
    and religious issue dimensions: coalition formation in
    ten western democracies, 1919-1979', European Journal of
    Political Research, 10, 201-211
McCormick, R. L. (1967) 'Political development and the Second
    Party System', in W. N. Chambers and W. D. Burnham
    (eds.), The American Party Systems, Oxford University
    Press, New York, 90-116

McCormick, R. L. (1974) 'Ethno-cultural interpretations of
American voting behaviour', Political Science Quarterly,
89, 351-77

O'Connor, J. (1973) The Fiscal Crisis of the State,
St. Martin's Press, New York

Osei-Kwame, P. and Taylor, P. J. (1984) 'A politics of
failure: the political geography of Ghanaian elections,
1954-1979' Annals, Association of American Geographers,
forthcoming

Orridge, A. W. (1983) 'The Blueshirts and the "Economic War":
a study of Ireland in the context of dependency theory',
Political Studies, 31, 351-69

Pirie, G. H., Rogerson, C. M. and Beavon, K. S. O. (1980)
'Convert power in South Africa: geography of the
Afrikaner Broederbond', Area, 12, 97-104

Rose, R. (1980) Do Parties Make a Difference? Macmillan,
London

Schattschneider, E. E. (1960) The Semi-Sovereign People,
Holt, Rinehart and Winston, New York

Sharpe, L. J. (1982) 'The Labour Party and the geography of
inequality: a puzzle' in D. Kavanagh (ed.), The Politics
of the Labour Party, George Allen and Unwin, London,
135-70

Taylor, P. J. (1978) 'Progress Report: Political Geography',
Progress in Human Geography, 2, 153-162

Taylor, P. J. (1981) 'Political geography and the world-
economy', in A. D. Burnett and P. J. Taylor (eds.),
Political Studies from Spatial Perspectives, Wiley,
Chichester, U.K., 157-74

Taylor, P. J. (1982a) 'A materialist framework for political
geography', Transactions, Institute of British
Geographers, NS7, 15-34

Taylor, P. J. (1982b) 'The changing political map', in
R. J. Johnston and J. C. Doornkamp (eds.), The Changing
Geography of the United Kingdom, Methuen, London,
275-290

Taylor, P. J. and Johnson, R. J. (1979) Geography of
Elections, Penguin, London

Chapter Nine

THE POLITICAL GEOGRAPHY OF ELECTORAL GEOGRAPHY

R. J. Johnston

Although recognised as a subdiscipline of political geography,
and generally allocated one or two chapters in textbooks
(e.g. Dikshit, 1982), electoral geography normally stands
alone as an autonomous field of study. This undoubtedly
reflects the weak theoretical base of most political
geography; the texts comprise a series of independent
chapters, linked only by their concern with space/environment
on the one hand and politics on the other. The major task
begun with this essay is to integrate electoral geography
into a coherent theoretical perspective on political
geography.

A major influence on the lack of clear links between
electoral and political geography is undoubtedly the ideology
prevailing in most countries where political geography is
(can be?) practised. These are the 'western democracies',
dominated by an implicit pluralist theory of the state
(Dunleavy, 1980; Johnston, 1982; Saunders, 1979).
Government is presented there as being by and for the people,
with elections providing the means for instructing
governments. Within this framework, attempts have been made
to link the geography of government activity with electoral
geography (Johnston, 1979, 1980a, 1980b). But such work
relates to a minority of the world's countries only. A
broader perspective is needed, and this is provided here by
an analysis of the nature of political activity (including
elections) in the context of a political-economy approach;
the foundation for the latter is provided by Taylor (1981,
1982a).

THE STATE AND THE WORLD-ECONOMY

The contemporary world comprises a single economic system. A
few countries (Albania, for example) have isolated themselves from it almost completely, and some others (most of
the COMECON bloc) are not fully participants. Nevertheless,

there is a single motor driving all 'national' economies - the capitalist world-economy.

This world-economy has a materialist base, and is driven by the need to accumulate wealth. Accumulation is advanced by those who benefit from it, using any available means that can stimulate production, distribution and consumption. The state is one of these means.

Some contemporary states preceded the modern, industrial world-economy, having been created to advance the interests of elite groups under other modes of production (Johnston, 1982). Many are relatively recent creations, however, having displaced the predecessors and created a new political map that exhausts the earth's land surface, plus an increasing proportion of maritime space. Thus there is not one state involvement but rather the involvement of a large number of states, pursuing similar goals in competition.

In a general sense, these states exist to stimulate the motor of capitalism. The state functions as a promoter of accumulation. Such promotional activity can take a great variety of forms. Capitalism is built on the buying and selling of resources, labour, commodities and services. The state oversees these transactions, providing an environment in which they will flourish, and in which capitalist investors will reap a substantial profit.

To make profits, capitalist enterprises exploit labour, so that increasing profits means increasing exploitation (otherwise known as increasing productivity). Such exploitation stimulates conflict between capital and labour, with the latter demanding greater real incomes in return for their contribution to greater profits. Such conflict is potentially very harmful to capitalist interests, so a means of defusing it is needed. This is provided by the state in its role as a legitimation agent, promoting the ideology of capitalism in a way that is acceptable to labour - by claiming that capitalist success is in labour's interests too. At times, this promotion of legitimation may involve the state winning concessions for labour from capital, as a way of ensuring social and economic stability.

The twin roles of the state are antithetical, for promotion of accumulation can threaten legitimation, and vice versa. The state must ensure a balance between the two, over the long term. For this reason, although it promotes the interests of capital it must be separate from it; if it were seen to be no more than an arm of capital its ability to legitimate exploitation would be slight. The state can only promote and maintain capitalism by being empirically separate from it.

Within the capitalist world-economy each state is a separate sovereign body, concerned with legitimation within its territory and with promoting accumulation there. But the separate states do not represent separate economic systems, neatly circumscribed by state boundaries. Each seeks to control a part of a world-economy - by domestic and foreign policies (Taylor and Johnston, 1983). It is in competition with all others, promoting the interests of local capital and labour.

Initially, the capitalist world-economy was dominated by a small number of states in northwestern Europe; its advance was sustained by increased exploitation of the resources and labour of other parts of the world. (On this, see Wallerstein, 1974, 1980). This involved the state through its promotion of colonialism, and a mosaic of colonial states was created from which surplus value was channelled back to the European hearths. This was followed by decolonisation, and increased commercial rivalry among a number of separate states.

During the colonial and initial post-colonial eras, most accumulation took place in the enterprises domiciled in particular countries (Europe and North America, plus Japan). Today, accumulation has no such clearly identifiable 'home base'. The dominant enterprises are trans-national in their scope, and states compete not only for their investment but also their profits; states create environments for both the exploitation of labour and the enjoyment of the fruits of that exploitation.

A capitalist world-economy dominated by trans-national enterprises provides the context for contemporary state activity. To attract investment, and to promote local accumulation, states must guarantee - as far as possible - that investments will yield suitable returns and/or that the returns on investments (wherever located) will not be taxed at punitive rates. Such guarantees, and especially the former, must cover the labour situation. Without an amenable labour force, not pressing its government to wring too many concessions from trans-national capital, investment may not be forthcoming - or may even be withdrawn. The state must legitimate the contemporary operation of capitalism with local labour, and this involves the use and/or non-use (plus occasional abuse) of elections.

POLITICS, ELECTIONS AND THE WORLD-ECONOMY

To the majority of practising political geographers, elections are integral to the operation of (their) modern states; elections are a part of the legitimation process (though not usually perceived as such) whereby, under a universal adult franchise, the population of the state 'directs' the running of society and economy. The constraints to that direction are severe, however, although they are only dimly perceived. When the constraints are most obvious, the state is involved in their legitimation. Recent British experience illustrates this. In 1976, the Labour government was forced to alter many of its social policies as a consequence of a foreign exchange crisis; cuts in public spending were demanded by the International Monetary Fund as the price of a loan, and the government had to justify these (Coates, 1980). Since 1979, the Conservative government has legitimated a rapid decline of industrial output and a growth in unemployment as both the consequences of world recession and the necessary price of economic management policies aimed at reducing inflation, encouraging investment, stimulating productivity increases, and eventually providing jobs and prosperity for all.

Elections as the source of directives to governments are typical of a minority of states only. According to a recent survey (Gastil, 1981:131), only twenty-four countries 'have a fully competitive electoral process and those elected clearly rule'; these are the 'free states'. A further twenty-seven are relatively free - 'although the electoral process works and the elected rule', factors such as 'extreme electoral inequality, illiteracy, or intimidatory violence' hinder the freedom. There are occasional elections in another forty-seven states, but these impose stringent limits to political freedom (e.g. on the right to participate). Finally, there are sixty-four states without basic political rights and lacking elected governments.

The countries lacking elected governments and experiencing severe infringements of basic individual liberties are, in most cases, ruled either by the military or by an unrepresentative elite backed by a strong military presence and other repressive apparatus. Why is this? What brings about rule by 'The man on horseback' (Finer, 1976)? The key to the answer was provided by Taylor (1982b). He contrasted the situation in relatively affluent First World countries (an affluence built on exploitation of the Second and Third Worlds), which are rich enough to enjoy high material living standards and 'liberal democracy', to that in the Third World where countries are too poor to buy the support of the exploited labour force (such buying including votes), and for which repression is the only viable programme. Thus the

> Third World elite ... although acting in their own self-interest, are also carrying out policies to the First World's general advantage. Their repressive regimes keep down labour costs so that even more of the world's material resources end up in First World pockets.

Accounting for the presence of authoritarian regimes in the Third World has attracted the attention of a variety of scholars. Most adopt an implicitly positivist philosophy, assuming that it is possible to develop general models whereby

a combination of independent variables can be used to predict
either the presence/absence of democracy or the 'amount' of
democracy present. Thus Coulter (1975), for example,
regressed his measures of 'liberal democracy' (a combination
of: political competitiveness in the country's legislature;
the level of political participation; and public liberties -
freedom of the press and of political opposition, political
participation by the military, and the political role of the
police) against measures of 'social mobilisation' (levels of
industrialisation, urbanisation, economic development,
education etc.). He concluded that 'Liberal democracy has a
fairly strong (positive) relationship to level of social
mobilisation', with the riders that 'Economic-development
level is most strongly related to liberal democracy ...
urbanisation is virtually not related to liberal democracy'
(Coulter, 1975:42). (His analysis of residuals led him to
identify countries such as Jamaica, India, Ireland and Israel
as 'over-democratised' and Spain and the United States, but
neither South Africa nor the U.S.S.R., as 'under-
democratised'!). A similar analysis by Bollen (1983), which
includes a useful review of 'theories' of the geography of
electoral geography, found significant positive relationships
between level of democracy and energy consumption (used as an
index of economic development), with countries outside the
core of the world-economy having significantly lower levels
of democracy than predicted from knowledge of their energy
consumption alone.

Such relatively crude, mechanistic quantitative
analyses are complemented by case studies which nevertheless
are based on the assumption that general laws relating
democracy to economic development, can be discovered. Thus,
for example, Hirschman (1981) has investigated an argument
of O'Donnell's (1979) relating the bureaucratic-authoritarian
state to economic conditions. In particular, he examines the
hypothesis that an authoritarian regime is necessary for the
process of 'deepening' that involves the establishment of
backward-linkage industries. Although he rejects the
hypothesis, Hirschman's whole approach suggests that
'explanation' is possible. He clearly locates the rationale
for the imposition of authoritarian regimes in the context
of the problems of the Third World economies and the role of
the state in encouraging accumulation. Economic development
will only occur, he claims, in a situation of predictability;
without this, investment, in particular investment from
foreign sources, will not be forthcoming:

> it is obvious that some degree of predictability
> is needed for any sort of development in countries
> where a large portion of savings, investment, and
> production decisions are made by private economic
> agents (Hirschman, 1981:68).

The state must generate this favourable economic environment by minimising labour demands, if necessary through repression.
    But what if the state fails in its repressive policies, and development with prosperity for all is not forthcoming? Legitimacy is under question and, despite its military backing, the government may find it necessary to democratise, despite the potential instability that this will bring. O'Donnell (1979:315) recognises the need for this, and also the inherent dangers; the sort of democracy needed is one in which class conflict is not allowed, but is not so farcical that it denies legitimacy. Elites fear mass politics, as McDonough (1982) illustrates for Brazil. They may see it as necessary to introduce democracy, however, even prior to any mass demands 'from below' (see Maravall, 1982, on Spain) but the likelihood that democracy will deliver the stability needed for accumulation in a trans-nationally dominated world is considered remote. ('One-party democracies' are favoured by some, usually with strong repressive backing).
    This suggests that neither an authoritarian nor a democratic regime is likely to promote accumulation in the contemporary Third World for very long, and indicates the need to study the nature of regimes over time (rather than the static, cross-sectional approach used by Coulter and Bollen). This can be done in the context of Habermas' (1976) work on crisis in capitalist societies. Two of the crises identified by him are relevant here: a rationality crisis occurs when the state cannot meet the demands of capitalist interests (i.e. it fails in its role as promoter of accumulation) whereas a legitimation crisis occurs when mass loyalty cannot be maintained. Many states today, especially those in the Third World, face both.
    The state can react to a rationality crisis in a variety of ways. Thus in Britain in the early 1980s, for example, the incumbent Conservative government follows a 'free-market' solution, the Labour opposition proposes an 'alternative economic strategy' based on import tariffs, control of capital flows, and planning agreements with capitalist firms, while the Alliance promotes a solution based on membership of the E.E.C., incomes policy, and worker participation in management (for a brief presentation, see Bogdanor, 1983). In each case, the goal is to increase capitalist accumulation. A legitimation crisis can be met either by yielding to worker demands (usually, though not always - France in 1958 and 1968? - long before the crisis deepens), or by repressing opposition; whichever course is taken, the state also acts as a cohesive force - arguing for national unity - and as an ideological mouthpiece for capitalism (as suggested in chapter eight - arguing that what is good for capital is good for all). Over the long term, as Taylor (1982b) suggests, 'advanced industrial' nations have yielded to worker demands by the granting of democratic freedoms and by curbs on

capitalism (the 'unacceptable face of capitalism' attacked by
the British Conservative government of the early 1970s).
Democracy and apparent control of government is the price that
the state has wrung from capital in order to legitimate its
operations.

But what happens when the state faces both a rationality
crisis and a legitimation crisis? Can it meet both
simultaneously, except by using repression to counter the
latter? Empirical evidence suggests not, and that repressive -
or, at least, authoritarian - regimes are the norm in the
Third World. But empirical evidence also suggests that this
'solution' to the legitimation crisis rarely helps to solve
the rationality crisis; in the early 1980s, Taiwan and South
Korea appear to have succeeded (in similar ways to those
employed earlier in Japan: Barrett and Whyte, 1982; Barone,
1983; Wade, 1983), but unrest in Argentina, Chile, Pakistan
and elsewhere provide examples of the failure of repressive
regimes to bring capitalist success.

What, then, is the response to failure to solve both
crises? As a model, it is possible to suggest a cyclical
sequence comprising: rationality and legitimation crises;
authoritarian regime; failure to bring prosperity; further
crises; a return to democracy; failure to bring prosperity;
further crises ... As an ideal type this has much to commend
it, for the insights it provides into the changing geography
of electoral geography. Empirically, however, it is readily
falsifiable - as the example of continuous democracy in
Jamaica shows (Manley, 1982). The capitalist world-economy
is extremely tolerant and robust, allowing a considerable
variety of strategies to be employed. (As the Jamaican
example shows, the empirical appearance of democracy can be
undermined by non-democratic forces). What is done, where,
and when, depends on contemporary interpretations of local
circumstances. There are no logical necessities in politics,
only historical necessities. Ideal type models such as that
outlined here inform the investigation of those historical
necessities, but cannot predict them.

The authoritarian/repressive solution to legitimation
crises is a common one, but a single ideal type - of the sort
implied by Hirschman's (1981) work - is insufficient. (This
is superbly illustrated in a work of fiction: Gordimer, 1971).
Luckhám (1981) has shown that legitimation crises are likely
in four separate types of dependent, Third World states, and
that in each a military solution to the crisis is 'sensible'.

Petty capitalist commodity producers. The main role of these
states in the world-economy is the production of resource-
based commodities, largely for export: most are dominated by
a single product (Johnston, 1976). The state must mediate
between producers and the world markets; it faces crises

because of internal conflicts and also economic problems brought about by world market fluctuations. Authoritarian/ military regimes may be the only way of creating national cohesion among the (tribal) fractions and of creating some internal stability in the face of external variability.

Enclave commodity producers. These countries also provide commodities for the world market, but by large-scale (probably international) investment rather than by petty producers. They face the same problems as the first type, but these are accentuated because of the need to promote long-term stability in order to attract very large investment by transnationals. Democracy is unlikely to provide that stability; authoritarian regimes are.

Import-substituting industrialisers. These are countries going through the 'deepening' process discussed above. Promotion of industrialisation requires the stability that is needed to encourage investment.

Export-promoting industrialisation. These countries are seeking to widen their export base, mainly by attracting foreign capital to low-cost producers. It is necessary to hold-down wages, hence the need for a repressive state apparatus.

In all of these types, reflecting the full range of Third World economies, authoritarian regimes seem the most likely to provide the stability and legitimation – via repression – necessary for the promotion (albeit rarely very successful) of economic development. Military governments are able to provide this. They may not side with inter-national capital, but may promote the interests of labour (as in Ghana); success is no more guaranteed, however. But

> The natural response of professional soldiers is
> to suppress class struggle when it appears
> because it divides the nation, undermines the
> international economic standing of the economy –
> causing flights of foreign capital – and imposes
> certain real costs ... upon the military
> establishment itself (Luckham, 1981:358)

DEMOCRACY AND LEGITIMATION

Class struggle is endemic to capitalist economy. The argument presented here is that in the Third World

authoritarian regimes have been introduced in order to
repress that struggle and promote accumulation, either by a
local elite or by international capital, from which the local
elite derives some benefits. In general, the Third World
cannot afford democracy in the face of rationality and
legitimation crises.

The counter to this argument is that the First can,
through its affluence founded on exploitation of the Third
World, allow legitimation to be secured by popular
participation rather than by repression. To what extent is
this really the case?

There have been many arguments that democracy offers
little in the way of real choice, that there is little
between the parties, in the policies that they enact if not
those that they propose. To many, these arguments provide an
accurate representation of reality. To others, they are
false because parties do act differently. 'Do parties
matter?' is a topic of considerable academic debate
(Rose, 1981).

In the United Kingdom it has been strongly argued by
some groups in the last two decades that parties do make a
difference, with unfortunate consequences for the country's
economy. Until the 1960s, it is contended, the two main
British parties, Conservative and Labour, occupied a
centralist position with regard to the fundamentals of
economic and social policy. (This was known as 'Butskellism':
Taylor, 1983; Bogdanor, 1983). Since then, however, inter-
party consensus has been replaced by what is known as
'adversary politics'. The nature of the British electoral
system makes a change of government very likely with only a
small inter-election swing in partisan support, so that,
given two parties of approximately similar levels of support
and major ideological and policy differences, each general
election is likely to result in a major shift of government
policy. This creates a situation of political instability,
according to Finer (1975:14):

> Given that the programmes of the Conservative
> and Labour parties will be unduly pushed away
> from the central consensus point by the influence
> of their right and left wing extremists
> respectively, the onset of the electoral season
> generates the expectation that current policies
> may be altered very radically indeed.

The economic costs of adversary politics, according to
Wilson (1975), relate to the declining consensus about the
means for achieving economic stabilisation. Regional policy
has also varied substantially between adjacent governments,
as have both pensions policy and incomes policy (Stout, 1975).
Both stability and constructive change are needed for

successful economic management, but, according to Wilson
(1975:115)

> the adversary system has not been helpful in
> achieving the most sensible trade-off ... between
> stability and change. Nor has the adversary
> system fostered serious consideration of basic
> objectives or of the techniques best calculated
> to achieve these objectives. For marginal votes
> at the next election have weighed too heavily in
> the balance.

Industrialists and financiers have expressed similar views:

> one of the greatest handicaps suffered by
> management in Britain has been the frequent and
> dramatic shifts in economic and industrial policy
> imposed by successive governments (National
> Committee for Electoral Reform, n.d.)

and

> The main disadvantage of the present system from an
> economic point of view is that it produces drastic
> changes in government policy at intervals which are
> far too short to enable industry to plan and
> operate efficiently (Caldecote, n.d.)

Examples of such changes are provided by Muggridge (1981).
    The solution, according to some academic analysts and to
the cited industrialists, lies in electoral reform, replacing
the British first-past-the-post system, with its tendency to
magnify swings and to 'manufacture' majorities (Rae, 1972;
Johnston, 1979), by one designed to produce proportional
representation. According to the National Committee for
Electoral Reform, the solution to the problems induced by an
electoral instability that is out-of-kilter with industrial
investment programmes

> would be the reform of our electoral system by
> introducing a system of proportional representation.

This would lead, according to Finer (1975:30), to

> greater moderation in policy since the extremes in
> either of the two main parties would no longer be
> able to exercise blackmail and pressure over their
> moderate colleagues.

Government would almost certainly be by a middle-of-the-road
coalition, reflecting the centrist views of the majority of

the electorate. As a result

> the alternations of government would not be as
> absolute and abrupt as at present ... the change
> would be "damped" by the necessity of both the
> major parties to coalesce with a party or parties
> of the centre (Finer, 1975:31)

This argument has been taken up by the centrist parties which
currently support electoral reform (Liberal/SPD Alliance,
1982; see also Hansard Society, 1979).

Adoption of electoral reform (involving a system aligned
to proportional representation)will assist the regeneration of
the British economy, it is argued, because it will provide
stable government. Unless there are major shifts in partisan
preferences towards extremist parties, elections will not
carry with them the fear of major policy changes.
Industrialists and others can invest, safe in the knowledge
that policy alterations in a few years will not undermine
those investments before they have borne their full fruit.

Put another way, this 'economic' case for electoral
reform is, in effect, a case for 'depoliticising' politics.
Stability is to be achieved by adopting an electoral system
which ensures that only in rare cases will elections lead to
major policy changes. The argument, then, is that to promote
accumulation (i.e. solve the increasingly severe rationality
crisis) the state must enact a particular policy. It must,
of course, legitimise such an action. The underpinning for
such legitimation is provided in many arguments that the
current system is 'unfair', whereas PR is 'fair':

> We want to make democracy really work in Britain,
> with a voting system which is fair to the voters
> and representative of public opinion (City Committee
> for Electoral Reform, n.d.)

The fairness is further promoted by statements such as

> electoral reform is an absolute priority for
> Britain, since we believe it to be a precondition
> both of national unity and of social and economic
> progress (Liberal/SDP Alliance, 1982)

What fair-minded person could disagree? (Although arguments
have been advanced that fair representation does not ensure a
fair distribution of power: Johnston, 1983a, 1983b).

According to the analyses in an earlier section of this
essay, electoral democracy is something that most Third World
countries cannot afford (at least for long) because it
threatens the stability that is so necessary for economic
development. According to the present section, it is argued

by some that Britain cannot afford a particular form of electoral democracy either, because that too threatens economic stability. Perhaps Taylor (1982b) was wrong in his claim that 'liberal democracy ... (is) enjoyed only in rich countries like Britain' because Britain is no longer rich enough to afford liberal democracy. It has too long a tradition of electoral democracy to encourage any move for abolition of elections to promote economic stability, but the decline (and the consequent alienation) is insufficiently deep to stimulate much thought of military takeover, given the ideological success of conservative elements within the society. So instead, a form of democracy is promoted which will hopefully be seen as legitimate (because it is 'fair') but whose main purpose will be to stimulate accumulation.

The parallels are quite striking; non-politics and de-politics will have the same effect, and so are presented for the same reason; electoral reform may be easier to legitimate than a military coup, however. Why, then, is it in Britain that the pro-PR lobby is so strong? In most of Europe, PR already exists and provides the models for replacing adversary politics by 'the politics of accumulation' (Finer, 1975; Bogdanor, 1983). And in the United States, it could fairly be claimed: (1) that adversary politics are not well-developed, for the two main parties do not have separate adversarial, class bases; (2) that, apart from the brief period during Johnson's presidency in the 1960s, Congress has had a continuous conservative coalition with a majority (comprising southern Democrats plus Republicans); and (3) that the nature of American politics places more emphasis on politicians than on party, and so differs substantially from Britain.

In any case, as argued earlier in this essay, a positivist view of political geography is not a sensible one. There is no one solution to any set of problems, and in any place at a particular time the chosen solution will reflect a combination of many factors, including inertia and the influence of key actors. All that can be argued here is that electoral politics as practiced in parts of the First World, and especially in Britain, is not apparently suited to the promotion of accumulation in the present economic situation. It is even less well suited to that role in the Third World countries, which does not mean that it cannot be practiced there. In most countries, some form of elections may be used - at some times - to legitimate the capitalist economic system. But where that system is faltering locally - as increasingly seems to be the case in the context of trans-national capitalism - elections, especially where they can result in major policy shifts, are not very sensible legitimising agents.

CONCLUSIONS

A map of the world showing which countries hold regular 'free elections' correlates strongly with a variety of other maps illustrating a range of economic and social variables. Such correlations suggest that the absence of democracy is a further characteristic of 'under-development', and can be accounted for by the same sets of variables that are used to suggest why certain areas are more developed than others.

Such (environmental and cultural) determinist arguments are readily falsified. So are positivist attempts at explanation, which claim that democracy can only be afforded in the metropolitan core of the world-economy. Counter-examples illustrate the fallibility of such arguments (which can always be 'explained away' by redefining democracy).

A satisfactory account of the current political geography of electoral geography must incorporate both a viable theory of the state and an historical perspective. The state exists to perform two main roles within the capitalist world-economy - to promote and to legitimate accumulation. This involves it in activities that produce a favourable environment for capitalist investment, including minimising the conflict between capital and labour. The latter (the legitimation role) involves the state as an ideological agent, promoting the benefits of capitalism among those who are the source of, but not the beneficiaries from, wealth.

Elections provide one possible element in a legitimation programme. They give the citizens of a state a part in its government, and hence a feeling (promoted in the state ideology) that they are controlling the future of their country. However, it is frequently the case that elections become a focus of the class conflict, with the development of electoral cleavages along class lines (Taylor and Johnston, 1979). This presents the possibility of either or both of: (1) control of the state apparatus falling into the hands of groups representing labour; and (2) the state awarding substantial concessions to labour (in high real wage levels, for example). Neither is conducive to accumulation, and may act as a deterrent to capitalist investment within the state territory.

It is because electoral democracy linked to class conflict (or to other cleavages, such as tribal, as in Zimbabwe) is not conducive to accumulation that most Third World and Second World countries have authoritarian-bureaucratic regimes. In the desperate fight for investment and economic growth, democracy cannot be afforded for much of the time, and a repressive regime may be advanced as necessary for 'the good of the country in the long term'.

In the First World, economic prosperity has allowed electoral democracy to be practised in many countries without fear of major harm to that prosperity and its foundation in

capitalist investment. This is because many First World
countries have based much of their accumulation of wealth on
exploitation of other countries, have operated electoral
systems which produce stability of government policy through
centrist coalitions, and have developed party systems that
are not linked to fundamental class cleavages. Democracy has
been an affordable luxury.

In Britain in recent years some have perceived that the
luxury can no longer be afforded. Accumulation is being
reduced; unemployment is increasing; and the long-term threat
to legitimation is substantial. Thus means are sought to
remove the potential harms of democracy, not by abolishing it,
because this would create a major legitimation crisis, but by
removing the degrees of freedom associated with the present
system. New centrist parties are being promoted, and with
them an electoral system which will virtually guarantee
centrist coalitions and thus provide the stability needed for
investment and accumulation. Such change is legitimated in
the promotions as being 'fair'.

This is but an initial, agenda-placing essay into the
political geography of electoral geography. It suggests that
a general level of explanation, for why some countries have
liberal democratic regimes at the present time whereas others
have authoritarian ones, must be sought in a theory of the
state which relates political activity to the materialist
base of the capitalist world-economy. Accounts for particular
cases must explore the historical situation, however,
including not only the political history of a state but also,
where relevant, its class structure and electoral system.
Explanation can be found only in the structure itself;
understanding of particulars must set the empirical situation
in its structural context.

REFERENCES

Barone, C. A. (1983) 'Dependency, Marxist theory and
        salvaging the idea of capitalism in South Korea',
        Review of Radical Political Economics, 15, 43-70
Barrett, R. E. and Whyte, M. K. (1983) 'Dependency theory and
        Taiwan', American Journal of Sociology, 87, 1064-1089
Bollen, K. (1983) 'World-system position, dependency and
        democracy', American Sociological Review, 48, 468-479
Bogdanor, V. (1983) Multi-Party Politics and the Constitution,
        Cambridge University Press, Cambridge
Caldecote, Viscount (n.d.) Industry needs electoral reform,
        Conservative Action for Electoral Reform, London
City Committee for Electoral Reform (n.d.) City committee for
        electoral reform, National Committee for Electoral
        Reform, London
Coates, D. (1980) Labour in power, Longman, London

Coulter, P. (1975) Social Mobilization and Liberal Democracy,
    Lexington Books, Lexington
Dikshit, R. D. (1982) Political geography: a contemporary
    perspective, Tata McGraw Hill, New Delhi
Dunleavy, P. (1980) Urban political analysis, Macmillan,
    London
Finer, S. E. (1975) 'Adversary politics and electoral reform,
    in S. E. Finer (ed.), Adversary politics and electoral
    reform, Anthony Wigram, London, 3-34
Finer, S. E. (1976) The man on horseback, Penguin, London
Gastil, R. D. (1981) Freedom in the world: political rights and
    civil liberties 1981, Clio Press, London
Gordimer, N. (1971) A guest of honour, Jonathan Cape, London
Habermas, J. (1976) Legitimation Crisis, Heinemann, London
Hansard Society (1979) Politics and industry - the great
    mismatch, Hansard Society, London
Hirschman, A. (1981) 'The turn to authoritarianism in Latin
    America and the search for its economic determinants',
    in D. Collier (ed.), The new authoritarianism in Latin
    America, Princeton University Press, Princeton NJ, 61-98
Johnston, R. J. (1976) The world trade system, Bell, London
Johnston, R. J. (1979) Political, electoral and spatial
    systems, Oxford University Press, Oxford
Johnston, R. J. (1980a) 'Political geography and electoral
    geography', Australian Geographical Studies, 18, 37-50
Johnston, R. J. (1980b) The geography of federal spending in
    the United States, Wiley, Chichester, U.K.
Johnston, R. J. (1982) Geography and the state, Macmillan,
    London
Johnston, R. J. (1983a) 'An unresolved issue for electoral
    reformers', Representation, 23, 6-10
Johnston, R. J. (1983b) 'Seats, votes, redistricting and the
    allocation of power in electoral systems', in B. Grofman
    and A. Lijphart (eds.), Choosing an electoral system,
    Sage, Beverly Hills
Liberal/SPD Alliance (1982) Electoral reform: fairer voting
    in natural communities, Poland Street Publications,
    London
Luckham, R. (1981) 'Militarism: force, class and inter-
    national conflict', in M. Smith, R. Little and
    M. Shackleton (eds.), Perspectives in World politics,
    Croom Helm, London, 350-363
McDonough, P. (1982) 'Repression and representation in Brazil',
    Comparative Politics, 14, 73-99
Manley, M. (1982) Struggle on the periphery, New Left Books,
    London
Moravall, J. M. (1982) The transition to democracy in Spain,
    Croom Helm, London
Muggridge, H. (1981) Industry and electoral reform, National
    Committee for Electoral Reform, London

National Committee for Electoral Reform (n.d.) Why industry
    needs electoral reform now, National Committee for
    Electoral Reform, London
O'Donnell, G. (1979) 'Tensions in the bureaucratic-
    authoritarian state and the question of democracy', in
    D. Collier (ed.), The new authoritarianism in Latin
    America, Princeton University Press, Princeton, 285-318
Rae, D. W. (1972) The political consequences of electoral
    laws, Yale University Press, New Haven
Rose, R. (1981) Do parties make a difference?, Macmillan,
    London
Saunders, P. (1979) Urban politics, Penguin, London
Stout, D. K. (1975) 'Incomes policy and the costs of the
    adversary system', in S. E. Finer (ed.), Adversary
    politics and electoral reform, Anthony Wigram, London
    117-142
Taylor, P. J. (1981) 'Political geography and the world
    economy', in A. D. Burnett and P. J. Taylor (eds.),
    Political studies from spatial perspectives, J. Wiley,
    Chichester, U.K., 157-174
Taylor, P. J. (1982a) 'A materialist framework for political
    geography', Transactions, Institute of British
    Geographers, NS7, 15-34
Taylor, P. J. (1982b) 'Democracies for the rich and
    dictatorships for the poor', The Guardian, 14 June
Taylor, P. J. (1983) 'The changing political map', in
    R. J. Johnston and J. C. Doornkamp (eds.), The changing
    geography of the United Kingdom, Methuen, London,
    275-290
Taylor, P. J. and Johnston, R. J. (1979) Geography of
    elections, Penguin, London
Taylor, P. J. and Johnston, R. J. (1983) 'Geography of the
    British state', in A. M. Kirby and J. R. Short (eds.),
    The human geography of contemporary Britain, Macmillan,
    London
Wade, R. (1983) 'South Korea's agricultural investment: the
    myth of the passive state', Pacific Viewpoint, 24, 11-28
Wallerstein, I. (1974) The Modern World-System, Academic
    Press, New York
Wallerstein, I. (1980) The Modern World-System II, Academic
    Press, New York
Wilson, T. (1975) 'The economic costs of the adversary
    system', in S. E. Finer (ed.), Adversary politics and
    electoral reform, Anthony Wigram, London, 99-116

Chapter Ten

FUTURE OF THE NATION-STATE SYSTEM

Stanley D. Brunn

Three key words in the title, future, nation-state, and
system, identify topics of interest shared by many political
geographers even though their major research foci may be in
the organisation of space, elections, policies, and
boundaries. The future is a time perspective. In studying
it we may plan for what our worlds and spaces may and will be
like as well as what we want and don't want in them.
Research into the study of the future is attracting
increasing attention among geographers, including political
geographers (Brunn, 1981). The second word, nation-state, is
recognised by most political geographers as the basic unit
of our investigations, even though it has been the focus of
limited conceptual and theoretical study (Taylor 1981;
Johnston, 1982). The third word, system, is a valuable
concept in geography (Coffey, 1981; Huggett, 1983) for
investigating what the political processes and spatial
structures might be in the future. Most previous studies on
geographic systems have dealt with economic transactions and
urban areas; the efforts by Cohen (1971, 1982 and 1983)
suggest the utility of the concept in examining political
events and processes at the regional and global scales.
    A missing but necessary ingredient in our examination of
the contemporary political world is what the state and state
system might be like or will be like in the future. That
future may be 2001, 2025, or 2084. There is no shortage of
material on the state either in book chapters or articles.
Recent books are beginning to examine the state within a
dynamic context (Muir, 1975; Cox, 1979; Gottman, 1980;
Muir and Paddison, 1981; Johnston, 1982; Short, 1982;
Paddison, 1983). The most comprehensive and detailed
statement on the state thus far by a geographer is Johnston's
(1982) treatise in which he draws on the contributions of
economic and social historians and political scientists to
investigate the origins, persistence, and characteristics of
the early and industrial states. A study on the state and
state system within a geographic context would not be complete

without some examination of what is happening now, will or might happen in the future, and what the consequences of on-going processes and specific events will or might be. The purpose of this essay is to present and identify some features of the state and the nation-state system in an emerging post-industrial space economy and society.

The following points are addressed:(1) the entrance of the developed (or core world) into a post-industrial economy and society; (2) the salient attributes of that economy and society and how it contrasts with the industrial world; (3) that the state or nation-state as we know and study it is an industrial era phenomenon; (4) that the emerging post-industrial space economy and post-industrial space society call for a re-examination and re-thinking about the functions and purposes of the state; and (5) the major features of a political system in the post-industrial world. This paper should not be considered a definitive statement on the subject, but more as a "think and discussion" piece.

EMERGING POST-INDUSTRIAL WORLDS

Numerous scholars, mostly non-political geographers, have discussed and identified major stages or periods of history. Early industrial or pre-industrial civilisations, societies, economies and stages have probably been the subject of as much inquiry as industrial periods of human history. In regards to the future, there certainly are only a few scholars writing about future societies, economies, and political worlds, and how they may be identified and defined and what are characteristics of transition periods to new periods or stages in human history. What studies are available to date are useful in helping us construct post-industrial space economies and societies (Bell, 1971; Spekke, 1975; Harman, 1976; Kahn et al., 1976; Feather, 1980; Toffler, 1980; Naisbett, 1982). These sources contain ideas about how the present may be considered as a time of transition and how specific events, processes, choices, and changes are helping shape new and somewhat different economies and societies. The single best geography source to date on the future is by Abler et al. (1975) on selected facets and impacts of rapidly shrinking worlds.

The most frequently used terms to label the society where rapid changes are being witnessed in the developed or rich world are the post-industrial economy (PE) and post-industrial society (PS). Those labels are used by Abler, Bell, Harman, Kahn, Toffler, and Naisbett among others. That period is also termed the post-city age, super-industrial age, tectronic era, communications era, and period of electronic social transformation. Whatever label is used, it is clear that the economic and social descriptors associated with this emerging society are in contrast to those attributes of the industrial world of the past two centuries. Toffler labels the post-industrial era The Third Wave. He posits that the present is a period of transition to the PE and PS. Toffler's first wave of human history represents our agrarian heritage, while the second is associated with our industrial orientation and emphasis. Each wave has a set of distinguishing characteristics that separate it from the previous one. Periods of transitions or watersheds in human history contain a mix of earlier and successive waves which remain complex and in a state of flux until the impress of the new wave is firmly established within new economies and societies.

CHARACTERISTICS OF POST-INDUSTRIAL ECONOMIES

What are the distinguishing characteristics of post-industrial space economies and societies and for that matter a post-industrial world? First, it is one in which more than half the labour force is in the services sector (Table 10.1). Transportation, wholesale and retail trade, communications, government, recreation, health and education professions comprise a much larger segment of the labour force than during the industrial era (Abler, 1975). Second, the key and growth industries in the PE are in the quaternary sector, that is, those related to information. Finance, real estate, journalism, telecommunications, and computer-based technologies are major components. Information collecting, analysis, dissemination, manipulation, packaging, and sales will be the major income generating elements of the PE in contrast to land or property which represented wealth and status in the first wave and the accumulation of industrial and energy resources and manufacturing which represented wealth and status in the second wave. We are already witnessing in the developed world examples of growth industries in the second wave diversifying their economic base by purchasing information technologies including radio and television stations, newspapers, magazine and book publishers, and companies on the frontier in telecommunications, computer hardware and software, and satellite data collecting and processing. A third characteristic has to do with human extensibility or the rapidity at which information is relayed over space and the high rate of human mobility (Warntz, 1966; Janelle, 1973). Frequent moves and long distance mobility are not uncommon for societies geared or accustomed to high speed change nor is instant contact with friends, colleagues, business or government offices half-way around the world. The shrinking world concept is ushered in by rapid and easy access to all points by television, telephones, computer, and even transportation. (It should

Table 10.1: Key Features of Post-Industrial Space Economies
and Societies

Employment in tertiary and quaternary sectors
Industrial growth in information industries
Time-space convergence (impacts of shrinking worlds)
   and human extensibility (at interregional and
   global scales)
Awareness of problems and issues at regional and
   global scales
Urban-oriented systems
Harmony with nature rather than conquering nature
Consumer-based society and quality of life issues
Greater affluence and a revolution of declining
   expectations
Sensate culture: cultural rather than material
   satisfaction
Pursuit of leisure
Acceptance of alternatives and choices rather than
   standardisation
Time perspective for examining problems: the future
Methodologies: Planning and Forecasting via
   abstract theories, models, systems analysis,
   simulations, etc.

---

not be inferred that all parts of the world "shrink"; by
contrast, some economies and societies, or even individual
members, may choose to retain traditions instead of adopting
innovative space-adjusting technologies). A fourth underlying feature of the PS is the emerging recognition of
problems at a continental and global scale. Few problems are
unique to any location. Instant reporting of major events in
small or large countries reach populations nearby and half a
world away at the same time. The result is that distance
(that is, linear distance) ceases to be a barrier to
knowledge (or ignorance) and even interaction. Satellite
reporting and visual coverage, instant telephone contact,
regional and interregional computer networks provide masses
of data summaries and visual displays about instantaneous
changes, environmental catastrophes, changes in money markets,
and political cultural conflicts that are long distances from
the receiver.

A fifth feature is the urban-oriented systems that are
emerging in both the developed and developing worlds (Brunn,
1983). Cities are growing closer together not only in time
but in space. The node of the past is being replaced by a
network in which large and small settlements are being
integrated into a series of tight transportation and
communications grids linking everyone to everyplace. The

sixth attribute is that there is a healthy respect for the natural environment and humankind's place within it. Rather than exploitation of the planet's waters, lands, air, and biota, humans strive to correct the imbalances associated with the exploitation of the natural worlds during our industrial histories. The seventh feature is that the PE and PS are basically consumer-oriented, again a sharp departure from the industrial society or the second wave in which the emphasis was on the production of goods for industries and consumers (material satisfaction). The economic climate then was one of growth as well. The major items of interest to consumers in the PS are likely to be related to quality of social programs (education, health), quality and safety of products (appliances, vehicles, homes, etc.), the quality of life for all ages and both sexes, and a general respect for the quality of the environment (workplace, recreation, etc.). A shift in emphasis is from the volume of goods produced and accumulated to the value of humans in society.

An eighth characteristic is the likelihood of greater affluence (at least absolutely) and at the same time a recognition that many expectations will never be achieved. Higher prices for some goods and services, limited supplies of some resources, global competition for nonrenewable resources and the unavailability of institutions (government included) to provide quality services will lead to a "revolution of declining expectations" in both the rich and poor worlds. Conservation ethics, recycling, doing more with less, and 'waste not-want not' may become trademarks or elements in the PE. A ninth feature identifies the emergence of a sensate culture. Humans will be valued as humans, not as objects as in industrial history. The pursuit of arts, leisure, knowledge, and advancement in the human enterprise will be valued. This more human world will lead, it is hoped, to a more humane world. The pursuit of leisure and emphasis on recreation activities is the tenth feature. Examples of the growth of sports, recreation, exercising, home crafts, and hobbies are already apparent in societies with more leisure time, higher incomes, shorter work weeks, and a support system for entertainment activities. The PS will put to rest the puritanical admonition of "the idle mind is the devil's workshop".

The eleventh feature of the PS is the acceptance of realistic alternatives or choices to specific problems. Rather than incorporating or attempting to instill standardisation and uniformity, whether in product design or institutional programs, alternatives or choices will have greater respect. The industrial mode or mold of doing things and solving problems coupled with the diffusion of industrial models, including the nation-state and democracy, is a trademark of the global Europeanisation of the past two

centuries. In part of the search for alternatives and
choices is related to the next, the twelfth feature. That is
the examination of problems within a future perspective.
Realistic and legitimate futures research and planning, while
not a salient feature of industrial history, possibly for
reasons of promoting standardisation (machine) and efficiency
(of humans and machines), reflect a society searching for a
variety of options to resolve short and long term problems.
Bell (1971) identifies future perspectives as characteristics
of post-industrial worlds in contrast to "ad hoc
adaptiveness" and "experimentation" in the industrial and
agrarian societies. The thirteenth and final attribute of
the PE and PS is the methodologies used to study problems.
Bell believes that there will be an emphasis on abstract
theory, models, simulations, decision theory, and systems
analysis. Again this is a marked departure from industrial
periods when empiricism and experimentation were accepted
methodologies. In the pre-industrial worlds, commonsense,
trial and error, and experience were the benchmarks used to
decide how to resolve problems. In summary, while the
thirteen characteristics listed in Table 10.1 and discussed
above are not mutually exclusive, they represent some of the
most salient features likely to be associated with the PE
and PS.

THE STATE AS AN INDUSTRIAL ERA PHENOMENON

The state or nation-state as an important governmental unit
in humankind's history is most strongly associated with
European exploration, discovery, and settlement, industrial
economies, and Europe's competitive and boundary conscious
governments. The transition of economies and societies from
those with an agricultural and rural orientation to those
with an industrial and urban focus was marked by changes in
marketing, transportation, communication, and the political
organisation of space. Each major period of human history
has associated with it distinct forms, organisation, and
functions of government. Salient features of the early state,
industrial state, and post-industrial state are summarised in
Table 10.2.
      The significance of territory or the demarcation of
political containers (to use Johnston's term) is one of the
most distinguishing characteristics of the industrial period
(Soja, 1971; Gottmann, 1973). Formal political units
represented an outgrowth of the centralisation of the economy
and political power. The delimitation and demarcation of
formal boundaries were also an important feature of the
industrial state. Political property or territory not only
became significant in emerging urban and industrial Europe
but in European overseas claims, colonisation, and expansion.

154

Table 10.2: State Societies: A Comparative Schema

	Early State	Industrial State	Post-industrial State
Initial Emergence	Early China, Central and South America, Middle East, India, and Europe	Europe	North America, West Europe, and Japan
Economy	Agrarian and pre-agrarian	Industrial (heavy and light) Natural resource base producer oriented accumulation of producer goods	Tertiary and quaternary sectors Information Human services Consumer oriented distribution of goods and services
Population	Slow growing Rural Little mobility	Rural depopulation Rural-urban migration Urban growth Voluntary and forced migration	Urban stability Slow or no growth High degree of mobility
Scale of Interaction	Local and regional	Local, regional, and continental	Regional, interregional, and global
Transportation and Communication	Road and water	Rail, water, road	Rail, road, water, air, satellite, and computer
Ease and Speed of Movement	Slow, very slow	Slow to rapid	Very rapid, instant

Table 10.2 (cont'd)

	Early State	Industrial State	Post-industrial State
Education	High illiteracy very few elites	Mass public education Standardised education	High literacy High levels of education Retraining; alternative modes of learning
Elites and Vested Power	Royalty and Nobility classes Military leaders Landed aristocracy Religious leaders	Holders of property (land, minerals, industries) Industrial corporations Political leaders Some church and military Organised unions The rich world	Information industries Technocrats Transnational corporations Cartels Professionals Organised unions Regional and global assemblies The North and South
Level of Awareness	Local	Continental, regional within state and territories Cores and peripheries	Extraterritorial Global
Boundaries	Local and land Ephemeral Formal	Local, regional, and global; land and coasts Persistence Formal and functional	High seas, air, outerspace Blurring of boundaries
Political organisations	Crude nodal structure Fuzzy frontiers	Creation of "container" spaces; mosaic of patterns	Functional administrative units; regional and interregional

		Refining territories Formal units based on nodes	
Loyalties	Chiefs Elites Church leaders Military leaders	Formal state Elites Central government Industrial corporations	Mixed: transnational corporations, extraterritorial units, interest groups
Pressure groups	Jealous and rival clans, neighbours and successors Rival empires	Neighbouring states Organised unions Emerging middle class Rival "world" powers	New Economic Order and Third World concerns Special interest lobbies (regional and extraregional) Resource cartels Emerging regional powers Disenfranchised minorities
Types of government	Chiefs Royalty and nobility Empires (regional) Church	New independent state Capitalist and socialist Totalitarian and democratic Global empires with colonies; imperialism	Superstates, alliances, federations, regional pacts, interregional trading blocks
Legal issues	Taxation Succession Preserving classes Loose and formal alliances	Equitable representation Property Protection of individuals Protection and responsibility of corporations Ownership of newly acquired spaces	Ownership of high seas and outer space Groups vs. individual Transnational corporations Protecting consumers Narrowing rich and poor gaps Accepting destandardisation and decentralisation

Table 10.2 (cont'd)

	Early State	Industrial State	Post-industrial State
Nature of Conflicts	Land neighbours Coastal neighbours Internal Local wars	Protection of monopolies and oligapolies Legalising trade unions Neighbouring state Rival states Protecting empire Boundary conflicts Regional and continental	Secession efforts Disenfranchised minorities Sea/air incursions State vs. transnational corporations Non-neighbours Surrogate wars Possible all-out nuclear war Disorder in periphery
Solutions to Conflict	Peace treaties Power (conquer adversary) Divide and conquer	Wars and treaties "Go it alone" even if unpopular Legitimise war (religion, state, economy)	Reluctance to use sheer force Use of economic power (credit, sanctions, etc.) Media pressure Use of non-governmental organisations
Concerns of Government	Survival Persistence of state Retaining elites Centralisation Protect elites	Acquisition of space Organisation of new space Maintaining bureaucracies Creating hierarchies	Adjusting to global system Consequences of widening rich-poor world Sharing for survival Equity and equality Placating secessionists

Mass health, education, etc.

Acculturation to national norms (homogenisation)

Eliminate differences and inequalities

Maintaining economic strength

Productivity (economic)

Disregard for natural environment

Maintain classes

Rights of individuals

Competition with rival states

Retaining empires and a formal state system

Problems dealt with in an economic context

Time orientation to protecting status quo

Dissolution of empires

Satisfying and protecting consumer

Permitting destandardisation

Protecting environment

Privacy and individualism

Quality of life measures

Flexible and functional political organisation

Impacts of technology on humans and environment

Dealing with problems in a human or social context

Concern for planning and the future

Parcels of space were seized in the name of a state and valued for what they could and did contribute to the nation-state's and empire's economic growth, political power, and military strength. The mosaic of political containers of varying size, shape, and ownership that has existed and persisted for the past two centuries and more is basically a reflection of how Europeans viewed territory and defined space.

The states carved out of Europe and Europeanised areas of the Americas, Africa, and Asia evolved during a time when the population was rural, the densities were low, there were few cities, the mobility over extensive areas was low, the transportation and communications networks were crude, and the awareness of national and international issues by the majority of society was not great. Loyalties to the state were strong, and political power was vested in the hands of the landed aristocracy, royalty and nobility, the military, and the emerging industrial elites. Boundaries and territories tended to be more formalised than earlier. It was important to know who owned and controlled what parts of space. The nation-state had a defined core and a definite territorial demarcation.

An important point in the investigation of the origin, development, and persistence of the nation-state or state is that in the perspective of human history, it represents only one of several forms of government and political organisation that has occurred and will occur. We know from our knowledge of the agrarian or pre-industrial era of history that the pre-state or state has a set of distinguishing characteristics dissimilar from the industrial state (Table 10.2). There is little reason to think or suggest that the forms and functions of governments or the territorial or spatial dimensions of political organisation at 2025 or 2075 will be like those existing in political space today. Contemporary world political maps and spaces and all the mosaic of containers (states, territories, colonies, etc.) are experiencing rapid changes at regional and global levels. Dynamism occurs within, between, and among political spaces even if the formal spatial structure remains or appears to remain static.

RE-EXAMINING THE INDUSTRIAL STATE

It is important to ask at this juncture exactly what are those ingredients of the political organisation of space that we need to use in studying the state through time. While Johnston (1982) and others might maintain who controls the mode of production is most important, I believe that the shaping of states and the organisation of space must consider as well the following: how distances (social and spatial) are measured and perceived, the nature of the transportation and communications networks and their extent and impress on the economy and society, and ongoing efforts to centralise and decentralise the decision-making machinery. Additional issues are the number and types of transactions with other areas and populations inside and outside the nation-state in question, the awareness groups in the population (voting and non-voting) have of political issues and their influences on policies, the mobility of the population, and the loyalties of individuals to the state, corporations, and organisations. Also the nature of boundaries; how they are perceived and affect internal and external movement, flows and organisation are important in assessing the viability of the present and the future of the nation-state system.

What I am suggesting is that the contemporary political worlds are markedly different in form and substance from the late 1700s, the 1800s, and the first half of this century. Because the worlds and all the spaces within them are different, so are the conditions that lead to the definitions of government, the role of national political units, the awareness of individuals, and the organisation of space. My reading of the contemporary political landscape suggests that the state or nation-state as a concept and as a specific political unit is found wanting both in trying to explain what is going on in much of the world and why. I see the present as a period of transition or a watershed in regards to global geopolitical organisation. The transition is marked by one of trying to adapt an industrial state typology and form into a post-industrial world. The space economies and societies of the industrial and post-industrial eras are markedly dissimilar in some facets and so are likely to be the politics associated with each.

Something is happening to the nation-state and what it is are changes in its form, function, organisation, and viability. Many current problems scholars, political leaders and parties, non-governmental and inter-governmental organisations, and citizens have in coming to grips with understanding what is going on in specific countries and much of the world is an outgrowth of trying to utilise an outdated concept and political form of organisation in new and rapidly changing worlds, viz., post-industrial societies and economies.

THE POST-INDUSTRIAL NATION-STATE AND STATE SYSTEM

The next questions that need to be discussed are: (1) what are some of the differences between the nation-state of the industrial world from that of the post-industrial world; and (2) what are the features of the post-industrial nation-state? Let me identify several for purposes of discussion

(Table 10.3). Those considered are not meant to be exhaustive, nor are features mutually exclusive.

First, the post-industrial world, as mentioned above, is a world of advanced and instant transportation and communications linking individuals, corporations, professional societies, non-governmental organisations, and governments (local, regional) to all parts of the world. This trans-national feature is most readily identified with corporations who have offices, subsidiaries, branches, and affiliates scattered on every continent.

Second, distance ceases to be a barrier to interaction between and among governments, organisations, corporations, or individuals. Existing and anticipated advances in telecommunications exert extraterritorial influences. The difference and distances between cores and peripheries are lessened. Even the core and periphery and states within them may need to be redefined. Nations or groups previously separated by distance or differences in language, religion, ethnicity and culture may be united. It merits mention that while telecommunications and computer technology may unite groups, they also may promote and exacerbate differences among groups and permit those identities and loyalties to surface (secession and regionalism).

Third, many boundaries (formal nation-state boundaries or cultural ones) are being blurred or eroded. A "world without borders" is ideal, but formal boundaries have lost much of their importance with instant telephone linkages, satellite images, computer processing of international data and images, and global television reporting. Few problems are considered unique to single political units. Even frontiers, buffers, and strategic areas associated with the industrial political maps and worlds lose much meaning in a time-space converging world and one of interregional and global human extensibility. Who controls the state as a unit will be more important in the future than control or claims of specific boundaries.

The fourth feature is related to the third and that is the levels of interest and awareness of problems meriting actions by government and policy bodies have intensified. Rather than individuals, voluntary organisations, or political parties focusing solely on local or regional concerns, many groups and parties in both developed and developing countries are addressing global problems and the implications of a nation-state's decisions on global societies. Support for co-ordinated government actions is bolstered by like-minded groups elsewhere. Amnesty International, Oxfam, World Wildlife Fund, and groups protesting nuclear weapons and environmental degradation attract supporters in many states. Governments represented in UNCTAD, the Group of 77, NEO, and various cartels demonstrate that distance (social or linear) need not be a barrier to resolving problems.

Table 10.3:   Characteristics of Post-Industrial Political
Worlds

Advances in rapid transportation and communication
   and in computer technology shrink spaces
Distance ceases to be a barrier to interaction
Boundaries and their significance is further eroded
Conflict over territory and areas more than
   boundaries
Recognition of transnational and international
   dimensions of problems
Shift of problems from production priorities to
   consumer issues, human rights, and quality of
   life
Loyalties are mixed (to states, transnational
   corporations, interests groups, and organisations,
   etc.)
Political organisation of new spaces - high seas,
   air space, outer space
Networks replace cores in hierarchy
Emergence of global and regional interdependent
   systems
Creation of super-states and emergence of
   regionalism and secession

Fifth, there is a marked shift in the priorities of the
PE and PS from a major focus on production of goods and
production economies to human-oriented issues. Civil rights
protecting minorities in employment, education and housing,
eliminating sex discrimination against women, the protection
of children and the elderly, and the quality of life are
associated with legislation and regulations in the post-
industrial state. There is also a concern for how energy,
chemical, computer and transportation technologies will
affect populations and areas. The social impacts of acid
rain, toxic and hazardous substances, nuclear waste and war,
and privacy (with vast computerised data bases and spy
satellites) were not considered of critical importance to
governments, political parties, or leaders previously. Human
services and rights replace the production of goods as top
priorities in the post-industrial society.
     Sixth, the loyalties of individuals are mixed. While
some citizens of nation-states may retain primary
allegiances to their state of birth and residence, others may
hold ties to transnational corporations, non-governmental
organisations, professional societies, and cultures (who are
dominant in an adjacent state). Alternative loyalties to
other states (refugees, foreign students), organisations,
corporations, and cultures will not only increase the levels

of awareness of a nation-state's residents but possibly lead
to some conflicts in language training, employment, housing
and political representation. Laws, regulations, and
policies may be changed to accommodate the loyalties of new
and existing groups. The loyalties of refugees (stateless
persons), whether related to voluntary or forced
immigration, will confront traditional global and emerging
regional powers.

Seventh, the political organisation of space has
entered new arenas, not of major importance to the land-based
industrial state. The ownership, demarcation, domination,
use, and exploitation of the high seas, the air above a
state, or even outer space represent jurisdictional questions
that are beginning to become critical in regional and
international bodies. Is the containerisation of the high
seas or air space or even the sectoral division of Antarctica
a satisfactory solution to resolve jurisdiction on
environments that are "the common heritage of all humankind"?
Common heritage legislation and jurisdiction aims to benefit
all populations and states, not simply those with the
technologies and military ability to exploit new-found
resource bases.

Eighth, the political world is becoming one because of
space-adjusting technologies; less important are cores and
boundaries. Rapid transportation and communication and
instant transactions between traditional cores, peripheries,
and semiperipheries lends this three-fold regional schema
virtually useless. Terms like centripetal and centrifugal
forces and influences also lose much meaning. The same holds
true for socialist and capitalist nation-states. Individuals,
offices, organisations, and governments whether in large or
small cities or near a world city half-a-world away are being
"hooked into" what goes on elsewhere. At the apex of the
global political hierarchy will be those nodes (cities) that
have the most intricate land and space transportation and
communications networks to cities in all parts of the world.
The rapid diffusion of some characteristics of the PE and PS
will mean some cities in the developing world will be more
tied into the rich world than into rural areas within their
own country.

Ninth, the new political orders that are emerging
represent systems of large, medium, and small sized nodes
being integrated across state boundaries, continents, and
oceans. The various trading blocs, cartels, economic unions,
federations, and alliances that have surfaced in the past
two decades are seen as harbingers of new forms of
governmental organisation. Even though the success record to
date of such intergovernmental and regional compacts is
mixed, the momentum exists within developed and developing
regions for different political forms and structures. The
functional nature of the post-industrial political world will

stand in marked contrast to the formal political organisation
of space in the industrial era. It seems likely that there
will be no single post-industrial state system, but a number,
as the system that evolves is a function of time, space,
culture, traditions, and government. While interdependence
and interregional political systems are trademarks of the new
state systems, remnants of earlier times will always remain,
as we see with monarchies and kingdoms today.

Tenth, the post-industrial political system will see the
existence of superstates, emerging regional powers (in the
developing world), cartel powers, transnational corporations
more powerful than nation-states, and the emergence of
regionalism and secession. Several decades are needed in
this present watershed or transition period before a more
formal and stable post-industrial state system gets sorted
out. Economic, social, and political changes are juxtaposed
in transition periods. It is one of the more curious twists
of globally interdependent and shrinking worlds that many of
the same economic and social transformations that serve to
bring groups together also tend to lead to social and
political alienation and separation among some groups.
Cultures and groups that have been traditionally disen-
franchised, either because they were an ethnic minority or
had culture traits (language or religion) different from the
ruling political authority, may ferret out commonalities with
groups in an adjacent state. Current political maps of Africa
and Asia contain examples of formal nation-states and legal
boundaries that are not based on the areal extent of dominant
or minority cultures. Sectionalism, self-determination and
secession have been voiced in numerous states in Europe,
North America, Africa, and Asia in recent years. New
political interest groups with interests in environmental
protection, banning nuclear weapons, or consumer protection
may form alliances across existing nation-states and
influence regional and global policies.

CONCLUSION

This paper addresses a question that political geographers
interested in the geography of the future need to consider
seriously: what is the future of the nation-state in the
emerging post-industrial world? That the formation,
organisation, functions, and transactions of states in the
post-industrial space society and economy are and will be
different from the industrial nation-state suggests that the
time is ripe for examining this topic. I have identified
above a number of salient features of the post-industrial
economies and the features of the emerging post-industrial
state system and delineated some basic differences with the
industrial state society and economy. It is clear that an

examination of industrial and post-industrial space economies
and societies is necessary for us to present models and
theories of the future nation-state system. The above
discussion is to serve as a vehicle for discussion and
research.

REFERENCES

Abler, R. (1975) 'Effects of Space-Adjusting Technologies on
    the Human Geography of the World', in R. Abler et al.,
    Human Geography in a Shrinking World, Duxbury Press,
    North Scituate, Ma, 35-56
Abler, R. et al. (1975) Human Geography in a Shrinking World,
    Duxbury Press, North Scituate, Ma.
Bell, D. (1976) The Coming Post-Industrial Society, Basic
    Books, New York
Brunn, S. D. (1981) 'Geopolitics in a Shrinking World:
    A Political Geography of the Twenty-first Century', in
    A. D. Burnett and P. J. Taylor (eds.), Political Studies
    from Spatial Perspectives, John Wiley, Chichester, U.K.,
    157-172
Brunn, S. D. (1983) 'Cities of the Future', in S. D. Brunn
    and J. F. Williams (eds.), Cities of the World: World
    Regional Urban Development, Harper and Row, New York,
    453-487
Coffey, W. J. (1981) Geography: Towards a General Spatial
    Systems Approach, Methuen, New York
Cohen, S. B. and Rosenthal, L. D. (1971) 'A Geographical
    Model for Political Systems Analysis', Geographical
    Review, 61, 5-31
Cohen, S. B. (1982) 'A New Map of Global Geopolitical
    Equilibrium: A Developmental Approach', Political
    Geography Quarterly, 1, 223-242
Cohen, S. B. (1983) 'American Foreign Policies for the
    Eighties', in N. Kliot and S. Waterman (eds.)
    Pluralism and Political Geography, Croom Helm, London,
    295-310
Cox, K. (1979) Location and Public Problems: A Political=
    Geography of the Contemporary World, Maaroufa Press,
    Chicago
Feather, F. (1980) Through the '80s: Thinking Globally,
    Acting Locally, World Future Society, Washington, D.C.
Gottmann, J. (1973) The Significance of Territory, University
    of Virginia Press, Richmond
Gottmann, J. (1980) Centre and Periphery: Spatial Variations
    in Politics, Wiley, Chichester, U.K.
Harman, W. (1976) An Incomplete Guide to the Future, San
    Francisco Book Co., San Francisco
Huggett, R. (1983) Systems Analysis in Geography, Claredon
    Press, Oxford

Janelle, D. (1973) 'Measuring Human Extensibility in a
    Shrinking World', Journal of Geography, 72 (5), 8-15
Johnston, R. J. (1982) Geography and the State: An Essay in
    Political Geography, St. Martin's Press, New York
Kahn, H. et al. (1976) The Next 200 Years, Morrow, New York
Muir, R. (1975) Modern Political Geography, Macmillan, London
Muir, R. and Paddison, R. (1981) Politics, Geography, and
    Behavior, Methuen, London and New York
Naisbett, J. (1982) Megatrends: Ten New Directions
    Transforming Our Lives, Warner Books, New York
Paddison, R. (1983) The Fragmented State: The Political
    Geography of Power, Basil Blackwell, Oxford
Spekke, A. (1975) The Next 25 Years: Crisis and Opportunity,
    World Future Society, Washington, D.C.
Short, J. R. (1982) An Introduction to Political Geography,
    Routledge and Kegan Paul, London and Boston
Soja, E. W. (1971) The Political Organization of Space,
    Association of American Geographers, Washington, D.C.
Taylor, P. J. (1982) 'Political Geography and the World
    Economy', in A. D. Burnett and P. J. Taylor (eds.),
    Political Studies from Spatial Perspectives, John Wiley,
    Chichester and New York, 1984, 157-172
Toffler, A. (1980) The Third Wave, Morrow, New York
Warntz, W. (1967) 'Global Science and the Tyranny of Space',
    Papers, Regional Science Association, 19, 7-19

Chapter Eleven

GEOGRAPHICAL PERSPECTIVES ON SELF-DETERMINATION

David B. Knight

Self-determination refers to the right of a group with a
distinctive politico-territorial identity to determine its
own destiny. This simple definition hides a multitude of
views on the concept. There exists today no universal
agreement on just what the concept means, to whom it
specifically applies, nor on how it might be achieved.
Although the dimensions of the concept have changed quite
markedly in the past sixty years, Robert Lansing's (1921:97)
phrase that the concept is "loaded with dynamite" still holds
true.
    The concept of self-determination is inherently
geographic inasmuch as it involves people, sense of place,
and bounded space (Knight 1982b). It is also a legal
concept, for the notions of sovereignty and recognition are
involved too, thus to focus on self-determination necessarily
involves an examination of international law (Knight, 1983a;
Davies, 1983a). Although the concept is all but ignored in
introductory political geography texts (Knight, 1983a,
footnore 1) some geographers have accomplished focussed
research on the process whereby self-determination has been
attempted or applied successfully (Burghardt, 1962;
Macdonald, 1975; Whebell, 1976; Boateng, 1978) but these
researchers have not been concerned with the same definitions.
Geographers also have focussed on some of the elements of the
concept, as with autonomy, links between identity and
territory, nation and nationalism, claims to territory,
territorial separation, and ethnic separatism (Adejuyigbe,
1980; Agnew, 1981a; Boateng, 1978; Burghardt, 1971, 1973,
1980; Knight, 1970, 1974, 1982a, 1982b, 1983b; Prescott,
1968; Smith, G. 1979; Whebell, 1973, 1976; Williams, C. H.
1980, 1981, 1982). Some of these same writers, with other
scholars (including political scientists and sociologists)
have reviewed some theories which seek to explain why there
has been a recent resurgence of ethnic regionalisms (Agnew
1981b; Connor, 1972, 1977; Johnston, 1982; Rokkan, 1980,
1983; Orridge and Williams, 1982; Smith, A. D. 1981, 1982;

Williams, C. H. 1979; Williams, S. W. 1977). This paper does not repeat what these various writers have said for it takes a different tack to the one previously taken by geographers.

The paper focuses explicitly on changing definitions and acceptances of the concept of self-determination and identifies contemporary problems relating to internal and external applications. Hopefully the reader will be challenged to think anew about some old and not so old problems by way of the numerous questions that are posed. Self-determination pertains to both intra- and inter-state relations, thus by focussing on the concept profound issues are identified which relate to state structures, international law, and the future of the international state system.

At the heart of my discussion is the concept of territory. Territory is area that is bounded, formally and informally, and includes terrain, flora and fauna, resources, and human inhabitants and their ways of life. Gottmann (1973:15) notes that territory is "a very substantial, material, measurable, and concrete entity" but too, it "is the product and indeed the expression of the psychological features of human groups." In this sense, as I have noted elsewhere, "territory is not; it becomes, for territory itself is passive, and it is human beliefs and actions that give territory meaning" (Knight, 1982a:517). Going further, as a political geographer concerned with self-determination, I feel that territory can be regarded "as space to which identity is attached by a distinctive group who hold or covet that territory and who desire to have full control over it for the group's benefit" (Knight, 1982a:526). The latter part of this statement is crucial, for it mentions control, control over the territory for the group's benefit. But control in what sense? Control of social and cultural policies? Economic control? Or political control? If one or more of these, to what extent is there autonomy? Or is autonomy enough, for it implies that there is another body which has ultimate control? If it is not enough then is there the desire to have full control over the territory, that is, to gain sovereignty?

Why is it necessary to raise these questions? The essential issue is that there is discordance between international political boundaries and the distribution of populations with distinct senses of self. Because of this discordance there is a preponderance of plural or multi-cultural societies in the world's state-structured system of territorial organisation. The existence of differences in definitions of self, if territorially distinct <u>within</u> states, can be referred to as regionalisms.[1] (I here set aside the issue of why these differences occur). Of course, all national governments will try to make persuasive use of the concept of "common territory" (that is, the total area of the respective states) in an attempt "to create the <u>illusion</u> of commonality for geographically diverse areas" (Potter, 1968: 41-42; my stress) and the various population groups located within the limits of the international boundaries. In so doing, a sense of national identity may be forged. The process of belonging is complex; for people to feel they belong to the state they must feel involved with a complex set of physical, economic, political, social, and especially psychological links with people who live in different parts of that common territory (Gottmann, 1952; Deutsch, 1953; Shafer, 1955). The sense of belonging being referred to here can be summed up by the concept of nationalism.

Nationalism involves the fundamental function of transferring loyalties from kinship groups or local and regional levels of attachment to the larger national group (Kohn, 1944; Shafer, 1972, 1982). It implies the attempt to give meaning to the commonality of interests of all who live within a state and to define the rights of membership in that national group of all those who are said to belong to it. A "we" versus "they" dichotomy comes into existence for nationalism also stresses antagonism to other national groups. This concept will not be expanded upon here; I have dealt with it elsewhere (Knight, 1982a). What I would like to stress at this point is that there are hundreds of groups within states, as the latter are territorially structured, which do not have an attachment to their supposed national territories and to the broader "nation". Many such groups remain with a consciousness that thus is regional within existing states. Some such groups can be said to have a sub-state "nationalism" or, perhaps, a "mini-nationalism", for their regional identities, like nationalism, also are rooted in a variety of emotional, historical, cultural, political, economic and psychological factors. Some of these groups may be content to live essentially as they are now, but others may seek fuller political expression for their distinctive sense of self. Indeed, many such groups desire to have a "nation-state", that is, where there will be a complete areal match between "nation" and its sovereign state. To this extent, the desire for achieving the ideal of "nation-state" is not dead.[2] However, to achieve the "nation-state" areal fit may well mean the break-up of existing multi-cultural states. Clearly, contrasting opinions concerning self-determination are likely to be held by different parties!

Before exploring something of the dynamics and range of opinions of today let me first more sharply focus on the concept of self-determination as it was in the past.

The concept of self-determination is ancient, going back to the first attempt by a people (or community) to control or subjugate another. But in recent centuries, we find that as the modern concept of nation developed, the concept of self-determination developed too. Essentially a revolutionary proposition, self-determination referred to the establishment of the idea of popular national sovereignty over the inhabited territory as the state-ruler relationship was replaced by that of state-nation. The source of all sovereignty was said to reside in the nation.

Many changes to the world's political map occurred as nationalistic ideas spread, with many independent states being created. By the nineteenth century, at least from the perspective of the dominant European powers, national self-determination was generally regarded as a unifying force because it involved the integration of people and territories into modern "nation-states". Some European nationalistic movements were suppressed because of this - they were regarded as being parts of existing states - and many peoples in African, Asian, and Pacific island territories were subjugated to colonial rule. Given that the European powers generally seemed favourable to the idea of self-determination, how was it that they felt so free to subjugate colonial peoples and their territories? Obviously this loaded question cannot be explored fully here, but may I suggest the following for food for thought?

The Peace of Westphalia of 1648 led to the modern system of states because it established the existence of an equality among territorial units; it asserted that each unit had no higher authority than its individual sovereign ruler. In short, states were said to be sovereign. The rulers, in recognising each other as equals, also accepted that they were equally independent in asserting control over the respective territories they ruled. Implicit in this was the concept of recognition. But Europeans generally did not acknowledge societies elsewhere as either organised (in the "civilised" way) or sovereign (in the European sense) so they felt morally and legally justified in taking those areas as colonial territories.

As suggested here, sovereign and supposedly equal European states existed within a system of international law. At least in theory, it was a law among states, not a law over states. The development of international law has been uneven since Vitoria's sixteenth century treatises (Scott, 1934; Davies, 1983a) and the Peace of Westphalia (Gottmann, 1973) although through time sovereignty, equality, and recognition have remained as essential principles. In the present century sovereignty and recognition have been achieved by many groups. There remain numerous groups who also desire the achievement of such goals.

The term "self-determination" gained political currency only near the end of World War I, first by the Bolsheviks and then by President Woodrow Wilson. Leninism and Wilsonianism, to use Arno Mayer's (1959:333) terms, were opposing ideologies through which self-rule came to have new meaning.

To the one ideology, world revolution of the oppressed peoples was called for, to the other, democracy for all was the sought after goal. The words self-determination thus had contrasting meanings to the people of different ideological persuasions: to Leninists they meant the overthrowing of bourgeois democracy and the rise of class self-determination, whereas to Wilsonians they meant the spread of bourgeois democracy; to Leninists they applied to the proletariat (who, ultimately, should achieve a stateless communist society), whereas to Wilsonians they applied to national minorities in Europe; to both Leninists and Wilsonians they meant reaching over the heads of governments to the people (Baker and Doff, 1927; Lenin, 1951; Shaheen, 1956; Pomerance, 1976; Ronen, 1979).

By self-determination, Wilson meant self-governed and government by the consent of the governed. He said at one point, "every people has a right to choose the sovereignty under which they live" (Pomerance, 1976:2). Not all of the participants in the Treaty of Versailles discussion following World War I were in agreement with this ideal (Cobban, 1944). Clemenceau, for instance, declared to Lloyd George "that he did not believe in the principle of self-determination, which allowed a man to clutch at your throat the first time it was convenient for him ..." (George, 1938:286). Wilson's Secretary of State, Robert Lansing, felt that considerations of national safety, historic rights, and economic interests should all have preference over the principles of self-determination (Lansing, 1921:97-98). It must be added that Wilson himself eventually came to question the principle because, as he put it, nationalities began appearing everywhere!

Wilson and his conference colleagues applied the principle of self-determination, but they applied it unevenly, with reference to the disintegration and dissolution of the Austro-Hungarian, German, and Turkish empires.[3] They denied "self-determination" to some European groups. Most certainly, self-determination was not intended, at that time, for the colonised world.

Between the two World Wars, some successful and unsuccessful efforts for self-determination were made. Following World War II the quest for self-determination became an especially powerful force in the Third World, a quest for the removal of control by alien Europeans, a quest for decolonisation and independence, a quest that was more or less met by the end of the 1960s (with some notable exceptions, including still today, Namibia) without altering the boundaries of then existing territories.[4] This latter point is one to which we will return.

The rush of Third World countries to achieve self-determination occurred with the blessings of, and not infrequent prodding by, the United Nations. Just what has been the perspective of the U.N.? The U.N. Charter and many subsequent documents make reference to self-determination, with the most explicit discussion being presented in U.N. Resolution 2625 (XXV) of October, 1970.[5] The latter resolution stated that all people have the right to self-determination. This "right" is boldly stated. Then, however, as Rupert Emerson has noted, "the small print takes over and becomes the big print which establishes the new and far more restricted guidelines" (Emerson, 1971:459). There are two points reflected in the "small print".

First, the Resolution declares that:

> every State shall refrain from any action aimed at the partial or total disruption of the national unity and territorial integrity of any other State or country.

This injunction has been blatantly ignored all too often since 1970.

Second, the resolution declares that:

> nothing (in the Declaration's discussion of self-determination) shall be construed as authorising or encouraging any action which would dismember or impair, totally or in part, the territorial integrity or political unity of sovereign and independent States conducting themselves in compliance with the principle of equal rights and self-determination of peoples ... and thus possessed of a government representing the whole people belonging to the territory without distinction as to race, creed or colour.

The U.N. position thus has been that whereas it is legitimate for peoples subjected to colonial rule to seek self-determination (i.e. the so-called salt water theory or external domination), it is not legitimate for people who form a minority within a national territory to seek self-determination, whether on their own initiative or with help from any outside power, for that would "dismember or impair, totally or in part" the existing state. There is a paramountcy of contemporary self-determination for the population of the total national territory over parts of either the population or territory within it. To affect any departure from this, under international law as so understood, must entail the free choice of the majority of the total population (or, can we ask, cynically, is it just the government in power - most notably in instances where a majority has been colonised and is subjected to minority rule, as in several Central American states?). The only currently acknowledged exception to the colonial limitation relates to those populations that are now subjected to rule by a minority who govern by an _apartheid_ philosophy.

Beyond the U.N. view, international lawyers are divided on whether or not self-determination is a right. Rosalyn Higgins (1963) and Antonio Cassese (1981), for instance, are two who believe that self-determination has developed into an international legal right, whereas Leo Gross (1975) and Gaetano Arangio-Ruiz (1979) are two who feel that practice (in Gross's words, 1975:141) "does _not_ support the proposition that the principle of self-determination is to be interpreted as a right ..." Whatever, we have recently witnessed the remarkable spread of the "right" to most former _colonial_ territories (i.e. external self-determination). But this action was "safe" in the sense that international boundaries were not further altered. In that sense, the _status quo_ was accepted.

To some, the creation of "new" states within the colonially-derived territorial frame provides the hope for the future, whereby culturally diverse societies are being brought to have a new level of identity, that is, whereby identification will increasingly be with the state as opposed to the lower level territorial attachments. To achieve this it is sometimes necessary to split former units of the state into smaller ones in an attempt to breakup competing units which may threaten the very existence of the total state or else to provide some legitimisation to smaller groups within the state, as in Nigeria (Adejuyigbe, 1974, 1980).

As further recognition of the "safety" of the _status quo_, vis-a-vis international boundaries and of the U.N. perspective, African leaders singly and together (through the Organisation of African Unity) have declared their opposition to any tampering with colonially-derived territorial partitioning, that is, as per international boundaries. Successor governments (to former colonial authorities) wish to have interstate unanimity so as to be better able to counter continuing demands for self-determination on the part of groups regional within the new states. African leaders thus have accepted the concept of "territorial integrity" as passed to them by colonial authorities - even though the bounding of the territories was decided in Europe nearly one hundred years ago with no Africans present. Will Africans ever be truly "free" of colonialism until they bring themselves to restructure the international political bounding of space on the continent? Such restructuring is not likely in the near future! Why? Because the concept of self-determination (as related above) is involved: it is legitimate for former colonial territories to seek and be granted self-determination; it is not legitimate for parts of existing states to seek self-determination. Or, to use the words of the Kenyan delegation to the 1963 OAU conference:

"The principle of self-determination has relevance where
foreign domination is the issue. It has no relevance where
the issue is territorial disintegration by dissident
citizens" (cited in Friedmann, et al., 1969:233). In short,
colonially-derived international boundaries are now "sacred"!
    The rationale for the U.N. and the O.A.U. stances are
not hard to appreciate. In Van Dyke's (1970:102) words, "the
United Nations would be in an extremely difficult position if
it were to interpret the right of self-determination in such
a way as to invite or justify attacks on the territorial
integrity of its own members". Thus, for instance, the U.N.
has ignored or rejected many claims for territorial
separation in post-colonial settings, including Biafra,
Katanga, and Kurdistan. There have been times, however, when
the U.N. stance has been suspect, as with the purposeful
ignoring of the wishes of the people of the Western Sahara
(Franck, 1976) or with the support given to Indonesia's
absorption of former Dutch New Guinea (West Irian), even
though the people there are ethnically and culturally
distinct. The U.N. justified Indonesia's claiming of West
Irian because of its former (Dutch) colonial status, yet U.N.
members have been divided over Indonesia's more recent
vicious taking over of (former Portuguese) East Timor where
the people were on record as wanting to remain apart from
Indonesia. Indonesia's claim is that the territory is being
"reintegrated" but this claim is not widely accepted (Clark,
1980a). With the two annexations, the West Irians and the
East Timorese are now "simply" sub-state regional identities
within Indonesia and, because they are now part of a
sovereign state (albeit the East Timor occupation is
disputed), the Indonesian government theoretically is free to
treat those people as it will; only lip service is paid to
human rights.
    Some territorial separations have occurred as self-
determination has been applied. The separations of Norway
from Sweden and Singapore from Malaysia were reasonably
peaceful. In contrast, the divisions of India in 1947 and
the more recent separation of Bangladesh from Pakistan were
violent, with terrible loss of life. The reasons for the
creation of Bangladesh were several-fold, but the call for
self-determination by the people was dominant. The
"sovereignty and territorial integrity" claims by Pakistan
as the basis for rejecting such a call were set aside by many
in the World community when there was the acceptance of the
fact that human rights deprivations were so severe that they
could no longer be tolerated. But if human rights claims can
be used in that case, cannot they also be used elsewhere?
Why is the U.N. not more actively supporting the people of
East Timor, or Afghanistan, or Cambodia, to name but three
places? Is it enough for individual countries to denounce
repression elsewhere? But perhaps this is a separate issue?

If states were to justify the recognition of self-determination for parts of existing states, then would there not be the potential for havoc on the international scene? Yes and No! Let us explore this ambivalent answer, in part by again focusing on international law. A stumbling block to endorsing rights to self-determination, if it is to involve secession, is the concept of sovereignty.

Robert Isaak has observed that the evolution of the legal notion of sovereignty led to a paradoxical development: while it provided a common principle upon which all states could agree, thus forming the foundation for the laws of nations or international law, it also recognised that the source of laws was invested within states (Isaak, 1981:81). This latter fact limited the effectiveness of international law because it maintained that political leaders could do whatever they chose within their own state boundaries. In other words:

> as long as the principle of sovereignty was
> considered to be primary, no principle of higher
> law could legally exist that allowed an inter-
> national organisation or any other foreign force
> to intervene in the domestic affairs of any
> country, regardless of how inhumane or immoral
> those affairs might be (Isaak, 1981:82)

Accordingly, in terms of international law as so understood, existing governments can legitimately use any means necessary to counter secessionist activities within the national territory. (We must note, however, that this interpretation of sovereignty increasingly is being challenged as questions about the morality of states are raised (Hoffmann, 1981) and as states - supposedly - have become bound by rapidly developing international human rights law (Henkin, 1981). Of course, no matter what perspectives are taken on sovereignty, the essential conflict that arises with respect to secessionist groups is that they seek their own sovereign status by the application of self-determination as they define it. The dilemma comes from the fact that every demand for self-determination involves some counter claim, involving the territorial integrity of some other "self".

A key problem thus seems to be one of definition - how is the group defined and by whom? A leading author on self-determination, Alfred Cobban (1944:48) said, "any territorial community, the members of which are conscious of themselves as members of a community, and wish to maintain the identity of their community, is a nation." Such a definition is volatile! If this definition were applied, with all groups who see themselves as being "nations" being granted statehood with sovereignty, then chaos would indeed reign.

Perhaps not surprisingly, the threat of such consequences thus has led many people to react conservatively. In 1921 the Commission of Rapporteurs rejected the Aaland Islanders' claim of legal right to separatist self-determination by declaring that:

> To concede to minorities either of language or religion, or to any fractions of a population, the right of withdrawing from the community to which they belong, because it is their wish or their good pleasure, would be to destroy order and stability within States and to inaugurate anarchy in international life; it would be to uphold a theory incompatible with the very idea of the State as a territorial and political entity (cited in Buchheit, 1978:71).

A group wanting to secede under the "right" of self-determination would counter this judgement by saying that the phrase "community to which they belong" is not that of the larger state but one they define as wanting to secede! Another typical conservative reaction was that of Mrs. Eleanor Roosevelt made when she was the U.S. representative to the U.N. in 1952:

> Does self-determination mean the right of secession? Does self-determination constitute a right of fragmentation or a justification for the fragmentation of nations? Does self-determination mean the right of people to sever association with another power regardless of the economic effect upon both parties, regardless of the effect upon their internal stability and their external security, regardless of the effect upon their neighbours or the international community? Of course not (cited in Buchheit, 1978:118).

But do secessionists really care about such a perspective? Not at all. The leaders of hundreds of sub-state regional groups simply do not accept such a view; agitation, some of it violent, continues for self-determination in its fullest sense in many parts of the world by groups regional within states.

One can identify dozens of present and potential instances in which claims for self-determination either do or could threaten existing states. There is as yet no fully comprehensive systematic comparison of these groups, although collections of studies are now appearing (Alexander and Friedlander, 1980; Dofny and Akiwowo, 1980; Hall, 1979; Rokkan and Urwin, 1982; Smith, A. D., 1976; Williams, C. H., 1982). From these various studies one thing stands out: such

identities, expressed politically, are difficult to control
because they feed on themselves. In that sense, to the
leaders of the larger state at least, claims by sub-state
groups for self-determination are not "rational" and are seen
to be quite incompatible with the notion of "oneness",
although, one must also note, leaders of states do use
elements of the regional identities as a means for causing
dissension amongst the regional population. Such certainly
has been the case in Canada over the past five years or so as
the Canadian Federal government has worked to undercut
Quebecois separatist plans (Knight, 1982b).

Some political systems can accommodate differences, most
notably federal systems. But is Alexandre Marc correct when
he states that "only a federal society provides the
conditions in which a complete freedom can blossom for all
ethnic groups, large or small, compact of dispersed"? Many
"sub-state nationalists" within certain federations would not
agree. For example, Rene Levesque and other Quebecois
nationalists/separatists "complete freedom can blossom" only
when Quebec is an independent state. In contrast, other
Quebecers are convinced that one can "at one and the same
time, be an authentic Quebecer and a true Canadian" (Quebec
Liberal Party, 1980:140). A basic dichotomy exists between
these two perspectives, for one is inward and the other
outward. As Canadian sociologist John Porter (1975:294) put
it:

> On the one hand, if they (i.e., a minority group)
> value and emphasise ethnic identity, mobility and
> opportunity are endangered; on the other hand, if
> they emphasise mobility and opportunity, it will
> be at the cost of submerging cultural identity.

Inward or outward; security versus opportunity. This
dichotomy, as an essential dilemma, also is inherent in the
concept of territory, as Gottmann (1973) has delineated it.
As applied to a group's concept of "self", inwardness can lead
to consistent self-glorification and self-congratulations and
to being so blinkered by petty and narrow nationalism that the
good to be gained from broader associations are ignored. In
ignoring the value of broader associations a sub-state
"nationalism" may come to feel that the only means for
providing a secure place for the distinctive identity is
through the creation of a separate sovereign state. However,
those who identify with the broader existing state can charge
that:

> It is always easier, in the short run, to live in
> a universe which conforms exactly to every aspect
> of one's personality. But the challenge of
> co-existence obliges each community within the

> state with a plural society to continually extend
> and surpass itself. It allows us to seek and
> achieve goals which, for each community taken
> separately, would never be attainable (Quebec
> Liberal Party, 1980:139).

In short, Quebec federalists, in this case, hold that there is
opportunity to be gained by reaching out and interacting with
others. The danger for the sub-state group in so doing is
that the narrow sense of "self" will thus be challenged and
may have to be incorporated into the larger concept of "self",
one which will tie one to the larger total group which also
happens to live within the state (although this attachment is
in the abstract, and does not necessarily force people to like
each other!).
      One of the continuing challenges that groups with
distinctive sub-state regionally-based identities face comes
from integrative modernising forces. Hand in hand with these
go anonymous technocratic bureaucrats who work for the state.
Is there a modern "political culture" that cuts across old
regional attachments to link notions of progress and orderly
government primarily to the areal limits of the total state?
Am I correct in suggesting that such technocrats are more
interested in the effective running of the state than in the
continued life of "romantic regionalisms"? If this is so -
and I base my comments principally on observations made in
Canada, the South West Pacific, and Botswana - then surely
there will necessarily be a spiral of conflict, conflict
between those who identify with the "rationalised",
technocratically "efficient" machine called the state and the
more subjective realities of sub-state politico-territorial
identities which, in response, desire and perhaps even demand
recognition.[6] If totally ignored or pushed to some limit -
but just what that limit is we cannot say with confidence -
then a sub-state regionalisms might pursue the goal of self-
determination. But in considering these thoughts, let us
also ponder upon the following: the rhythm of modernisation
over the past several decades has been neither constant nor
unilinear; there has been no single path, no equal pace, no
single goal. Equally, with the concept of self-determination
is no single path, no equal pace, and, beyond the words and
perhaps some vague notions as to what they mean, not even a
common goal.
      Does the "nation" always need its own sovereign state to
fully develop? Many sub-state or mini-nationalists would say
yes! The leader of Quebec's separatist party has declared
that "self-determination is an absolute necessity for the
growth to maturity of a society which has its own identity"
(Levesque, 1978:110). To him, self-determination means
sovereign control over the territory by the "nation" for the
"nation". Of course, there are problems in defining who is

in the "nation" and who is not (Knight, 1983b). For now, the majority of Quebecers are against the separation of Quebec from Canada for they, with other Canadian federalists, feel that the distinctive French-Canadian identity is protected by Canadian federalism.

Federalism can indeed provide for differences within the state, but does it necessarily provide for all politico-territorially distinct groups within the state? Not so in Canada. The indigenous peoples' cultures have generally not been well protected and fostered by the federal structure. At the First Ministers' Conference on Aboriginal Rights held in Ottawa in March, 1983, Indian political leaders referred to two centuries of frustration and broken promises. Repeating their oft-made call for "self-determination" they demanded "sovereignty". The twist is that they wanted these two concepts applied to themselves within Canada, not apart from it! Likewise, the Inuit (Eskimo) of the Northwest Territories have called for "self-determination" in Nunavut, a new territory to be created out of the northeast portion of the N.W.T. In mentioning "self-determination" and "sovereignty" here we again touch on the issue of definitions. As Dawson (1983:40) noted:

> The recent First Ministers' Conference on aboriginal rights illustrated that one of the most difficult obstacles facing natives is the absence of an accepted theoretical framework for much of the debate. Confusion of the meaning of such concepts as sovereignty, self-government, self-determination, nations, territory and identity was agonisingly obvious to all of the participants in the conference and to Canadians who watched the proceedings on television at home.

Conceptual confusion and the problem of definitions is not confined to Canada. In New Zealand, for instance, Maoris have formed a political party called Mana Motuhake, which means self-determination, but its purpose is not oriented to territorial separation.

Maoris have a term, turangawaewae, which, literally, means standing place for the feet and implies "the rights of a tribal group in land and the consequential rights of individual members of the group" (Kawhara, 1979:3). Identity, territory, group rights, control - these four concepts go together. And they go together for more than just Maoris for, as suggested earlier, indigenous populations in numerous states have called for such a linking. There are problems, however. Just what is meant by self-determination in the varied cases of indigenous people? Do they want control over natural resources and the opportunity to govern themselves or, in short, to be separate so as to protect their way of life? But separate in what sense and degree, socially and politically? Not all indigenous peoples live on "reserves", so what of the people who live elsewhere within the state? If rights are to be granted to people within designated territories within the state - where some degree of autonomy might be granted - are those living elsewhere to be asked/told to go "back" to those territories? (The horrors of apartheid loom). If they do not move to the designated areas are they to be categorised as guest workers or will they legally lose their minority identity? Will the - generally marginalised - territories be eligible for economic assistance? From whom? The state? From outside the state? What will the international standing be of such territories? Falsely "independent" in the manner of the so-called "Homelands" in the Republic of South Africa or perhaps operating more as local municipalities within the state?[8]

Perhaps this all too brief mention of some indigenous peoples and some related questions is a side issue? It surely cannot be central to any contemporary discussion of self-determination? Not at all! It is central. For so long pushed aside, native peoples in numerous countries are now finding their voices and increasingly are demanding their collective human rights under international law, that is, "the right to physical existence and the right to preserve a separate identity" (Opekokew, 1982:7). Many indigenous peoples individually within their states and collectively at the international level are seeking the recognition of their right to "self-determination" (World Council of Indigenous People 1981). The International Labour Organisation and the U.N. Working Group on Indigenous Populations[7] also are addressing these claims, but several states are against such international explorations of what they hold are purely "internal" issues.

Full self-determination (with territorial separation and sovereignty) is highly unlikely for any indigenous peoples anywhere. Some of them claim they were "colonised" and so they want to be "de-colonised" in like manner to other former colonial territories (Watkins, 1977), but the territorial integrity claim of existing states rules against this as does the salt-water theory of colonisation.[9] But is separation of territory essential to secure the future needs of a people? The question remains open. What is meant by self-determination? The answer remains fuzzy. The World Council of Indigenous Peoples (1981) has, among other things, declared in a draft covenant that:

> One manner in which the right of self-determination can be realised is by the free determination of an Indigenous People to associate their territory and institutions with one or more states in a manner involving free association, regional autonomy,

home rule or associate statehood as self-
governing units.

<u>Their</u> territory. And within that territory they want such
things as water rights, land rights, hunting and fishing
rights, the right to deal internationally with other like
groups and with international organisations, and most
especially (and related to all other points), the right to
recognition of the group's distinctive identity and ways of
doing things. Why is it necessary for them to demand the
latter? Because such a right has rarely been recognised
anywhere, especially in matters of law. There has been a
clash in law when European-originated societies deal in
courts with indigenous peoples' claims (Raby, 1974). Concepts
of territory, ecology, and communal as opposed to individual
rights are in conflict. Generally, to date, "European law"
has won out because of the difficulties of communication,
in part due to a lack of respect for and understanding of the
cultural frameworks of indigenous populations, but also
because the formats are European <u>per se</u>.

And so I could continue, but it is necessary to begin to
conclude. At this point I would like to suggest that the
major stumbling block to "self-determination" being achieved
by sub-state regional groups - whether indigenous peoples or
not - is the state, that is, the state as it is currently
known, with sovereignty, territorial integrity, and so on as
essential elements. Because of the centrality of the state
in our contemporary world it seems that the attaining of
statehood generally is perceived to be the only means whereby
self-determination can be <u>fully</u> institutionalised. What are
the alternatives?

Some forms of autonomy already exist in some states for
parts of their territories (Sutton, 1976; Clark, 1980b) and
territorial restructuring is possible (Knight, 1983a, 1983b;
Adejuyigbe, 1974, 1975). Alternatively, cannot there be a
freeing of the concept of the state so as to better accommodate group political identities that remain vibrant but
discordant within existing state boundaries? Is federalism
the answer, or, indeed, the only answer? What other forms of
governmental structures are there which could be used to
permit differences to flourish without destroying existing
states - and without destroying viable identities? Or should
we simply encourage the secession of all groups desiring such
action? Or are these the wrong questions? Should we not be
asking how to do away with differences so that a classless
one-world community emerges? I do not accept the premise of
this last question! Even if, theoretically, political and
cultural differences could be wiped out, people in different
parts of the world would retain a sense of place. They would
always have and want <u>turangawaewae</u>, a place for the feet -
and thus we return to the very foundations of self-determin-

ation!

The quest for self-determination is one of the fundamental forces of our day. It is a centripetal force in the sense that it bonds people of a particular regional group by means of a shared target of aspirations. However, it is also a centrifugal force in that for that target to be met fully it pulls part of a state's population away from the total and can even lead to territorial separation. If the latter stage is reached by the many groups that currently or potentially desire it then there would be the disintegration of the politically structured world as we now know it. Leopold Kohr, who felt that the underlying cause for human misery was bigness, suggested that economic chaos need not result from political fragmentation. He suggested that the abandonment of the present large unified-area state system in favour of a small-state world "would not necessarily mean the destruction of all existing kinds of economic unity ... Political particularism does not automatically entail economic particularism" (Kohr, 1957:166-67). This is an interesting perspective to consider and is one that still deserves exploration.

There are many other points that could be discussed, including the links between terrorism and self-determination (Alexander, 1976) and considerably more on the relationship between human rights and self-determination (Davies, 1983a, 1983b; Henkin, 1981). Hopefully, however, this paper has challenged the reader to think afresh about "regionalisms", that is, by way of suggesting that they be considered from the perspective of self-determination. Many questions have been posed in this paper. Some of them have been wrestled with by scholars from different disciplines although satisfactory answers have not always been forthcoming. The critical issue of definitions still remains to be solved. But people wanting "self-determination" will not wait for scholars to decide on meanings! Perhaps scholars should focus on what people mean when they say they want self-determination? Perhaps then scholars could provide better understanding of both peoples' demands and governments' responses? Perhaps the issues are beyond understanding?! I feel not, yet there is still much to learn.

The challenge of self-determination remains as a vital and sometimes bothersome one in numerous states. Potential for both accommodations and conflicts are many, yet all too little is known about both sorts of outcomes and the processes whereby they can result. Clearly, however defined, the concept of self-determination remains "loaded with dynamite".

ACKNOWLEDGEMENTS

This paper is based on research that is partially funded by
the Dean of Graduate Studies and Research and the Dean of
Social Sciences, Carleton University, and the Social Sciences
and Humanities Research Council of Canada. I am extremely
grateful for the continued support.

NOTES

1. It should be recalled that a regionalism is
recognisable only when it represents but a part of a larger
territorial whole, the latter being, in this context, the
areal extent of the state.
2. The "nation-state" is often held to be the ultimate
expression of a people. It implies a complete areal fit
between the "nation" and the "state". However, as Cornelia
Navari (1981:13) has observed, "actual nation-states rather
approximate to an ideal type than mirror it, and do so in
very different degrees." We can ask, is there any true nation-
state today? I have difficulty thinking of any. There is
doubt even with respect to instances of states that are held
to be good approximations of the ideal, as with Britain and
France, because of the existence therein of potent sub-state
"nationalisms". Do nation-states only exist in theory? Can
we develop a sliding scale and say that above a certain point
on a line means a people are a nation while those below it
are not? Or a parallel territorial scale which would measure
the areal fit between "nation" and "state"? Not at all!
Such scales would be meaningless for, as Hans Kohn (1944:13)
noted, "nationalities are groups ... of the utmost complexity.
They defy exact definition." Perhaps, at minimum, we can
accept that the nation, or those who claim to speak for it
(as an existing or hoped-for reality), desire to form or
maintain what is perceived to be a "nation-state". Certainly,
in Asia and Africa today diverse peoples grouped within
colonially-derived state boundaries generally have such
profound cultural differences that the "new" state polities
do not qualify as nation-states, even though there may be the
hope by some leaders that such an ideal may become a reality
as groups regional within the national territory increasingly
give priority of belonging to the new "nation".
Since it is so difficult to identify existing "nation-
states", has the time come to throw out the concept of
"nation-state"? I admit that the phrase is still often used,
but it is used quite incorrectly (even by political
geographers) when the terms "state" or "national societies"
(as opposed to "nation") would be more appropriate. Support
for dumping the phrase also comes from the belief by some
that widespread diffusion of ideas and material culture and
ever increasing time-space convergences on a world scale are

leading to a convergence of world culture (Spencer and
Thomas, 1969:559-560). Will a new universalism result from
such convergence? If "space-ship" earth is to survive, some
say, then there must be increased attention paid to global
interests over parochial concerns. Despite the ideals that
lie behind such hopes there is ample evidence to suggest that
such a universalism is not widely adhered to, for people still
tend to give priority of attachment to their particular state
or to a community within their state rather than to a
nebulous supra-state one-world ideal. But perhaps the latter
is necessary only as an ideal to guide positive interaction
between states, on a state to state basis or through the
United Nations? Most clearly what has still to be achieved is
mutual respect and trust between peoples within all states
and between all states. Tragically, on most days, these
basic ideals seems barely to be visible.

3. For an interesting examination of how "the self-
determination of national adherence by the local population"
was a factor in the placement of boundaries for Burgenland,
Austria, in the 1920s see the work by geographer Andrew
Burghardt (1962).

4. Over eighty newly independent states came into
existence after 1943: fourteen in the period 1943-51; twenty-
four during the years 1956-60, all but one in Africa and most
being in French Africa; twenty-eight during the period
1961-70, all but four having been granted independence from
Britain and other members of the Commonwealth of Nations;
and about twenty since 1971 (Pearcy, 1977; and newspapers and
other sources).

5. Resolution 2625 (XXV) of 24 October, 1970, is
entitled "Declaration of Principles of International Law
Concerning Friendly Relations and Co-operation Among States
in Accordance With the Charter of the United Nations."

6. For a discussion of different orientations of
Allegiance as suggested by de Vos (that is, present-
functional, present-specific, past familial-cultural, and
future-ideological) see Knight (1982a:521-523).

7. The Working Group on Indigenous Populations was
established in 1982 under the Subcommission on the Prevention
of Minorities which, in turn, is a subcommission of the U.N.
Human Rights Commission.

8. These questions have suddenly ceased to be of only
academic interest within Canada for since these questions
were first posed by this author the Federal Parliamentary
Special Committee on Indian Self-Government has recommended to
Parliament that the right of Indian Peoples to self-
government should be explicitly stated and entrenched in the
Constitution of Canada and that these rights should become
reality for Indians living on their own lands (Canada, House
of Commons, 1983).

9. That is, where colonies had to be geographically

separate and continentally distant from the metropolitan power.

REFERENCES

Adejuyigbe, O. (1974) 'Ethnic Pluralism and Political Stability in Nigeria', in L. J. Evenden and F. F. Cunningham (eds.), Cultural Discord in the Modern World: Geographical Themes, Tantalus, Vancouver, 83-107

Adejuyigbe, O. (1975) Boundary Problems in Western Nigeria: A Geographical Analysis, University of Ife Press, Ile-Ife

Adejuyigbe, O. (1982) Social Considerations in Political Territorial Organization of Society, University of Ife Press, Ile-Ife

Agnew, J. A. (1981a) 'Political Regionalism and Scottish Nationalism in Gaelic Scotland', Canadian Review of Studies in Nationalism, 8, 115-29

Agnew, J. A. (1981b) 'Structural and Dialectical Theories of Political Regionalism', in A. D. Burnett and P. J. Taylor (eds.), Political Studies from Spatial Perspectives, Wiley, Chichester, U.K. 275-89

Alexander, Y. (1976) Terrorism: National, Regional and Global Perspectives, Praeger, New York

Alexander, Y. and Friedlander, R. A. (1980) Self-Determination: National, Regional and Global Perspectives, Boulder, Westview

Arangio-Ruiz, G. (1979) The United States Declaration on Friendly Relations and the System of the Sources of International Law, Sijthoff and Noordhoff, Alphen aan den Rijn

Baker, R. S. and Doff, W. E. (1927) War and Peace: Presidential Messages, Addresses, and Public Papers (1917-1924), Harper and Row, New York

Boateng, E. A. (1978) A Political Geography of Africa, Cambridge University Press, Cambridge

Buchheit, L. C. (1980) Secession: The Legitimacy of Self-Determination, Yale University Press, New Haven

Burghardt, A. F. (1962) Borderland: A Historical and Geographical Study of Burgenland, Austria, University of Wisconsin Press, Madison

Burghardt, A. F. (1971) 'Quebec Separatism and the Future of Canada', in R. L. Gentilcore (ed.), Geographical Approaches to Canadian Problems, Prentice-Hall of Canada, Toronto, 229-35

Burghardt, A. F. (1973) 'The Bases of Territorial Claims', Geographical Review, 63, 225-45

Burghardt, A. F. (1980) 'Nation, State and Territorial Unity: A Trans-Outaouais View', Cahiers de geographie du Quebec, 24, 123-34

Canada, House of Commons (1983) Indian Self-Government in
    Canada: Report of the Special Committee, Queen's Printer
    for the House of Commons, Ottawa, (First Session of the
    Thirty-second Parliament, Issue No. 40).
Cassese, A. (1981) 'The Self-Determination of Peoples', in
    L. Henkin (ed.), The International Bill of Rights,
    Columbia University Press, New York, 92-113, 416-427
Clark, R. S. (1980a) 'The 'Decolonization' of East Timor and
    the United Nations Norms on Self-Determination and
    Aggression', Yale Journal of World Public Order, 7, 2-44
Clark, R. S. (1980b) 'Self-Determination and Free
    Association - Should the United Nations Terminate The
    Pacific Islands Trust?' Harvard International Law
    Journal, 21, 1-86
Cobban, A. (1944) National Self-Determination, Oxford
    University Press, London
Connor, W. (1972) 'Nation-Building or Nation-Destroying?'
    World Politics, 24, 317-55
Connor, W. (1977) 'Ethno-nationalism in the First World: The
    Present in Historical Perspective', in M. J. Esman (ed.),
    Ethnic Conflict in the Western World, Cornell University
    Press, Ithica, 19-45
Dawson, E. (1983) 'Identity and Territory: The Case of
    Nunavut', unpublished paper, Department of Geography,
    Ottawa
Davies, M. (1983a) 'Aspects of Aboriginal Rights in
    International Law', in B. Morse (ed.), Aboriginal People
    and the Law, Carleton University Press, Ottawa
Davies, M. (1983b) 'Aboriginal Rights in International Law:
    Human Rights', in B. Morse (ed.), Aboriginal People and
    the Law, Carleton University Press, Ottawa
Dofny, J. and Akiwowo, A. (1980) National and Ethnic
    Movements, Sage Publications, Palo Alto
Deutsch, K. W. (1953) Nationalism and Social Communication,
    M.I.T. Press, Boston
Emerson, R. (1971) 'Self-Determination', American Journal of
    International Law, 65, 459-75
Franck, T. M. (1976) 'The Stealing of the Sahara', American
    Journal of International Law, 70, 694-721
Friedman, W. et al. (1969) International Law: Cases and
    Materials, West, St. Paul
George, D. L. (1938) The Truth About the Peace Treaties,
    Victor Gollancy, London
Gottmann, J. (1952) La politique des etats et leur
    geographie, Armand Colin, Paris
Gottmann, J. (1973) The Significance of Territory, The
    University Press of Virginia, Charlottesville
Gross, L. (1975) 'The Right of Self-Determination in
    International Law', in M. Kilson (ed.), New States in the
    Modern World, Harvard University Press, Cambridge,
    136-57

Hall, R. L. (1979) Ethnic Autonomy, Pergamon, New York
Henkin, L. (1981) The International Bill of Rights, Columbia
    University Press, New York
Higgins, R. (1963) The Development of International Law
    Through the Political Organs of the United Nations,
    Oxford University Press, New York
Hoffmann, S. (1981) Duties Beyond Borders: On the Limits and
    Possibilities of Ethical International Politics,
    Syracuse University Press, Syracuse
Isaak, R. (1981) Individuals and World Politics, (2nd ed.),
    Duxbury Press, Monterey
Johnston, R. J. (1982) Geography and the State: An Essay in
    Political Geography, St. Martin's Press, New York
Kawhara, I. H. (1979) Land as Turangawaewae: Ngati Whatua's
    Destiny at Orakei, New Zealand Planning Council,
    Wellington, (Planning Paper No. 2).
Knight, D. B. (1970) 'Changing Orientations: Elements of
    New Zealand's Political Geography', Geographical
    Bulletin, 1, 21-30
Knight, D. B. (1974) 'Racism and Reaction: The Development of
    a Botswana 'raison d'etre' for the Country', in
    L. J. Evenden and F. F. Cunningham (eds.), Cultural
    Discord in the Modern World: Geographical Themes,
    Tantalus, Vancouver, 111-26
Knight, D. B. (1982a) 'Identity and Territory: Geographical
    Perspectives on Nationalism and Regionalism', Annals
    of the Association of American Geographers, 72, 514-31
Knight, D. B. (1982b) 'Canada in Crisis: The Power of
    Regionalisms', in D. G. Bennett (ed.), Tension Areas of
    the World, Park Press, Champaign, Ill, 254-79
Knight, D. B. (1983a) 'Self-Determination as a Geopolitical
    Force', Journal of Geography, 82, 148-52
Knight, D. B. (1983b) 'The Dilemma of Nations in a Rigid
    State Structured World', in N. Kliot and S. Waterman
    (eds.), Pluralism and Political Geography: People,
    Territory and State, Croom Helm, London, 114-37
Kohn, H. (1944) The Idea of Nationalism, Macmillan, New York
Kohr, L. (1957) The Breakdown of Nations, Rinehart, New York
Lansing, R. (1921) The Peace Negotiations: A Personal
    Narrative, Houghton Mifflin, Boston
Lenin, V. I. (1951) The Right of Nations to Self-Government,
    Greenwood Press, Westport, Conn.
Lévesque, R. (1978) La passion du Quebec, Editions Quebec/
    Amerique, Montreal
MacDonald, B. (1975) 'Secession in Defense of Identity: The
    Making of Tavalu', Pacific Viewpoint, 16, 26-44
Marc, A. (1963) 'Preface', in G. Heraud, L'Europe des
    ethnies, Presses d'Europe, Paris
Mayer, A. J. (1959) Political Origins of the New Diplomacy
    1917-1918, Yale University Press, New Haven

Navari, C. (1981) 'The Origins of the Nation-State', in
    L. Tivey (ed.), The Nation-State: The Formation of
    Modern Politics, Martin Robertson, Oxford, 13-38
Opekokew, D. (1982) The First Nations: Indian Government in
    the Community of Man, Federation of Saskatchewan,
    Saskatoon
Orridge, A. W. and Williams, C. H. (1982) 'Autonomist
    Nationalism: A Theoretical Framework for Spatial
    Variations in its Genesis and Development', Political
    Geography Quarterly, 1, 19-39
Pearcy, G. E. (1977) World Sovereignty, Plycon, Fullerton, Ca.
Pomerance, M. (1976) 'The United States and Self-
    Determination: Perspectives on the Wilsonian Conception',
    American Journal of International Law, 70, 1-27
Porter, J. (1975) 'Ethnic Pluralism in Canadian Perspective',
    in N. Glazer and D. P. Moynihan (eds.), Ethnicity:
    Theory and Experience, Harvard University Press,
    Cambridge, Ma., 267-304
Potter, D. M. (1968) The South and the Sectional Conflict,
    Louisiana State University Press, Baton Rouge
Prescott, J. R. V. (1968) The Geography of State Policies,
    Hutchinson, London
Quebec Liberal Party (1980) A New Canadian Federation, Quebec
    Liberal Party, Montreal
Raby, S. (1974) 'Aboriginal Territorial Aspirations in
    Political Geography', Proceedings of the International
    Geographical Union Regional Conference, New Zealand
    Geographical Society, Palmerston North, 169-74
Rokkan, S. (1980) 'Territories, Centres, and Peripheries:
    Towards a Geoethnic-Geoeconomic-Geopolitical Model of
    Differentiation Within Western Europe', in J. Gottmann
    (ed.), Centre and Periphery: Spatial Variation in
    Politics, Sage, Beverly Hills, 163-204
Rokkan, S. and Urwin, D. W. (1982) The Politics of
    Territorial Identity: Studies in European Regionalism,
    Sage, London
Rokkan, S. (1983) Economy, Territory, Identity: Politics of
    West European Peripheries, Sage, London
Ronen, D. (1979) The Quest for Self-Determination, Yale
    University Press, New Haven
Scott, J. B. (1934) The Spanish Origin of International Law,
    Part I, Francisco de Vitoria and his Law of Nations,
    Clarendon Press, Oxford
Shafer, B. C. (1955) Nationalism: Myth and Reality, Harcourt,
    Brace & World, New York
Shafer, B. C. (1972) Faces of Nationalism: New Realities and
    Old Myths, Harcourt Brace Javanovich, New York
Shafer, B. C. (1982) Nationalism and Internationalism:
    Belonging in Human Experience, Krieger, Malabar, Florida

Shaheen, S. (1956) The Communist (Bolshevik) Theory of
    National Self-Determination, N. V. Uitgeverij W. Van
    Hoeve, S'-Gravenhage
Smith, A. D. (1976) Nationalist Movements, Macmillan, London
Smith, A. D. (1981) The Ethnic Revival, Cambridge University
    Press, Cambridge
Smith, A. D. (1982) 'Nationalism, Ethnic Separation and the
    Intelligentsia', in C. H. Williams (ed.), National
    Separatism, University of British Columbia Press,
    Vancouver, 17-41
Smith, G. (1979) 'Political Geography and the Theoretical
    Study of the East European Nation', Indian Journal of
    Political Science, 40, 59-83
Spencer, J. E. and Thomas, W. L. Jr. (1969) Cultural Geography
    Geography: An Evolutionary Introduction to Our Humanized
    Earth, John Wiley, New York
Sutton, I. (1976) 'Sovereign States and the Changing
    Definition of the Indian Reservation', Geographical
    Review, 66, 281-95
Van Dyke, V. (1970) Human Rights: The United States and the
    World Community, Oxford University Press, New York
Watkins, M. (1977) Dene Nation: The Colony Within, University
    of Toronto Press, Toronto
Whebell, C. F. J. (1973) 'A Model of Territorial Separation',
    Proceedings of the Association of American Geographers,
    5, 295-98
Whebell, C. F. J. (1976) 'Non-national Separatism: With
    Special Reference to Australian Cases Past and Present',
    in W. H. Morris-Jones (ed.), Collected Papers on the
    Politics of Separation, University of London, Institute
    of Commonwealth Studies, London, 19-29
Williams, C. H. (1979) 'Ethnic Resurgence in the Periphery',
    Area, 11, 279-83
Williams, C. H. (1980) 'Ethnic Separatism in Western Europe',
    Tijdschrift voor Economische en Sociale Geografie, 71,
    142-58
Williams, C. H. (1981) 'Identity Through Autonomy: Ethnic
    Separatism in Quebec', in A. D. Burnett and P. J. Taylor
    (eds.), Political Studies from Spatial Perspectives,
    Wiley, Chichester, U.K., 389-418
Williams, C. H. (1982) National Separatism, University of
    British Columbia Press, Vancouver
Williams, S. W. (1977) 'Internal Colonialism, Core-Periphery
    Contrasts and Devolution: An Integrative Comment', Area,
    9, 272-78
World Council of Indigenous Peoples (1981) Draft of an
    'International Covenant on the Rights of Indigenous
    Peoples', United Nations, New York

Chapter Twelve

GEOGRAPHY AND WAR/PEACE STUDIES

H. van der Wusten

INTRODUCTION

As the new <u>Political Geography Quarterly</u> was launched in 1982,
several research agendas were pieced together in order to
present a general overview of the path this part of the
discipline was taking (Editorial Board, 1982). The result
looks like a fireworks: lots of noise and flashy lights in all
sorts of directions. It is a long way from the moribund
backwater where political geography was supposed to lay at
rest some time ago.

The following sections fall under two headings of the
aforementioned research agendas: 'the future of the state
system' and 'the revival of geostrategic studies'. In
passing I will make some remarks with regard to 'the concept
of the nation state', 'the variable nature of international
boundaries' and 'bringing history back in'. I consider
geography - and political geography in particular - as a
distinct tradition mainly within the social sciences. Its
future depends on the relevance of the contributions its
practitioners are able to make to the body of knowledge of
the social sciences and on the fruitfulness of its tradition
to present-day researchers.

In the field of war/peace studies the relevance of
geographical factors seems to be large. But not much
attention is paid to this theme by geographers. In any case
geographers are rarely heard in the general fora of the
social sciences. A glance through relevant interdisciplinary
journals like the <u>Journal of Conflict Resolution</u> and the
<u>Journal of Peace Research</u> shows an extremely small number of
contributions by geographers (Laponce, 1980). On a more
mundane level it is appropriate to remark that 'geopolitics'
is a trendy word again, but it now seems to be in use for
very general ideas on world politics without much specific
geographical content. For example, Marie-France Garaud, a
former official and presidential candidate has recently
established the 'Institut international de geopolitique' in

Paris, which apparently concerns itself with the study of
East-West problems in general terms (Amalric, 1983). And
former British ambassador in Washington, Peter Jay, at an
already earlier stage used the same idiom for a <u>tour d'-
horizon</u> of current issues (Jay, 1979).
    In the following sections I want to derive the relevance
of geographical factors for the explanation of the
occurrences of war and for the discussion on strategies for
war avoidance from general social science literature. In the
course of this presentation I will try to suggest the sort of
problems geographers may want to tackle in this field. In
the end this will hopefully give a better grasp of research
priorities in a domain where geography has a diverse and
disputed history.

EXPLAINING WAR

The study of war/peace problems has made progress during the
last two decades or so, if only for the major data collection
efforts that have taken place. These data allow much more
precise comparisons of different cases of large scale
violence over sometimes extended periods of time and
consequently open up possibilities for the testing of
theories in this field. In any case they close possibilities
for the retention of easy generalisations that can not be
contradicted on a factual base. One of the most fruitful
efforts in this field has been the <u>Correlates of War Project</u>
directed by J. David Singer (Singer and Small, 1972; Small
and Singer, 1982; Singer, 1981). It covers the period since
1816 and so facilitates that history be brought back in.
Apart from handbooks and data tapes the project has
generated a large number of interpretative research reports
that have brought to fruition a tradition of war/peace
studies instituted by such figures as Sorokin, Wright and
Richardson. Other large-scale data bases have been
established by Rummel and Choucri & North for their studies
on the <u>Understanding Conflict and War</u> and the outbreak of
World War I respectively (Rummel, 1975–81; Choucri and North,
1975). More general datasets like the Conflict and Peace
Data Bank (COPDAB) and the World Handbook III tape are also
highly relevant in this regard.[1] Although problems of war
definition and measurement are by no means settled I will
leave them alone for the moment and concentrate on research
results irrespective of the data base from which they have
been gathered.
    In a recent progress report Singer (1981:12) indicates
that for the whole period "such basic geo-strategic factors
as location and strength seem to be of importance, but that
despite persuasive arguments to the contrary ... domestic
factors of a less material sort would appear to be rather

neglible in accounting for the war proneness of individual
nations". Compared to for example diversity of ranks of a
country on material and diplomatic capabilities ('status-
inconsistencies on the national level') or regime type,
traditional geographic interests in location and strength as
predictors of war involvement are well-founded. On the other
hand relevant characteristics of dyads like the behavioural
and interactional patterns that eventually lead to war or are
conducive to it (think of arms races and trade patterns) seem
to be neglected items in geographical research with regard to
this problem area. Besides the internal dynamics of an arms
race and the inevitability of it leading to war, a
geographical perspective on arms races would lead to the
question of whether specific combinations of countries enter
an arms race on account of their position in the ecology of
the interstate system. As to trade patterns a good question
would be to what extent they can diviate from political
orientations and preferences for different types of countries
without leading to strain. And when the deviation leads to
strain, under what circumstances will this lead to war? Cases
in point are Finno-Soviet relations (Kwaasteniet and Wusten,
1982) and the links between South Africa and its neighbours.
    Wallensteen (1981) has tried to find relations between
basic characteristics of members of the interstate system and
the frequency of wars between them. Incompatibilities as
regards these basic characteristics of two members within a
pair would facilitate the outbreak of war between them.
Territorial claims, pursued military power positions,
economic growth trends and legitimising principles of
government may be perceived as incompatible and lead to
military confrontation and war. Wallensteen labels these
four conditions Geopolitik, Realpolitik, Kapitalpolitik and
Idealpolitik. His results show ideological differences
(Idealpolitik) to be the most important condition that leads
to war for the 1816-1976 period that his study covers, but all
incompatibilities contribute to some extent. It should be
stressed that he studied only major powers, but the effort to
look for the relative strength of different possible war
conditions is worthwhile.
    Another significant direction in which further studies
may be done is Wallensteen's periodisation of stages of the
interstate system: an essentially European-centered system
for the nineteenth century; the opening up of this system to
the rest of the world by recognising two outer European
countries as major powers - the US and Japan around the turn
of the century; and the end of this transitional system after
World War II by the institution of a global system dominated
by a few superpowers. Whereas the number of military
confrontations increases from stage to stage irrespective of
the extension of the system, the frequency of wars is
largest in the transitional system and decreases in the global

system. But this pattern of conflict between majors does not
apply to all system pairs.

In a number of studies the significance of geographical
factors in the explanation of war has been indicated for the
period of the global system. Russett (1967) found that
whereas 26 per cent of all pairs of states consisted of
neighbours, 63 per cent of all warring pairs between 1945 and
1965 shared boundaries. This does not necessarily mean that
border disputes are the cause of the fight. In fact Russett
(1967:201) emphasises other aspects: "Proximity is not a
cause of war, but it makes nations salient to each other,
providing them with issues over which they can fight if other
capabilities are low and with the opportunity to make their
own power felt on each other's territory".

The study of the spatial ordering of degrees of salience
for different countries, to some extent comparable to the
information field of individuals, is a task geographers
should be able to shoulder. But it is quite possible that
Russett has underestimated the importance of territorial
disputes as a cause of war. The respective contributions of
geographical propinquity to the explanation of war, as a
source of incompatible territorial claims and creating
opportunities to bring other incompatibilities to the
foreground, should be further clarified. A note of caution
should be added as to any simple equation of the possibility
of territorial claims and adjacent territories as the
Falklands/Malvinas conflict has highlighted.

Weede (1985) has already gone some way in this direction.
He studied the instances of war and several of its
concomitants for the twentieth century but particularly for
the post-1945 period. For our actual purposes it is interesting to note that his analysis is not only based on
neighbouring and non-neighbouring states and their wars but
on an effort to determine if incompatible claims are now
discernible or have led to conflict in recent history. One
important conclusion is that territorial disputes are among
the most potent causes of war after as well as before 1945.

Finally a number of studies argue that large scale
violent conflict is now for the most part a question of
different parties within a single state. One talks of
internal wars with or without external intervention.
Problems of data and classification are extremely acute here.
Kende (1978) concludes that more and more the most common
type of war has become an internal war somewhere in the third
world with foreign intervention (increasingly by other third
world countries). The geographical distribution of these wars
is not stable nor is their frequency in time. Between 1945
and 1976 there has been a general rising trend of organised
violence to about 1968 and a general decrease after that date.

Kende supposes some connection with the acceptance of
the principle of peaceful coexistence and the realisation of

some elements of detente. But it is not clear how these
factors could explain a process that manifests itself
primarily in the third world. Nor is it clear to what extent
the sequal to this period (the years after 1976) supports the
hypothesis. From a geographical perspective the following
questions may be relevant. Do circumstances like the spatial
split between opposing parties and the limited degree and
scope of penetration of state authorities in different parts
of a country or, perhaps, the efforts of state authorities to
widen these, bear on the breakdown of the rule that the state
holds the monopoly of legitimate force? In what niches of
the interstate system do we particularly find governments who
are murdering their own population by extra-judicial
executions and efforts in the direction of genocide? (Kuper,
1981). Do territorial claims or specific patterns of
spatially ordered salience in terms of Realpolitik,
Idealpolitik and Kapitalpolitik induce countries to interfere
in internal conflicts elsewhere? The overextended use of the
so-called domino-theory provides several examples of the ways
in which spatially ordered patterns of Idealpolitik-changes
in the perceptions of American decisionmakers have formed the
background for some of the most fateful decisions in postwar
history (Draper, 1983).

The apparent ebb and flow of war occurrences in some
regions in recent times is an illustration of one promising
avenue of further research in the general explanation of war
outbreaks. In his progress report Singer (1981:7) states that
"evidence for addiction to war on the part of the system or
any nation seems weak". But a close reading of some papers
"suggests that more complex models of diffusion and
contagion ... might well stand against the empirical test".
An as yet unpublished study of Houweling and Siccama (1983)
has uncovered evidence of a recurrent tendency of war
outbreaks to be concentrated in time and space. Explanations
are still highly tentative in terms of imitations and
opportunities created by ongoing wars for third parties. They
do not yet answer the question why such phenomena would be
more frequent at particular stages in certain regions. But it
is evident, that such distributions, isomorphous to sequences
of innovation-diffusion although by no means necessarily
propelled by the same forces, deserve close attention of
geographers.

WAR AVOIDANCE STRATEGIES

In spite of the progress made in the field of war/peace
studies war still is an elusive phenomenon. It is a rather
rare event each case having its own singular features. But
war is also a catastrophe so that much attention may be given
by policymakers to lower even a small risk of terrible cost.

Given the state of knowledge, however, the contribution of specific steps to the aim of war avoidance may be debatable. For example the evidence on the effects of alliance bonds to war involvement is extremely varied. Nevertheless there are a few general policy types that are supposed to have a direct bearing on the issue of war avoidance. It is of course clear that war avoidance is not necessarily a goal of government policy and that it has to compete with other aims, primarily with the aim on continued national independence.[2]

As stated, alliance bonds have a different bearing on war chances in different circumstances. Even so we can ask the question under what conditions countries opt for nonaligned security policies or get them imposed, be they with a relatively high (Yugoslavia) or a low (Austria) military posture. There is no question that geography played an important role in the eventual distribution of non- and less-aligned countries in postwar Europe, e.g. as a stage for the enactment of World War II which constrained the number of viable military choreographies of the major contenders.

States may also opt for collective forms of security policy. Apart from worldwide arrangements any collective security policy has specific internal and external functions for the set of countries involved. Therefore the boundary of the collective system is extremely important. Internally security may be maintained and war avoided by what is variously called subordination or a security community. Externally war may be avoided by deterrence or by detente policies. Packages of these lines have been tried (official NATO policies since the late sixties).

Collective security arrangements in which superpowers participate have acquired a new dimension in the nuclear age. As long as nuclear weapons are in a class of their own, deterrence in particular may be empowered by threats with the use of this class of weapons. All military action implying transgression of the external boundaries of the collective security system are enormously consequential. This boundary therefore is also in a class of its own. However, its precise delimitation is in fact far from clear as soon as we leave the well-trodden paths of treaty obligations. For example, Weede (1975:169) quoting Schelling reckons that a number of European states outside NATO and without bilateral treaties with the US are in fact under the American nuclear umbrella according to what he calls 'cartographic psychology'. If a secret or informal arrangement to that effect exists or if the US would feel obliged to respond in kind once a country in this situation was attacked by the other side, is well nigh impossible to prove. Some years ago Falk (1975) saw Central America and the Caribbean as the clearest example of a US sphere of influence. At the same time Gochman and Ray (1979) compared the relationship of all Latin American countries with the US to the relationship of the East

European countries with the USSR implying that they studied two comparable spheres of influence. In sum, the question of the boundaries of the global empires deserves careful attention.

Another vexed question is the role of nuclear weapons in the collective security arrangements. Weede describes the relationship not only of the USSR and its Warsaw pact allies but also of the US and other NATO members as one of super- and sub-ordination. He speaks of blocprovinces to express the limited sovereignty of smaller powers in the field of nuclear weaponry. However, the question of whether the nuclear guarantee applies equally to all parts of the territory of the alliances has been answered in a number of ways during the last few years.

For a number of reasons the stability of the situation of mutual deterrence has increasingly been questioned along with the credibility of nuclear deterrence against attacks not on one's own territory. There has always been persistent doubt in some quarters in the realism of military and political doctrines regulating the threats with and eventual use of nuclear weapons although deployment and targeting practices were real enough. This feeling seems to be spreading. Instead of doctrines - logically related and explicit sets of rules based on chosen values, preferences and technical constraints - saving the world from aggression and nuclear disaster, it is now stated that in fact only 'existential' deterrence blocks the way to total war: primary feelings of awe and fright outside any strategy, policy or commitment about the destructive capacity of nuclear armaments (Rothschild, 1983). Such attitudes would normally result in cautious policies by those who own nuclear arms or who have them on their territory. The nuclear umbrella could in due course shrink accordingly. In this respect it would be worthwhile to study more precisely to what extent, where and when force has been used or the use of force threatened by the superpowers. Such a study could bring the possibilities to delimit spheres of influence a lot nearer.[3]

To the extent that superpowers are in fact restrained by their own overextended military armories, the question of the ranking of superpowers in a more general hierarchy of countries gets new relevance. As a matter of fact the additivity of several types of resources and capabilities to bring about one index of power has often been questioned (Jonsson, 1979). For this reason alone one may have doubts about the possibilities of discerning a general trend towards the formation of a new world order built up as a nested hierarchy of primary, secondary, etc. power centers with their respective regional hinterlands of varying size.

The process of a cluster of countries becoming a collective security system internally is supposed to happen along two not necessarily exclusive lines. The countries concerned may formalise their common aims through treaties, alliances and the like. They may on the other hand through increased interaction in different spheres of life and the development of capabilities to cope with the strains arising out of their relationship, create what may be called a community. If this is a security community its members - not only governments but people as a whole - share the expectation that their conflicts will be solved peacefully. The work of Karl Deutsch and his followers aims particularly in this last direction. Since Deutsch started to think along these lines in the fifties a lot of work has been done but the conditions of international community-building and its consequences for the avoidance of war still remain open-ended questions.[4] It is an alternative, probably complementary way of looking at the internal part of sphere of influence problems. Russett's (1967) early effort to map the ecology of political macro-regions still points in a direction which geographers could pursue.

Finally war may be avoided by diminishing the level of armaments or curbing its increase. Geographers can contribute to the practical task of the design or evaluation of arms control and disarmament measures and the construction of non-violent defense systems. In particular past and current proposals for the denuclearisation of zones (the Nordic areas, Central Europe, the Mediterranean) may be assessed (Berg and Lodgaard, 1983). Also, the study of the use of troop withdrawals and the dismantling of military installations from certain regions may be undertaken as a confidence building measure and from the perspective of risk analysis. The importance of territory has been slighted compared to the preservation of the integrity of the social system in discussions on non-violent defense systems (Galtung, 1968). Geographers are aware that one can only very imperfectly separate the social system from its territorial base. The question how territory should be taken into account when constructing a non-violent defense system or the non-violent part of a defense system is still largely open.

CONCLUSION

The editors of Deutsch's Festschrift call the modern nation-state "that now almost universal instrument of social control, source of reward and punishment, bringer of security and insecurity" (Marritt and Russett, 1981:1). As indeed the model of the nation-state has diffused over the earth, the model has been transformed in its practical functioning in different forms of institutionalised social life that to some extent defy classification (what should Chad be called or revolutionary Iran?). On the other hand states are to such an extent linked by all sorts of ties that new forms of

political institutions and politically relevant behaviour
result. In the field of war/peace studies as in all other
fields where relations in the system of states are studied,
it is the geographer's task to propose complements to "the
billiard-ball model of international politics" (Lijphart,
1981:239). Not only are states very much more constrained to
move, they are also part of the table, the table itself is
by no means isotropic, and finally the whole system and its
parts have a history, some of it shared.

NOTES

1. Both data sets are available on tape from ICPSR,
Ann Arbor, Michigan.
2. For a recent plea that the search for a certain
kind of stability is the general focus of political geography
see Gottmann (1982). The question that arises is whether
this stability is equal to a state which allows peaceful
change.
3. Sources would be the published lists of cases where
the nuclear alert has been used by at least one of both
superpowers, and also where conventional armed forces have
been deployed to put pressure on weaker states. From
Blechman and Kaplan (1978) and Kaplan (1981) it can be seen
that both superpowers have used their armed forces in this
'quiet' way about 200 times each since 1945.
4. Recent appraisals from within the tradition are to
be found in Merritt and Russett's (1981) collection of essays
in honour of Karl Deutsch; see especially Lijphart (1981) and
Puchala (1981).

REFERENCES

Amalric, J. (1983) 'Un colloque de l'Institut international
    de geopolitique. Les democraties face au totalitarisme',
    Le Monde, 7th June
Blechman, B. M. and Kaplan, S. S. (1978) Force without War,
    Brookings Institute, Washington D.C.
Berg, P. and Lodgaard, S. (1983) 'Disengagement zones: a
    step towards meaningful defence', Journal of Peace
    Research, 20, 5-16
Choucri, N. and North, R. (1975) Nations in Conflict:
    National Growth and International Violence, Freeman,
    San Francisco
Draper, T. (1983) 'Falling dominoes', The New York Review of
    Books, 27th October, 6-18
Editorial Board (1982) 'Editorial essay: political geography -
    research agendas for the nineteen eighties', Political
    Geography Quarterly, 1, 1-18
Falk, R. A. (1975) A Global Approach to National Policy,
    Harvard University Press, Cambridge, Ma.

Galtung, J. (1968) 'Niet-militaire vormen van verdediging',
    in M. Albruski et al. Cahiers voor Vredesvraagstukken,
    Romen, Roermond, 53-120
Gochman, C. S. and Ray, J. C. (1979) 'Structural disparities
    in Latin America and Eastern Europe 1950-1970', Journal
    of Peace Research, 16, 231-54
Gottmann, J. (1982) 'The basic problem of political geography:
    the organization of space and the search for stability',
    Tijdschrift voor Economische en Sociale Geografie, 73,
    340-9
Houweling, H. W. and Siccama, J. G. (1983) 'Time-space
    interaction in warfare: some theoretical and empirical
    aspects of the epidemiology of collective violence
    1816-1980', paper presented at the European Consortium
    for Political Research, Frieberg
Kende, I. (1978) 'War of ten years (1967-1976)', Journal of
    Peace Research, 15, 227-41
Kuper, L. (1981) Genocide, Penguin, London
Kwaasteniet, M de and Wusten, H van der (1982) Finlandisering,
    de Voorloper van de Hollanditis, SGI, Amsterdam
Jay, P. (1979) 'Regionalism as geopolitics', Foreign Affairs,
    57, 485-514
Jonsson, C. (1979) 'The paradoxes of superpower: omnipotence
    or impotence', in K. Goldman and G. Sjostedt (eds.),
    Power, Capabilities, Interdependence, Sage, Beverly
    Hills, Ca.
Kaplan, S. S. (1981) Diplomacy of Power, Brookings Institute,
    Washington, D.C.
Laponce, J. A. (1980) 'Political science: an input-output
    analysis of journals and footnotes', Political Studies,
    28, 401-19
Lijphart, A. (1981) 'Karl Deutsch and the new paradigm in
    international relations', in R. L. Merritt and
    B. M. Russett (eds.), From National Development to
    Global Community, Allen and Unwin, London, 233-51
Merritt, R. L. and Russett, B. M. (1981) From National
    Development to Global Community, Allen and Unwin, London
Puchala, D. J. (1981) 'Integration theory and the study of
    international relations' in R. L. Merritt and
    B. M. Russett (eds.), From National Development to
    Global Community, Allen and Unwin, London, 143-64
Rothschild, E. (1983) 'The delusions of deterrence;
    McGeorge Bundy, the bishops and the bomb', New York
    Review of Books, 14th April, 40-50
Rummel, R. J. (1975-1981) Understanding Conflict and War,
    Sage, Beverly Hills, (five volumes)
Russett, B. M. (1967) International Regions and the
    International System, Rand McNally, Chicago
Singer, J. D. (1981) 'Accounting for international war: the
    state of the discipline', Journal of Peace Research,
    18, 1-21

Singer, J. D. and Small, M. (1972) The Wages of War: a
    Statistical Handbook, 1816-1965, Wiley, New York
Small, M. and Singer, J. D. (1982) Resort to Arms, Sage,
    Beverly Hills
Wallensteen, P. (1981) 'Incompatibility, confrontation, and
    war: four models and three historical systems, 1816-
    1976', Journal of Peace Research, 18, 57-89
Weede, E. (1975) Weltpolitik und Kriegsursachen im 20.
    Jahrhundert, Oldenbourg Verlag, München and Wien

Chapter Thirteen

GEOGRAPHIC MODELS OF INTERNATIONAL CONFLICTS

John O'Loughlin

INTRODUCTION

My aim in this paper is to attempt to synthesise two
approaches to the geography of international conflicts. One
approach, can be designated as geostrategy, a traditional
concern of political geographers, while the other is derived
from the burgeoning field of quantitative international
relations (QIR). While the former is predominantly idiographic in research and normative in policy, the latter is
characterised by descriptive and mathematical models, with
a special interest in interstate conflict among major powers.
I will attempt to summarise and merge the theories and
empirical results from both fields, and then suggest a
modelling scheme for international conflicts based on a
space-time-structural framework. This work is motivated by a
concern that the neglect of international relations,
particularly conflicts resulting in war, is hindering the
full blossoming of political geography. A cursory literature
survey indicates a greater concern for the explanatory role
of nation-state separation, location and contiguity by
international relations researchers than by geographers. It
is time to reclaim our birthright, based on both recent
methodological and technical developments in geography and
on our continuing, though controversial, legacy of
geopolitics.
    The paper is organised in seven sections. After the
introduction four theoretical perspectives on world politics
are reviewed. The tradition of geopolitics is analysed
separately before three major research projects in QIR are
evaluated. Explicit consideration is given to the role of
space in explaining war outbreaks. World conflicts are then
summarised by five overarching theories before they are set
in a spatial diffusion framework. A tentative time-space-
structural model of international relations is proposed in
an effort to stimulate further work by geographers on this
critical problem of our time.[1]

Geographic Models of International Conflicts

Some researchers will hold that relations between units
as large and diverse as nation-states cannot be modelled:
each event is the product of the complicated historical,
geographical, political, economic and legal structures of the
states and the particular psychological and ideological views
of the decision-makers. Indeed, strong feelings on this
issue have led to a distinct split in international relations
research between the idiographic and nomothetic schools and
is reflected both in the journals (compare Foreign Affairs
with the Journal of Conflict Resolution) and in a distinction
between micro and macro explanations of interstate relations.
Thus, while a traditionalist would examine the unique
domestic and international circumstances leading to a
particular event, (e.g. the incursion by U.S. forces into
Grenada in October 1983), the QIR approach stresses the
causality of systemic forces, in Grenada, in the United
States and in First World-Third World relations. Political
geography studies of inter-state relations have been highly
individualistic and historical, particularly in the case of
frontier and boundary studies.

Two small but growing literatures with increasing
geographic components are not included in this review.
Analytic procedures for the management of international
conflict, called peace science, have been advocated by
Walter Isard for two decades. Quantititative methods are
drawn from economics, operations research, regional science
and methematics while qualitative procedures stress cost-
benefit accounting and examination of basic values having a
conceptual basis in public administration, psychology and
law (Isard and Smith, 1983). Attempts by quantitative
geographers to adapt their techniques to political topics in
examining issues of territorial partition, population
pressure and expansion, and idealistic notions of spatial
justice have suffered from both a lack of practical
application and a predisposition to substitute methodological
rigor for sound assumptions grounded in reality. Nevertheless, peace science provides an important signpost for
political geography on its circuitous route toward global
model development through the Scylla of areal uniqueness and
the Charybdis of unwarranted and unrealistic mathematical
symbolisation. More recently, geographers are turning their
attention to the issue of nuclear war and the spatial
ramifications of total destruction (Openshaw and Steadman,
1983; Pepper and Jenkins, 1983, Bunge, 1982). Nuclear
destruction is intrinsically a spatial issue with both human
and physical geographic elements. Both groups of
geographers are expected to develop simulations of the
devastation of nuclear war as they combine academic and
citizen roles in examining this pressing problem of our age.

to 1976, Wallensteen found that while the other three models explained 20-30 per cent, only the "idealpolitik" model managed to account for two-thirds of all international conflict. Unfortunately, he did not explore the interconnections between the models. Similarly, most research in the political geography of international relations has relied too heavily on a univariate approach. "Geopolitik", for its theory to the exclusion of complementary approaches.

The essential unity of all perspectives can be seen in contemporary world conflicts. Although frequently expressed in simplistic "domino theory" jargon, few can doubt that current American foreign policy in Central America reflects a mix of all four perspectives. In one sense, by imposing an orthogonal axis of an east-west scale on a north-south scale, we visualise a quadrapartite division of the globe in "Kapital" and "Ideal" politico-geographic spaces (Alker, 1981). Grouping nations in this two-dimensional space can be the basis for either geopolitical analysis through maps or power-political analysis through the simple addition of the strength of the various blocs (Cline, 1980). Alker uses Lenin's 16 point dialectical statement on the development of capitalism to formulate eight hypotheses on the problems of continuity, conflict and change in the global economic-political system. All international relations, not just conflict in the form of war, should be examined in such an encompassing framework. Likewise, political geography should be concerned with "structural" violence as well as with interstate conflict. This "maximalist" position (Galtung, 1964) examines states as actors on a large ever-changing stage and the apparent maximum entropy in the actors' linkages is actually highly ordered because international relations are subject to macro-systemic forces, of which economic relations in an evolving spatio-temporal setting is the most important regulating mechanism (Krippendorff, 1981). To reiterate the editorial in the first issue of the Political Geography Quarterly, "What is clear is that new geostrategic modelling will require an integration of economic and military considerations in ways not considered by early workers in their field" (Editorial Board,1982:9).

THE GEOPOLITICAL LEGACY

Rather than concentrating on the historical accuracy or alternative policy applications of the global geopolitical formulations proposed by Mackinder, Kjellen, Haushofer, Spykman, de Seversky or Cohen, I will confine my attention to criticism of the research tradition and methodological issues inherent in geostrategic study. Consistent problems continue to plague work in this specialty. First, each researcher brings a distinctive ethnocentric bias to his/her world-view, be it Germany in the European cockpit, Britain on the world-island fringe or the United States as the centre of the western alliance. Second, the research is designed to generate normative policy judgements, such as the proper U.S. response to the French defeat at Dien Bien Phu or to the Nicaraguan revolution in 1979. Since the empirical and theoretical evidence supporting the geostrategic formula is weak, reliance by decision-makers on these normative statements for policy requires a good deal of faith. Third, the deterministic tone of geopolitics, sometimes coupled with ideological statements, lowers the level of debate to gut-feelings and precludes the development of a common ground of objective research based on a theme of the implications for international relations of the location of nations. In particular, neglect of the domestic bases of international behaviour has led to the absurd implication that nations have foreign policies that are unchanging, unyielding, unwieldly, and unsympathetic to contemporary global economic developments.

There are two further implications of these criticisms. Fourth, foreign policy in the form of spatial expression of geopolitical objectives is naturally simplistic in the extreme. Thus, "containment of Soviet expansionism" during the Cold War involved the United States in a dozen or more armed conflicts on the "Heartland-Rimland" divide (Gaddis, 1982; Cohen, 1982). While some authorities wish to return to the days of simple, consistent, aggressive response to anti-Western trends in Rimland nations (Cline, 1980; Gray, 1977; Lowe, 1981), others (Cohen, 1982) advocate avoidance of a "crude form of locational determinism and uncritical acceptance of the domino theory" in favour of a flexible, hierarchical military response in relation to the intrinsic global significance of the local conflict and the causes of its outbreak. Finally, the pseudo-scientific justification given to military action by the geopolitical framework has rendered an intrinsically valuable concept worthless and raised doubts about the judgement of the term's advocates. While political geographers search for alternative semantics to summarise the important roles of the location of and distances between nations in international relations, we have not addressed adequately the issue of the existence of a "geographical cause" or whether spatial structure in international relations is simply the geographical expression of some underlying social, economic, military, psycho-locational or political variables. While other human geographers have moved from spatial pattern to social process explanations of geographical patterns and view spatial arrangements as a consequence, not a cause, of social conflict, some traditional political geographers remain locked in 1930s environmental deterministic moulds. As will be shown later in this paper, spatiotemporal arrangements of

FOUR PERSPECTIVES ON INTERNATIONAL RELATIONS

While at first glance a myriad of research perspectives
characterises work in international relations, a closer
examination reveals four broad nonexclusive views.
Wallensteen (1981) has "Germanised" the perspectives because
of their origins in nineteenth-century Germany. "Geopolitik"
needs no introduction to political geographers and stresses
the evolving spatial setting as an environmental determinant
of state relations, foreign policy and the probability of war.
"Geography is the most fundamental factor in the foreign
policy of states because it is the most permanent" (Gray,
1977:1). "Realpolitik" or power politics, devotes itself to
the question of achieving military or political victory.
Military strength, alliance behaviour, arms technology and
resources are its key variables and all states, regardless of
ideology, are assumed to act according to their hierarchial
power ranking, (Incidentally, most research in QIR is
premised on "Realpolitik"). J. David Singer (1982:42)
reviewing two decades of QIR research asks "what is the
driving force behind a government's foreign policy decisions?"
His review of results suggests that "classical realpolitik
factors typically become dominant with a remarkable homogeneity across nations, cases and time ... Geographic,
military, alliance and diplomatic factors dominate."

"Kapitalpolitik", under its more common designation of
economic relations, also needs little introduction to
political geographers. In this view, political, diplomatic
and military relations between states are driven by each
state's economic self-interest, particular as expressed in
trade and resource exploitation. The popularity of
Wallerstein's (1979) world systems model has led researchers
to examine the links between Kondratieff (long) cycles of
economic growth and decline, resource competition and
exploitation and foreign policy. Purely economic
explanations of foreign policy actions have been disappointing
and political factors must be added to the examination
(Zolberg, 1981). The simple protective relationship posited
by Barnet (1972) between a state's domestic economic needs
and foreign policy has been expanded by Krasner (1978) to
incorporate "a statist" element and by Agnew (1983) and Beer
(1981) to incorporate regional and historical perspectives.
Finally, "Idealpolitik" examines the principles of legitimacy
on which the state is founded and by which the state
justifies its actions, both domestically and internationally.
Numerous policymakers have found it convenient to label their
actions as an effort to supress a competing ideology (e.g.
Fascism, Communism, Capitalism, Zionism, Imperialism) and
conflict in this century can be viewed as a chess match
between competing ideologies on the checkerboard of nations.
Using international conflicts between major powers from 1816

international relations can act as both a synthesis of a complicated network of contact and as a method of relating and evaluating the various structural and systematic forces operating to produce a dynamic spatial distribution of interstate linkages.

QUANTITATIVE INTERNATIONAL RELATIONS (QIR)

Given the limited perspective and methodological narrowness of traditional political geography, we must look to other social scientists for guidance in examining international relations. In particular, a macrolevel perspective on conflict characterises the three major QIR projects of the past two decades. All three are based on the premise that to account for war, researchers must first discover what its incidence has been and what conditions correlate with its presence, absence or magnitude. The research design derives from Wright (1942) and Richardson (1960a, b) and the work generally has searched for consistent correlates of conflict in the absence of strong theoretical formulations.

Singer (1979), the leader of the Correlates of War (COW) project, feels that formal articulation of complex theories of international conflict is premature because of the weak knowledge base of the discipline and that the best prospects lie in a systematic "brush-clearing" operation of some magnitude. Consequently, basic concepts from the "Realpolitik" model (alliance behaviour, international organisation, diplomatic links, military and economic capabilities) are correlated with war indices for major power (systemic) conflict from 1816 to 1965. Despite a profusion of tests, no consistent theories of conflict are emerging from this large project. Either no theories exist due to the random, idiosyncratic nature of war or the COW methodology has not allowed theoretical development. Before the former explanation can be accepted, the latter must be examined. It seems evident that theory cannot develop because the COW researchers do not examine the international structures or totality within which conflict takes place. Essentially, they focus on "Realpolitik" to the exclusion of the other three perspectives and their purely inductive approaches have led to some interesting findings (Singer and Wallace, 1979). In particular, Wallace's findings, that while 85 per cent of arms races ended in war, only 7 per cent of wars were not preceded by an arms race and its extension, that engaging in an arms build-up is more likely to increase a nation's chances of going to war than of avoiding it, have clear policy implications and are the subject of much discussion in the peace research field. However, since most post-World War II conflict is "extra-systemic", frequently territorial disputes between minor powers, the findings of

the COW project may not be relevant to the largest set of
wars in the contemporary world (Mandel, 1980).

The Dimensionality of Nations (DON) project, headed by
Rudolph Rummel, began with a proto-theory, called social
field theory. Nations are social units that interact in a
social field and this behaviour can be analytically divided
into two spaces, behaviour and attribute. In attribute
space, nations are located in terms of their characteristics
(social, political, economic, military, etc.) and in
behaviour space, dyads of nations are located in terms of
their interactions (co-operation, conflict, avoidance, etc.).
Then, the locations of dyads in behaviour space is a function
of their locations in attribute space. (A well-known
geographic example of this factor analytic approach is
Berry's (1967) study of commodity flows in India.) Wealth,
politics and power were the three most important national
attributes in explaining dyadic behaviour while Catholic
culture, domestic conflict and density were important
secondary factors. A later version of the model allowed
dyadic assymetry as each policy-maker weighs national
attribute distances in deciding on his/her own international
behaviour. Although Rummel did not specify a priori which
attributes are related in which way to international
behaviour beyond a general expectation that the greater the
sum of the distances in the attribute spaces, the greater
the possibility of dyadic conflict, his model offers a way
forward for political geography. Its strong points are its
measures of absolute and relative distances between states,
its relationship of domestic to international events, its
technical sophistication, its incorporation of a behavioural
element in policymakers' evaluations, its clear tests of
hypothesised causes of international conflict and its
examination of formal and functional regions at the global
scale. Its major weaknesses are the nonspecification of
individual attribute-behaviour responses, its confinement of
tests to a small sample of nations and its neglect of underlying (substructural) global political economic trends.

The third large QIR project, termed the 1914 project
(Choucri and North, 1975), focussed on the major structural
forces leading to the First World War. After reviewing a
lengthy list of possible causes of war, the researchers
reduced their list to three, population growth, new
technologies and the search for resources. Lateral pressure
by nations (Lebensraum?) is the major element in leading to
an arms race and eventual war. Ample domestic resources
lead to increasing population which in turn demands more
resources eventually exceeding domestic supply. Concurrently,
new technology allows exploitation of resources and
contributes to both economic and population growth. After
expending readily available domestic resources, major powers
turned their attention abroad in the late nineteenth century

to colonial development. Nations came into conflict over
diminishing international booty, leading to alliance
formation, arms races and, eventually, war. While the
assassination of Archduke Ferdinand at Sarajevo provided the
spark that set off the European tinderbox, by a series of
simultaneous regression equations, calibrated for each nation
and modified to account for temporal autocorrelation,
Choucri and North were able to show that, despite intentions
to the contrary, a crisis environment emerged. The more
nations are involved in the crisis, the more likely they
respond to threats and hostility with similar behaviour
leading to an upward spiral of conflict, frequently resulting
in war.

The importance of the 1914 project lies not only in the
historical domain. If we add Galtung's structural forces to
Choucri and North's causal factors, the outlook for international peace is distinctly gloomy. Competition between
major powers for resources, formation of power blocs based on
ideology, power politics or economic ties, the domestic
interaction between technology, demography and growth leading
to global search for resources, the inevitable "dependence"
of small states on large powers reflected in a clear global
division, and the perceptions and threat behaviour of
politicians suggest a continued state of global strife.
While conflicts in the form of war is thankfully rare,
structural violence is continuous. Consequently political
geographers should turn their attention to endemic "non-war
conflict" within and between nations as well as continuing to
examine the geographic element in the causes of war.
Simplistic environmental deterministic models must be
avoided (e.g. countries with high population densities will
invade their neighbours) but the interconnections between
environmental, economic, demographic, political, geographic
and military attributes identified by the Stanford
researchers should be further explicated for a larger sample
of nations in the contemporary world.

FIVE THEORIES OF INTERNATIONAL CONFLICTS

Models of international relations, though often giving lip
service to a "global system", focus on one aspect of
international affairs such as power and dominance, on a
unidirectional link between national and international
events, on the influence of ideology on strategy or on
decision-making theory. Singer (1979) has strongly
criticised univariate models of international conflict and
has urged the development of models that link structural
(political, social and economic) predictors of conflict to
war behaviour and international relations. In previous
research, spatial influences are assumed to be non-existent,

randomly distributed, held constant or are treated in an
elementary fashion after other explanations fail. It
appears as if five general approaches or explanations for
international conflict exist. Each theory has links with
the four perspectives outlined above and the three QIR
projects. All five theories have spatial analogues and when
combined together into an interconnecting model, they provide
a useful beginning for a comprehensive approach to international conflicts.

Boulding's (1962) _theory of viability,_ a "realpolitik"
model derived from Morgenthau, examines zones in which a
nation is dominated or dominant. In naked power terms,
foreign policy is viewed as an effort to decrease the former
area and expand the latter. Frequently referred to as a
"sphere of influence" approach, it can be examined by the
gravity model (O'Sullivan, 1982). Intensity of power
declines with the inverse square of the radius of the
territorial limit of the state and by extension, the larger
the net of power cast by a state, the greater the force
required to sustain it. Smaller states can exist within the
larger power spheres of influence. Competition between major
states will be magnified if they are proximate. If a state
over expands, it can collapse under the pressure of the cost
of power maintenance and the emergence of rival powers at the
interstices. Some geo-realpoliticians urge a bipolar sphere
of influence for its ability to reduce conflict when
accepted by both nations (Cohen, 1973). Despite its
potential mathematical extension, this formulation reduces
complex international interactions to a simplistic and
debatable notion that all that matters is power because
aggression is basic to human nature, regardless of other,
varying character traits.

Rummel's (1977) _field theory_ has already been
elaborated and its emphasis on the domestic attribute-
international behaviour linkage parallels a growing feeling
in political geography that local, national and global events
are strongly linked so that seemingly distant macro-
developments are reflected in local changes (Taylor, 1982).
Thus, in one sense, the "barrio" dweller in Latin American
cities is paying for the current American military build-up
because high American military expenditures have helped to
produce a $200 billion budget deficit and to keep interest
rates high. Borrowing by Latin American nations at the high
interest rates has led to huge debts ($90 billion for Brazil,
$85 billion for Mexico) and near-default. Strong measures
by the International Monetary Fund (IMF) has forced Latin
American governments to reduce domestic spending, reducing
the quality of life for poor urban residents. The relations
between the global and local political economies are
becoming stronger and even the isolated African farmer is
affected by domestic political decisions in Washington D.C.,

or Paris both directly, such as American or French import
limitations on foodstuffs or military actions or indirectly,
through the operations of the international financial markets
(Harris, 1983).

The Sprouts are responsible for making explicit the
environmental theme in international politics. "In any
period of history, the results of international statecraft ...
are reflected in political terms with strong geographic
connotations such as balance of power, bipolarity, political
orbit, satellite, bloc, coalition, alliance, the Monroe
Doctrine, the Atlantic Community, the Near East and many
others" (Sprout and Sprout, 1965). They, too, were concerned
with the domestic-international linkages and they argued that
a second element, the intervening perceptions of individual
policymakers, should be added to the environment (attributes)-
global behaviour link. Rummel's Model II, in effect, adopted
this suggestion and the Choucri-North 1914 study, with its
environment-behaviour focus combined with the work of another
Stanford researcher (Holsti, 1972) on the changing
perceptions of decision makers in crises, illustrate the
application of the Sprout model to international relations.

The fourth theory of international relations, power
politics, is an extension of the sphere of influence
"Realpolitik" model. As advocated most forcefully by Cline
(1980) it provides a simple and controversial foreign policy
formulation. Each nation's power index is computed. Cline's
formula is $P_p = (C+E+M) \times (S+W)$ where P_p = power potential;
C = critical mass, the size of a nation; E = economic
capability; M = military capability; S = national strategy;
and W = national will. Each nation is evaluated both on
ideological and strategic grounds and an alliance strategy for
the United States is advocated, based on the sum of the power
indices. The world view is bipolar and the security of
Western "vital interests" is maintained by overlooking
questionable domestic policies of allies and by support for
governments in trouble from left-wing movements. A strong
geographical element is added to the scenario through control
of strategic pathways (e.g., Strait of Hormuz), support of
strategically located allies (South Africa, Israel) and a
clear demarcation of the globe into two competing geographical
blocs in classic "geopolitik" fashion.

The fifth and final theory of international relations
also derives from geopolitik and reflects geography's
traditional concern with cultural realms. Cohen (1973, 1982)
has suggested that certain regions, because of their complex
ethnic, religious, political, ideological, economic and
physical composition are intrinsically areas of tension,
called Shatterbelts. Major external powers are attracted
by the region's strategic location and internal resources.
Dominated by neither pole (west or east), they display
regional levels of power hierarchies because of local

divisions and major power competition, and so will remain
regions of international conflict. Cohen (1982) identified
three Shatterbelts: Sub-Saharan Africa, the Middle East and
Southeast Asia. He identified second-order powers and
advocated a foreign policy for the U.S. through support of
key regionally-dominant nations. Regardless of the policy
formulation, this view is extremely useful because it
stresses the nonuniformity of the globe, the diverse
composition of the actors (states), the parallel continuation
of local conflicts and world power competition, the alliance
behaviour of major powers in regional wars (e.g., the Horn of
Africa), and the fact that territorial boundary disputes in
these Shatterbelts has been the most frequent cause of war
over the past 30 years. While QIR researchers view space as
a minor element in conflict between major powers, a return to
traditional geographical concerns, the regional mosaic,
offers an excellent opportunity for political geographers to
establish themselves in the forefront of international
conflicts research. Since all five models are valid, though
frequently limited, representations of world conflicts, the
possible links between them are examined following the next
section in the effort to provide a more complete theoretical
formulation.

BOUNDARY AND CONTAGION STUDIES OF INTERNATIONAL CONFLICTS

A brief glance at the literature on the causes of war will
convince a reader that consistent explanations of war
occurrences in space and time are still far off. The
results are frequently contradictory, reflecting in part,
the ideological biases of the researchers but, more usually,
the result of differences in the measurement of state
attributes and conflict scales, and subjective definitions of
participant's conflict behaviour. A reappraisal of two
decades of QIR research continues as Rummel's DON project is
ending and the COW project re-evaluates its research design.
Variables which have not been consistently examined for their
effect on interstate conflict are now subject to greater
scrutiny. The location of states with respect to each other
is one such variable. Three statements by leading QIR
researchers illustrate the growing awareness of location as
an explanation in international conflicts.

Zinnes (1980), in her presidential address to the
International Studies Association, examined the "war
proneness of nations". An apparent contradiction exists.
The domestic attributes of nations do not make them warprone
on the one hand, yet consistent results have been found
between defense expenditures and the likelihood that a nation
will go to war on the other hand. Zinnes (1980:328) thinks
the key to the puzzle is contiguity. "Borders are an

attribute, borders produce contact, contact generates conflict, conflict leads to international violence. It would seem that the puzzle is on its way toward a solution". Klingman (1980:131), in attempting to form a general model of social change, finds that "apparently no one has yet suggested using auto-regression models to describe spatial diffusion cross-sectionally". (He clearly was unfamiliar with the geographic literature on the subject.) He proceeds to advocate "a new approach", a primitive space-time auto-regressive model with additional regressors to analyse social change across space and time. Singer (1981:1) saw a growing consensus in QIR research that "much research on periodicity in the occurrence of war has yielded little result, suggesting that the direction should now be to focus on such variables as diffusion and contagion".

Relatively few studies have explicitly made location the focus of study in examining international conflicts. The pioneers of research in this subject, Sir Lewis Richardson (1960a, b) and Quincy Wright (1942) both thought that the location of states was a key element in the global patterns of conflict. Their early work showed that there was a strong inverse relationship between the distance separating states and their likelihood of going to war and that the probability of confrontation escalating into war is greatly increased if the participating nations are contiguous. While the trends are clear, the explanation is not. Geography per se is not deterministic so that contiguity of states does not cause wars. However, nations that are close to each other are likely to interact and perceive each other's behaviour and condition as important. Nations possessing many neighbours are given many targets or opportunities for uncertainty, leading them to form alliances, in turn increasing the likelihood of being dragged into a war. "The evidence ... is consistent with the hypothesis that the process of infectious contagion which characterises war initiation between 1815 and 1965 was influenced by the pre-war alliances linking war coalition members" (Siverson and King, 1979:47). In this light, location operates as an important intermediary modifying a nation's attribute-foreign policy relationship.

A focus on major power tends to obscure the most important single cause of wars between states, border and territorial disputes. Mandel (1980), in his examination of 66 border disputes between 1945 and 1974, found that war conditions were ripe when the states were about equal in power, had low levels of technology, have border disputes reflecting ethnic divisions and are members of the two state mutually contiguous set. Third parties tend to become involved when the two warring states belong to different ideological blocs. Russett (1967) found that whereas 26 per cent of all pairs of states consisted of neighbours, 63 per cent of all warring pairs between 1945 and 1965 shared boundaries.

Weede (1975) concluded that territorial problems induced arms races between the disputants, in turn increasing the chances of war and that contiguity provides opportunity for territorial problems to arise and, so, indirectly is a cause of war. In the two most complete studies of the geographic element in interstate conflicts, both Houwling and Siccama (1983) and Most and Starr (1980) have found that wars are clustered in both space and time. While the methodologies differed, the results were similar. For their war sample 1816-1980, Houweling and Siccama concluded that wars are not independent events and that the dynamics within regional sub-systems seem to outweigh the processes of war causation in the world system as a whole. They use David and Barton's Q statistic, developed for examining epidemiological contagion, to show that conflicts between major powers (n=193) and between all nations (n=435) are highly auto-correlated in both space and time. When the sample is broken down by region, high and significant Q values are present for Europe at all time periods but insignificant Q values for the Americas. Most and Starr (1980) use a contingency table analysis to examine the pattern of new war participation from 1945-1965 in a diffusion framework. They found that tests of the accuracy of four diffusion-related processes (positive and negative spatial diffusion and positive and negative reinforcement) support their arguments that certain types of wars (border conflicts) have tended to diffuse across space, (positive spatial diffusion) just as other researchers have indicated for coups d'etat. In essence, their framework is an endogenous time-space model of first order lags. "Mean transition rates indicated that having a warring border nation increases the likelihood that a subsequent new war would occur over 3 times in the SIPRI data set and over 5 times in the COW set" (Most and Starr, 1980:944). It would appear that the time is right for a comprehensive time-space interaction model of international conflicts that would also incorporate explanations from the four perspectives described by Wallensteen. A time-space model without structural elements is as confining as the reverse, the typical QIR structural model in a time-space vacuum.

A TIME-SPACE MODEL OF INTERNATIONAL CONFLICTS

Having reviewed the nature and direction of research in quantitative international relations and political geography, a synthesis of both sub-disciplines with a general model of international conflicts in a space-time framework is proposed. The ideal conditions for such a model are elaborated, the principle elements of its construction are defined and possible tests of the model using existing data banks are suggested. Hopefully, these suggestions will spur

other researchers to continue development of this approach.
A political geography model of international conflicts should
include as far as possible seven conditions, drawn from the
QIR, political geography and the world political economy
literatures.

On the methodology side, the model should contain
variables that derive from the four perspectives identified
above such as power and distance measures, economic data and
political views. In a sense the analysis would test the
ability of each perspective. Second, the model should view
the world as a system with feedback loops, externality
effects, stimuli and responses, and dynamic change as key
elements. Third, the model should be multivariate, a clear
requirement as a result of the shortcomings of QIR univariate
tests. In a theoretical vein, the model should accept the
principle that international events are responses, in part, to
domestic conditions, modified through the filter of policy
decision-makers. Consequently, domestic attributes and international behaviour are measured as in Model II of field
theory. Fifth, the model would be a reflection of a
"maximalist" approach to international conflicts reflected not
only in non-military concerns, but which uses the triangular
requirements of peace research; acceptance of empirical data
analysis, a value commitment to peace research and a concern
for the relationship of structures to violence with a view to
changing structures so as to reduce violence (Dunn, 1979).
Of foremost concern is the need to deal with both east-west
political competition and north-south economic, military and
political conflicts. Sixth, borrowing from econometrics, we
can view the model as having both exogenous (structural) and
endogenous (time-space) predictors. The basic data
arrangement is three-dimensional. Both rows and columns are
nations with the data consisting of distance and interactive
measures. Additional domestic attributes are included for
each nation. The third dimension is time. Structural
explanations refer to field theory analyses while endogenous
explanations adopt the view that international relations are
ordered in both their temporal and spatial elements, or
stated another way, that significant positive space-time
autocorrelation is present. These regularities can be
modelled using STARIMA methods (Cliff et al., 1981) and such
topics as the impact of legislation, periodicity, higher-
order spatial lags and trend can be readily examined. By
adding the structural variables to the equation, we obtain a
mixed space-time-structural explanation, called STARIMAR
(Space-Time Auto-regressive Integrated Moving Average Model
with Additional Regressors) (Haggett, Cliff, Frey, 1977:525),
of the form

$$\nabla Y_{it} = \alpha_1 + \alpha_2\, X_{i,t-1} + \beta \nabla Y_{i,t-1} + \gamma \sum_j W_{ij}\, \nabla Y_{j,t-1} + U_{it}$$

where $U_{it} = \epsilon_{it} + b\epsilon_{i,t-1} + c\sum_j W_{ij} \epsilon_{j,t-1}$ is a random component called the moving average;

α_1, α_2, β, γ, b and c are parameters to be estimated;

$X_{i,t-1}$ is a structural predictor drawn from the list of variables listed below;

$Y_{i,t-1}$ is a first order (endogenous) temporal auto-regressive term;

$\sum_j W_{ij}\nabla Y_{j,t-1}$ is a first order endogenous spatial auto-regressive term; and

∇Y_{it} reflects the repeated differencing or integration of dependent variable (international conflict measure) to remove trend and periodicity and to ensure stationarity. While model identification and parameter estimation are time-consuming, they have been successfully calculated for other similar data sets (O'Loughlin, 1983; Martin and Oeppen, 1975). A similar estimation of the cultural, economic and spatial effects on insurgency in the Phillipines is given in Cliff and Ord (1981)

An example of a research procedure required to calibrate this space-time structural model is outlined here. The research proceeds in three phases. It is necessary to determine the presence or absence of significant space-time interaction effects in the conflict data set. Previous research has shown interaction to exist at a variety of scales. Spatial correlograms will be used for this initial exploration, with both space and time logged from 0 to 5. Examination of the correlograms will suggest appropriate temporal and spatial lags for the auto-regressive models to be calibrated. Generally lags less than 2 are appropriate. Regional and time period differences in autocorrelation will be examined since Houweling and Siccama (1983) found large regional variation in conflicts between meighbours. The choice of weights (the w_{ij} matrix in the equation), measuring the propinquity, contiguity or interaction between nations, poses a vexing problem. Previous measures have been simplistic, such as first order contiguity, and airline distance between capitals. It is possible that conflicts may be clustered using one weights matrix and not another. This finding would have serious methodological implications for contiguity studies of international conflicts as well as posing interesting questions, such as why are nations clustered in one space metric and not another. Both absolute measures such as contiguity, length of shared boundary, proportion of shared boundary to all the nation's boundary lengths, distance between centroids, and distance-shared boundary index, and relative measures such as diplomatic

distance, ideological distance as reflected in UN votes,
economic distance as reflected in trade flows, language and
culture distance, and non-Euclidean distances such as multidimensional scales (Gatrell, 1979) will be tested. Starr and
Most (1976) have argued that large states tend to have many
small neighbours and wars between states of unequal sizes are
infrequent. Consequently, they claim that the net effects of
the two trends is to cancel out any neighbouring effect in
inter-national conflicts. The sample of states will be
divided into size classes and space-time correlograms
constructed for the different classes. The data series is
examined for spatial and temporal non-stationarity and trend
to determine whether detrending of differencing is needed.

The second phase is most familiar to QIR researchers,
the construction of a multiple regression model in which
international conflict is seen as a function of the
characteristic of the nations. A large body of results
suggests key indicators that would avoid the problem of
multicollinearity. As with the correlograms, the model would
be fitted for different regions. The four perspectives
previously outlined of this paper will guide the selection of
variables with each "politik" represented. Possible
individual measures under "Kapitalpolitik" are per capita
income, economic growth indices, import/export ratios,
colonial/excolonial links and status, population density,
foreign investment, and technology level. Under "Geopolitik",
regional location (Heartland or Rimland), number of
neighbours, and Shatterbelt location are obvious choices.
Under "Realpolitik", power is measured by military
expenditures per capita, absolute military strength, military
expenditure of regional nonallies, alliances and diplomatic
links, fields of dominance (dominant or dominated), area and
populations. "Idealpolitik" is more difficult to measure but
would include legitimation (type of government), national
will and strategy (Cline, 1980, population composition, and
indices of civil unrest. International conflict can be
scaled on a co-operation-conflict scale (Azar, 1980) or
measured by war casualities (Small and Singer, 1982).
Residuals from the structural multiple regression will be
examined to determine if additional regressors are needed.

The third and final phase involves the calibration of
the time-space structural model. Only significant
structural predictors from the multiple regression will be
included in the model as well as only significant temporal
and spatial lags. As earlier, this model will be fitted for
different regions. The relative contribution of temporal,
spatial and structural explanations of international
conflicts can be determined from this comprehensive model.
In geography, a good empirical example of the type of model
proposed here is the study by Cliff et al., (1981) on the
diffusion of epidemics in Iceland. Previous attempts in

international relations have separately verified the utility
of both spatial contagion and temporal auto-regressive
approaches as well as structural explanations to conflict but
they suffered from methodological and technical deficiencies,
simplistic assumptions about proximity and restricted views
of diffusion processes.

The final requirement is clearly the acquisition of an
adequate data set. Luckily a number are readily available
through the Inter-University Consortium for Political
Research at the University of Michigan, among them the QIR
data sets discussed above (Beattie, 1979). The Conflict and
Peace Data Bank (COPDAB) (Azar, 1980; ISQ, 1983) is probably
the most complete data bank for international relations
because it holds over a half-million events reported in 70
scores about 135 nation states between 1948 and the present.
Each record contains variables describing the actions,
reactions and interactions of nation-states. It offers the
best collection of data for this study.

This tentative spatial diffusion model sees individual
states as possible sites of conflict and focuses on both their
individual characteristics, links with other states, the role
of conflict-generating agencies and events, and spatial
proximity, to calibrate models based on past events and
forecast future conflicts. Following Hagerstrand (1967), the
procedure is to conceptualise the diffusion process, develop
techniques for operationalising the concept and identify
empirical regularities in diffusion. This diffusion framework has 6 elements that demonstrate clear parallels with the
study of international conflicts. The event being analysed
has the following properties: (1) spatial elements;
(2) temporal elements; (3) a specific character (e.g. war);
(4) places where the event is located at the start;
(5) places where the event is located at the end of time
interval; and (6) paths of movement, influence or interaction
between states. When viewed in an individualistic mode, the
pattern of conflicts seems random but, like other diffusion
analyses, as we examine the aggregate pattern of numerous
individual conflicts, order and regularity may appear in the
diffusion surface.

A research effort should be devoted to explicating the
ties between the five theories of international relations and
space-time models. The five conflict theories can be viewed
as having causal influences on international conflicts under
the rubrics of distance, attributes, attitudes/beliefs,
hierarchy, and location, respectively. These elements have
been examined in spatial diffusion studies and shown to have
important effects, both individually and collectively.
Diffusion processes are stochastic rather than deterministic
so that the influence of distance is modelled through
distance-decay functions, the equivalent of spheres of
influence in international relations. In general, the

greater the power of the state, the larger the distance over which it extends its influence. Attribute (domestic conditions) of the receiving and sending states will influence their view of conflict, a consistent finding of the social field theory approach. Likewise, the role of access to resources, economic relations, political ideology and historical experience in international conflicts can be incorporated into the diffusion model. Perceptions refers to the national capability and values which allocate national resources and determine technology, just as certain farmers, by virtue of their attitudes, perceptions and beliefs, accept agricultural innovations while others reject them. Policy choice responds to these forces both directly and indirectly through the filter of policymakers' perceptions. Threats, fears, balance of power thinking, national commitment and alliance behaviour work in concert to regulate a state's international behaviour. The meshing of objective measures, such as military strength and subjective factors, such as perceptions, provide the context for international conflicts.

It is frequently suggested that states can be classified according to power, 1st order (U.S., USSR), 2nd order (South Africa, China, Japan, etc.), 3rd order (Spain, Mexico, Phillipines, etc.), 4th order (Malaysia, Tanzania, Zaire), and 5th order (Mali, Bangladesh, Ireland, etc.). Each level in the hierarchy corresponds to a zone of influence, global, continental, regional, local and none. Just as innovations move down the urban hierarchy as well as through spatial contagion, so, too, do international conflicts have both local (contagion) and extra local (regional or global) ramifications. In this view, major powers, through their alliances and geostrategies are seen as the prime movers behind local conflict or as causing expansion and prolongation of local rivalries. Conflicts, unlike most diffusion processes, may move up the hierarchy of power. Finally, certain locations seem more prone to conflict, akin to corridors of movement in diffusion research, because of their historical rivalries, contemporary disputes, economic resources and geographic situation. Southern Africa and the Middle East provide good examples. Other areas are presently stable, similar to barriers to diffusion, such as North-Western Europe and North America. I believe the parallels between these theories of international conflict and spatial diffusion represent much more than coincidence but are representations of the same set of causal processes, a dynamism that lends itself ideally to space-time process models (Cliff and Ord, 1981).

There are clearly some contentious issues in equating the changing distribution of international conflicts to the common spatial diffusion model. The logistic curve, so evident in the diffusion of innovations, does not reflect trends in international conflict as nations repeatedly become involved in wars since no global saturation point exists. A more accurate analogy is disease diffusion examined by a general epidemic model (Cliff et al., 1981). Distance computation, dyadic relationships, barrier and corridor definition, and goodness-of-fit tests represent only computational or definitional difficulties. In general greater emphasis should be given to the market/infrastructure perspective on diffusion, rather than the more common adoption perspective (Brown, 1981). For political geographers, so long accustomed to working with individual states, limited temporal and spatial set of conflicts, and an idiographic perspective, the proposal made in this section is a major break with tradition. However, its adoption would help bridge the divide that currently isolates global political geography from quantitative international relations and mainstream human geography.

GEOGRAPHY AND INTERNATIONAL CONFLICTS: A SUMMARY

The beginnings of a concern with the roles that distance, location and contiguity play in international conflicts are now evident in the QIR literature. Although both Wright (1942) and Richardson (1960b) showed that states tended to become involved in war in proportion to the number of states with which they shared a common border, contiguity was not directly examined by the COW researchers or other QIR adherents until other predictors showed inconsistent or non-significant relationships with conflict. A retest of Richardson's findings showed that most interstate wars are between nations that are not only close together geographically but quite similar in most other attribute dimensions. A confounding factor seems to be alliance formation, generally over short distances. (The enemy of my enemy is my friend). However, the univariate approach adopted by the COW research team does not allow an adequate test of the importance of independent effects of the geographic dimension, after controlling for cultural and economic variables and alliance behaviour.

The research called for in this paper requires a major commitment but it would appear that unless political geographers move in the direction of nomothetic research, their contributions will continue to be ignored by political scientists (Laponce, 1980). This neglect seems to be particularly worrisome in the area of global political geography. Only Mackinder and the German geopoliticians are referred to in power bloc studies and the QIR researchers seem intent on rediscovering the wheel of space-time models. Nevertheless, they have progressed much farther in the study of the spatial element in international relations than political geographers although their technical definitions and measurements are very rudimentary. After the methodological breakthrough to nomothetic research takes place in global political geography, lines of communication are opened to other branches of the geographic discipline and more researchers might be attracted into the field. The merger of traditional political geographic concerns such as border conflicts and geostrategies, with modern geographic and social scientific methods is long past due.

NOTES

1. Only major theoretical and empirical works are cited in the body of the paper. Further references can be found in the accompanying bibliography. Individual studies are rarely cited: they are summarised in the recent books by Beer (1981), Choucri and Robinson (1978), Gurr et al., (1982), Hoole and Zinnes (1976), Kegley and McGowan (1983), Rosenau (1976), Russett and Starr (1981), Singer (1979), Singer and Wallace (1979), Weede (1975), Zinnes (1976) and Zinnes and Gillespie (1976).

REFERENCES

Agnew, J. A. (1983) 'An excess of 'national exceptionalism': towards a new political geography of American foreign policy', Political Geography Quarterly, 2, 151-166

Alker, H. A. Jr. (1981) 'Dialectical foundations of global disparities', International Studies Quarterly, 25, 69-98

Amin, A. et al. (1982) Dynamics of Global Crisis, Monthly Review Press, New York

Azar, E. E. (1980) 'The conflict and peace data bank (COPDAB) project' Journal of Conflict Resolution, 24, 143-152

Barnet, R. J. (1972) Roots of War, Penguin, New York

Beattie, R. (1979) 'ICPSR: resources for the study of conflict resolution', Journal of Conflict Resolution, 23, 337-345

Beer, F. A. (1981) Peace Against War: The Ecology of International Violence, Freeman, San Francisco

Berry, B. J. L. (1967) Essays on Commodity Flows and the Spatial Structure of the Indian Economy, University of Chicago, Department of Geography, (Research Paper No. 111), Chicago

Brown, L. (1981) Innovation Diffusion: A New Perspective, St. Martins, New York

Bunge, W. (1982) The Nuclear War Atlas, Society for Human Exploration, Victoriaville, Quebec

Chatfield, C. (1977) 'International peace research: the field defined by dissemination', Journal of Peace Research, 16, 163-179

Choucri, N. and North, R. (1975) Nations in Conflict: National Growth and International Violence, Freeman, San Francisco

Choucri, N. and Robinson, T. (1978) Forecasting International Relations: Theory, Methods, Problems and Prospects, Freeman, San Francisco

Cliff, A. D., Haggett, P., Ord, J. K. and Versey, G. R. (1981) Spatial Diffusion: An Historical Geography of Epidemics in an Island Community, Cambridge University Press, Cambridge

Cliff, A. D. and Ord, J. K. (1981) Spatial Processes: Models and Applications, Pion Ltd., London

Cline, R. S. (1980) World Power Trends and U.S. Foreign Policy for the 1980s, Westview Press, Boulder

Cohen, S. B. (1973) Geography and Politics in a World Divided, Oxford University Press, New York

Cohen, S. B. (1982) 'A new map of global geopolitical equilibrium: a developmental approach', Political Geography Quarterly, 1, 223-242

Day, A. J. (1982) Border and Territorial Disputes, Longman, London

Dunn, D. J. (1978) 'Peace research' in T. Taylor (ed.), Approaches and Theory in International Relations, Longman, London, 257-279

Eberwein, W. D. (1982) 'The quantitative study of international conflict: quantity and quality' Journal of Peace Research, 18, 19-38

Editorial Board (1982) 'Research agendas for the nineteen eighties', Political Geography Quarterly, 1, 1-18

Gaddis, J. L. (1982) Strategies of Containment: A Critical Appraisal of Postwar American National Security Policy, Oxford University Press, New York

Galtung, J. (1964) 'A structural theory of aggression', Journal of Peace Research, 1, 95-119

Garnham, D. (1976) 'Dyadic international war, 1816-1965: the role of power parity and geographical proximity', Western Political Quarterly, 29, 231-242

Gatrell, A. C. (1979) 'Autocorrelation in Spaces' Environment and Planning A, 11, 507-516

Gochman, C. S. (1976) 'Studies of international violence: five easy pieces', Journal of Conflict Resolution, 20, 539-560

Gochman, C. S. and Leng, R. J. (1983) 'Realpolitik and the road to war: an analysis of attributes and behaviour', International Studies Quarterly, 27, 97-120

Gray, C. S. (1977) The Geopolitics of the Nuclear Era, Crane Russak, New York

Gurr, T. R. et al. (1982) World Patterns of Conflict, Sage, Beverly Hills, Ca.

Harris, N. (1982) Of Bread and Guns: The World Economy in Crisis, Penguin, London

Henrikson, A. K. (1980) 'The geographical 'mental maps' of American foreign policy makers', International Political Science Journal, 1, 495-530

Hoffman, G. (1982) 'Nineteenth century roots of American
    power relations: a study in historical political
    geography', Political Geography Quarterly, 1, 279-292
Holsti, O. R. (1972) Crisis, Escalation and War, McGill-
    Queens University Press, Montreal
Hoole, F. W. and Zinnes, D. A. (1976) Quantitative
    International Politics: An Appraisal, Praeger Publishers,
    New York
Houweling, H. W. and Siccama, J. G. (1983) 'Time-space
    interaction in warfare: some theoretical and empirical
    aspects of the epidemiology of collective violence,
    1816-1980', paper presented at the European Consortium
    for Political Research, Frieburg
ISQ (1983) 'Symposium on Events Data Collection',
    International Studies Quarterly, 27, 147-178
Isard, W. (1979) 'A definition of peace science: the queen of
    the social science, parts I and II', Journal of Peace
    Science, 4, 1-49 and 97-132
Isard, W. and Nagra, Y. (1983) International and Regional
    Conflict: Analytical Approaches, Ballinger, Cambridge, Ma
Isard, W. and Smith, C. (1983) Conflict Analysis and Practical
    Conflict Management Procedure, Ballinger, Cambridge, Ma
Jackman, R. W. (1978) 'The predictability of coups d'etat: a
    model with African data', American Political Science
    Review, 72, 1262-1275
Kegley, C. W. Jr. and McGowan, P. (1981) The Political Economy
    of Foreign Policy Behaviour, Sage, Beverly Hills, Ca
Kende, I. (1971) 'Twenty five years of local wars', Journal
    of Peace Research, 1, 5-22
Klingman, D. (1980) 'Temporal and spatial diffusion in the
    comparative analysis of social change', American Political
    Science Review, 74, 123-137
Krasner, S. D. (1978) Defending the National Interest: Raw
    Materials Investments and U.S. Foreign Policy, Princeton
    University Press, Princeton, N.J.
Krell, G. (1980) 'Capitalism and armaments: business cycles
    and defence spending in the United States, 1945-79',
    Journal of Peace Research, 18, 221-240
Krippendorff, E. (1981) 'The victims - reflections on a
    research failure', Journal of Peace Research, 18, 97-102
Krippendorff, E. (1982) 'Review of Russett/Starr, World
    Politics: the Menu for Choice', Journal of Peace
    Research, 19, 197-202
Laponce, J. A. (1980) 'Political science: an import-export
    analysis of journals and footnotes', Political Studies,
    28, 401-419
Li, R. P. Y. and Thompson, W. R. (1975) 'The 'coup contagion'
    hypothesis', Journal of Conflict Resolution, 19, 63-88
Lowe, J. T. (1981) Geopolitics and War: Mackinder's
    Philosophy of Power, University Press of America,
    Washington, D.C.

Mackinder, H. J. (1962) <u>Democratic Ideals and Reality</u>, Norton, New York

Mandel, R. (1980) 'Roots of the modern interstate border dispute', <u>Journal of Conflict Resolution</u>, <u>24</u>, 427-454

McGowan, P. J. and Kordan, B. (1981) 'Imperialism in world-system perspective: Britain 1870-1914', <u>International Studies Quarterly</u>, <u>25</u>, 43-68

Merritt, R. and Russett, B. (1981) <u>From National Development to Global Community: A Festschrift to Karl Deutsch</u>, George Allen and Unwin, Boston

Midlarsky, M. I. (1976) 'Power and distance in international conflict behaviour' in D. A. Zinnes and J. V. Gillespie (eds.), <u>Mathematical Models in International Relations</u>, Praeger, New York, 132-155

Midlarsky, M. I. (1978) 'Analysing diffusion and contagion effects', <u>American Political Science Review</u>, <u>72</u>, 996-1008

Modelski, G. (1978) 'The long cycle of global politics and the nation state, <u>Comparative Studies in Society and History</u>, <u>20</u>, 214-235

Morgenthau, H. J. (1973) <u>Politics among Nations: The Struggle for Power and Peace</u>, (5th ed.), Alfred Knopf, New York

Most, B. A. and Starr, H. (1980) 'Diffusion, reinforcement, geopolitics and the spread of war', <u>American Political Science Review</u>, <u>74</u>, 932-946

Nincic, M. (1982) <u>The Arms Race: The Political Economy of Military Growth</u>, Praeger, New York

Nye, J. S. and Keohane, R. (1977) <u>Power and Interdependence</u>, Little, Brown, Boston

O'Loughlin, J. (1983) 'The geographic distribution of foreigners in West Germany, 1964-1981', unpublished paper, Department of Geography, University of Illinois at Urbana-Champaign

Olson, M. (1982) <u>The Rise and Decline of Nations</u>, Yale University Press, New Haven

Openshaw, S. and Steadman, P. (1983) 'The geography of two hypothetical nuclear attacks on Britain', <u>Area</u>, <u>15</u>, 193-201

O'Sullivan, P. (1983) 'A geographical analysis of guerrilla warfare', <u>Political Geography Quarterly</u>, <u>2</u>, 139-150

Parker, W. H. (1982) <u>Mackinder: Geography as an Aid to Statecraft</u>, Clarendon, Oxford

Partem, M. G. (1983) 'The buffer system in international relations', <u>Journal of Conflict Resolution</u>, <u>27</u>, 3-26

Pearson, F. S. (1974) 'Geographic proximity and foreign military intervention', <u>Journal of Conflict Resolution</u>, <u>18</u>, 432-460

Pepper, D. and Jenkins, A. (1983) 'A call to arms: geography and peace studies', <u>Area</u>, <u>15</u>, 202-208

Rosenau, J. N. (1976) <u>In Search of Global Patterns</u>, Free Press, New York

Richardson, L. F. (1960a) Arms and Insecurity: A Mathematical
    Study of the Causes and Origins of Wars, Boxwood,
    Pittsburgh
Richardson, L. F. (1960b) The Statistics of Deadly Quarrels,
    Boxwood, Pittsburgh
Rummel, R. J. (1977) Field Theory Evolving, Sage, Beverly
    Hills, Ca.
Russett, B. (1967) International Regions and the International
    System: A Study in Political Ecology, Rand-McNally,
    Chicago
Russett, B. and Starr, H. (1981) World Politics: The Menu for
    Choice, Freeman, San Francisco
Singer, J. D. (1968) Quantitative International Politics,
    Macmillan, New York
Singer, J. D. (1979) Explaining War: Selected Papers from the
    Correlates of War Project, Sage, Beverly Hills, Ca.
Singer, J. D. (1981) 'Accounting for international war: the
    state of the discipline', Journal of Peace Research, 18,
    1-18
Singer, J. D. (1982) 'Confrontational behaviour and
    escalation to war, 1816-1980: a research plan', Journal
    of Peace Research, 19, 37-48
Singer, J. D. and Small, M. (1968) 'Alliance aggregation and
    the onset of war, 1815-1945', in J. D. Singer (ed.),
    Quantitative International Politics, Free Press, New York,
    247-286
Singer, J. D. and Small, M. (1972) The Wages of War 1816-1965:
    A Statistical Handbook, Wiley, New York
Singer, J. D. and Wallace, M. D. (1979) To Augur Well: Early
    Warning Indicators in World Politics, Sage, Beverly
    Hills, Ca.
Siverson, R. and King, J. (1980) 'Attributes of national
    alliance membership and war participation, 1816-1965',
    American Journal of Political Science, 24, 1-15
Small, M. and Singer, J. D. (1982) The Resort to Arms:
    International and Civil Wars 1916-1980, Sage, Beverly
    Hill, Ca.
Soppelsa, J. (1980) Geographie des Armaments, Masson, Paris
Sprout, H. (1963) 'Geopolitical hypotheses in international
    perspective', World Politics, 15, 187-212
Sprout, H. and Sprout, M. (1965) The Ecological Perspective on
    Human Affairs, Princeton University Press, Princeton, N.J.
Spykman, N. J. (1970) America's Strategy in World Politics:
    The United States and the Balance of Power, Archon Books,
    (first published, 1942), Hamden, Conn.
Starr, H. and Most, B.A. (1976) 'The substance and study of
    borders in international relations research',
    International Studies Quarterly, 20, 581-620
Szymanski, A. (1981) The Logic of Imperialism, Praeger,
    New York

Taylor, P. J. (1982) 'A materialist framework for political
    geography', Transactions, Institute of British
    Geographers, NS7, 15-34
Taylor, T. (1978) Approaches and Theory in International
    Relations, Longman, London
Taylor, W. J. Jr. and Maaren, S. A. (1983) The Future of
    Conflict in the 1980s, Heath, Lexington, Ma.
Thorndike, T. (1978) 'The revolutionary approach: a marxist
    perspective', in T. Taylor (ed.), Approaches and Theory
    in International Relations, Longman, London, 54-99
Vayrynen, R. (1979) 'Economic and military position of the
    regional power centers', Journal of Peace Research, 16,
    349-369
Wallace, M. D. (1979) 'Arms races and escalation: some new
    evidence', Journal of Conflict Resolution, 23, 3-16
Wallace, M. D. (1981) 'Old nails in new coffins: the para
    bellum hypothesis revisited', Journal of Peace Research,
    18, 91-95
Wallensteen, P. (1981) 'Incompatibility, confrontation and
    war: four models and three historical systems, 1816-1976'
    Journal of Peace Research, 10, 57-90
Wallerstein, I. (1974) The Modern World System, Academic
    Press, New York
Wallerstein, I. (1979) The Capitalist World Economy,
    Cambridge University Press, New York
Wassmund, H. (1982) Grundzüge der Weltpolitik: Daten und
    Tendenzen von 1945 bis zur Gegenwart, Beck, Munich
Weede, E. (1975) Weltpolitik und Kriegsursachen in 20.
    Jahrhundert, R. Oldenbourg Verlag, Munich
Whittlesey, D. (1942) German Strategy of World Conquest,
    Robinson, London
Wohlstetter, A. 'The illusions of distance', Foreign Affairs,
    46, 242-255
Wright, Q. (1942) A Study of War, University of Chicago
    Press, Chicago
Zinnes, D. (1976) Contemporary Research in International
    Relations: a Perspective and Critical Appraisal,
    Macmillan, New York
Zinnes, D. (1980) 'Three puzzles in search of a researcher',
    International Studies Quarterly, 24, 315-342
Zinnes, D. and Gillespie, J. (1976) Mathematical Models in
    International Relations, Praeger, New York
Zolberg, A. R. (1981) 'Origins of the modern world system:
    a missing link', World Politics, 33, 253-281

Chapter Fourteen

POLITICAL PHILOSOPHY AND POLITICAL GEOGRAPHY

G. H. Pirie

INTRODUCTION

As shown in other chapters of this book, the new political
geography leans heavily on either positivist political
science or on critical political economy for its subjects and
its analytical procedures. The potential association between
political geography and political philosophy has not been
dismissed; it has scarcely been investigated. Although
discussion of ethics and values in geography at large
(Buttimer, 1974; Sayer, 1981), and of equity, freedom and
justice (Claval, 1983; Pirie, 1983) do represent some initial
departures, it remains substantially true that "contemporary
geography is out of touch with contemporary philosophy"
(Tuan, 1974:58, footnote 15). Certainly there have not been
systematic attempts to sketch areas of co-operation and
borrowing between political philosophy and political
geography in the same way as historians and sociologists have
sought to do (Strauss, 1949; Partridge, 1965).
    The following presentation sets out to persuade political
geographers about the merit of paying closer attention to the
work of political philosophers. The argument is largely that
political philosophy offers conceptual tools for critical and
imaginative reflection on the present organisation of the
world political map and on the values which structure and
emerge from it. The methodological presupposition is that
"making rationally defended 'value-judgements' is an
essential element of any rigorous social inquiry" (Sayer,
1981:29).

POLITICAL PHILOSOPHY

In 1957 political philosophy was declared dead (Laslett and
Runciman, 1956). The subject appeared that way because of
the claim that discussion of values could only ever be
subjective and beyond the realms of rationality. Part of the

227

difficulty was that of reasoning from an 'is' to an 'ought' proposition, from the positive to the normative. As such, political philosophy was linked to "a taste for ice-cream. One can only state one's taste and go away - there is no point in arguing" (Runciman, 1963:156). Political philosophers were said to have been shown that many of the problems with which they traditionally grappled were "spurious, resting on confusions of thought and the misuse of language" (Plamenatz, 1960:37). Evidence for the claim came at least in part from the observation that "no commanding work of political philosophy has appeared in the twentieth century" (Berlin, 1962:1). The points of reference here were, for example, Plato's Republic, Aristotle's Politics, Hobbes' Leviathan, Locke's Treatise on Civil Government, Rousseau's Social Contract, Mill's Liberty and Hegel's Philosophy of Right. All of these major tracts had displayed concern for the nature of collective life and the institutions which it comprised; for the problem of political obligation to the state (Quinton, 1967; Parekh, 1982).

Opinion on the fate of political philosophy was by no means universal and several scholars sought to point out fallacies and oversights which punctuated the epitaphs. It was suggested, for one, that reports of the slackening of a moral urge in society were grossly exaggerated and that there remained a lively interest in, and need for, moral reflection: for "elaborating and advocating conceptions of the good life", and for "describing the forms of social action and organisation necessary for their achievement" (Partridge, 1961:219). The argument was put forward despite growing despondency that 'large moral intimations' had apparently come to nought and had even had pernicious effects. In similar vein, another defendent of political philosophy contended that with the weakening of moral principles derived from theological and metaphysical doctrines about human nature, humanity required a coherent and practical philosophy: it was "... part of man's need to be his own master, to make up his own mind how he shall live and what he shall be" (Plamenatz, 1960:46, footnote 1). Finally, curiosity itself was said to protect political philosophy from demise:

> it would be a gratuitous abdication of our powers
> of reasoning ... not to want to know what we
> believe, and for what reason, what the metaphysical
> implications of such beliefs are, what their
> relation is to all other types of belief, what
> criteria of value and truth they involve, and so
> what reason we have to think them true or valid
> (Berlin, 1962:33).

In the revivification of political philosophy actions

spoke louder than words and the 1960s and 1970s saw an increasing number of publications in the field. Toward the close of the 1970s it was clearly possible to remark that political philosophy was flourishing (Laslett and Fishkin, 1979). Journal-length papers on freedom, equality, rights and justice (see, for example those reprinted in Flathman 1973) were expanded into book form, most notably in the case of Rawls' (1972) Olympian A Theory of Justice - 'a contemporary classic' (Laslett and Fishkin, 1979). The list of major works which were prompted by a Rawls-led revival in political philosophy is too long to be included here. It must suffice to select a few titles to convey a flavour of the new research: Anarchy, State and Utopia (Nozick, 1974), The Practice of Rights (Flathman, 1976), The Idea of Freedom (Ryan, 1979), Social Justice in the Liberal State (Ackerman, 1980), Rights, Justice and the Bounds of Liberty (Feinberg, 1980) and A Critique of Freedom and Equality (Charvet, 1981).

A considerable proportion of the contemporary literature in political philosophy is dense, difficult and esoteric, inaccessible to most of those outside the discipline. As part of the subject's own 'relevance revolution', interpretative books, new journals and new courses were launched. The intention was to produce tractable and more prescriptive work. Among the publications are texts by Barry (1980), Petit (1980) and Goodwin (1982), and the periodicals Philosophy and Public Affairs and Applied Philosophy. A Centre for Philosophy and Public Affairs has been established at the University of Maryland, and a graduate programme in Values and Social Policy at the University of Colorado. An inter-disciplinary research project into distributive justice in Australia is being undertaken currently at Australia National University. These various initiatives make it clear that in both theoretical and concrete senses significant steps have been taken on the path to recovering questions of value from the inscrutable realms of intuition and feeling and placing them firmly in the realm of political reason (Petit, 1980). Issues in the evaluation of social organisation which had lain dormant since the heyday of nineteenth century utilitarianism have been vigorously reopened. In the new world order

> such questions as whether and what obligations one
> has to men struggling for survival, freedom or
> justice in other countries, how these relate to
> one's obligations to one's own community, how
> mankind's common stake in survival and freedom can
> be institutionally articulated, the nature of
> sovereignty and the character of global citizen-
> ship become central to political philosophy
> (Parekh, 1982:201).

POLITICAL GEOGRAPHY

Neither anticipation nor encouragement of a philosophically better informed political geography has been prominent in reviews of and agenda for the new political geography. In some cases there has been total neglect of the issue (Kliot, 1982; Editorial Board, 1982), while in others, reference has been only slight. Both Gottmann (1982) and Busteed (1983) acknowledge politico-geographical elements in Plato, Aristotle and Montesquieu, but they fail to extend their presentations to an argument for also using modern political philosophy as critique and as a visionary guide as to how territory ought to be organised. Mindful perhaps of Smith's presentation of justice concerns in human geography (Smith, 1977:131-157), Taylor (1983) hints at the emergence of a welfare-linked 'philosophic-liberal' component in political geography. The point is well taken, but it must be noted that contemporary political philosophy is not an exclusively liberal edifice (see, for example, Cohen, Nagel and Scanlon, 1980; Canadian Journal of Philosophy, 7 (supplement), 1981; Cohen, 1981; Buchanan, 1982; Graham, 1982; Sandel, 1982).

There are at least two ways in which political geography may be aligned more closely with political philosophy. One of these would involve application (and perhaps modification) of principles such as equity, freedom, justice and rights in adjudication of the spatial outcome of decisions taken privately and publicly. Rapprochement might also be used by political geographers to enhance their use of non-evaluative concepts such as legitimacy, power and state. These two possible associations between political philosophy and political geography are discussed below.

There is no shortage in geography of empirical studies of incidental or deliberate discrimination and favouring related to facility location, service area delimitation, zoning and gerrymandering. The debilitating real-income effects of, or windfall gains from, highway construction, decentralisation, property-rating adjustments and transport fare revisions have also been explored. In these, and other instances, statistics are often left to speak for themselves as evidence valued according to a simple rule of thumb such as 'more is better'. Alternatively, the impersonal calculus from welfare economics might be invoked: do the gains of the gainers exceed the losses of the losers? Politicians may judge in terms of votes lost and gained. Others rail and remonstrate without any clear indication of which values and which evaluation criteria are used and why. For example, work on the race zoning which has butchered cities, properties and social relations in South African cities (Pirie, 1984) is written in vituperative tones but shows no clearly developed politico-philosophical defence of the virtues of property rights and freedoms of association and

230

choice, either in general, or in the particular socio-economic environment of the Republic.

The sketchiest acquaintance with nuances of concepts such as freedom, justice and rights is, in practice, not a disqualification from peddling these notions. Experts blithely parade redistricting, refugee resettlement, transit subsidisation, drought relief, slum clearance and public housing with shallow reference to 'the common good', 'fairness' and the like. On the receiving end, a huge proportion of the world's discarded people cry out against injustices in state development priorities and aid programmes, appeal for equal or preferential consideration, for attention to their rights, for compensation for hardships inflicted by nature or war. Judgments about what is right and wrong are made with half an eye on the public purse and the expediency of party or national politics. In the hands of ideological rivals, evaluative principles become pliable standards, and contrasting solutions vie as best, fairest and most humane. Principles of adjudication are compromised and contradicted. They are chosen at random without reflecting on their pertinence to the issue at hand, or their consistency with other standards. Worst of all, political philosophical concepts are relentlessly manipulated and prostituted to shore up dubious claims. Only in certain quarters are the concepts 'essentially contested'; more usually they are inadequately contested.

Against this displeasing backdrop of whimsical and unprincipled planning and protest, geographers have two exacting duties. For some of us, the first is to instruct ourselves in our own vaguely held values and to prepare as properly political geographers. The second is to illuminate, devise and appraise evaluation criteria appropriate to geographical concerns, and to comment on and guide others in the selection and application of these in particular instances. A preliminary excursion into this matter (Pirie, 1983) suggests that criteria of judgment cannot be made to incorporate spatial elements (e.g. distance, accessibility) very easily, if at all. The problem does not however preclude application of aspatial criteria to evaluation of geographical patterns and the forces which shape them. Hopefully, political geographers could also demonstrate senses in which the theory of political philosophers is deficient because of its 'head-of-the-pin' character. A start may be made by investigating the way in which territoriality, property rights and locational freedom are treasured and protected, and how they enter into and weigh in the equation of 'the common good'. Historical and cross-national empirical comparisons would cast light on the dominance of certain formulations and their similarities/ differences in diverse contexts.

Far from being obsessed with justice, rights, equality

and liberty, political philosophers have also written extensively on allied subjects such as the legitimacy of the state and law. At a time when political geographers are showing increasing interest in the rationale and workings of the judiciary, the legislature, the executive and the bureaucracy, study of the limits of law and state from a political philosophical perspective may be fruitful. It would be prudent though to remember that political philosophy remains strongly wedded to the categories and assumptions of the nineteenth century. Totalitarian governments, communist regimes, quasi-democratic and tribally constituted one-party governments cannot be subsumed under those forms theorised by political philosophers (Parekh, 1982).

On a conceptual plane, the outpourings of political philosophers also permit close inspection of the integrity of everyday interpretations of power and obligation. The use made by political geographers of notions of legitimacy, consent, authority, representation, community and privacy would also benefit by careful scrutiny of their domain. Conceptual analysis corrects, but is also provokes new ways of thinking about events, and thereby, invites research into new dimensions of an issue. One example involves some recent work which has urged rethinking of justice in relation to the subjective, personal sense of being done-down rather than in terms of some more objective, universal criterion. Rival interpretations of the notion of power (Lukes, 1974) furnish another good example of theorising in political philosophy as a spur for innovative case studies. Lively arguments among political philosophers about the concept of property (Macpherson, 1978; Pennock and Chapman, 1980) offer the enticing prospect to the geographer of elevating ideas about property into a new organising concept for politically informed urban studies. The appeal resides in the many connotations of property and its material and institutional volatility. 'The urban' is nothing else but property, in the broadest sense of the word. Cities are made of parcels of land and buildings, all of these involving titles to possession, rights or private and public use and disposal, and contingent social and economic relations making for independence and dependence, rich and poor, owners and workers, wages, rents and interest payments. Viewing the city in terms of widely conceived notions of property automatically forces individual liberty, interpersonal equality, appropriation and exploitation to the fore. This brings in train matters of their mediation and adjudication by law and state; the disjuncture between social-scientific conceptions of the city and political-philosophical conceptions of propriety and proprietary is avoided.

CONCLUSION

The crafting of philosophically better informed research and
teaching in political geography is an important addendum to
the subject's full agenda. Although no claim is made that
political philosophy should be the touchstone of a less
fragmented political geography, it does seem that the former
field of inquiry may be tilled to useful effect. The task
will be difficult and must involve more than the customary
genuflection and flirtatious dabbling:

> those who butterfly their way around some of the
> most complex and difficult philosophical material
> of the twentieth century, severing passages from
> their immediate context of concern, and remaining
> in unrelieved ignorance about the larger body of
> thought of which each work is an integral and
> connected part, appear to feel that 'doing
> philosophy' is rather like picking currants out of
> a bun (Gould, 1983:433).

Conceptual analysis within modern political philosophy
has produced a vast and intricate literature on the
contextually proper use, coherence and limits of key
evaluative and non-evaluative concepts which are all too
easily invoked and (mis)used. The opportunity to tap this
work as a source for sensitive and informed politico-
geographical judgment ought not to go begging. Political
philosophy also offers a way of filling the values-vacuum in
terms of which countless lives are lived, decisions
inflicted and futures circumscribed. The importance of
tying action to clearly understood and consistently held
values cannot be stressed enough to apologists or to those
contesting legitimacy and morality. For the scholar of
political geography an abstract, conceptual approach affords
a means of critical appraisal which is detached from existing
society. Criticism may be directed at better adjudication or
at exposure of the myths by which privilege and oppression
are justified, revolts conducted and conflict resolved. As
Goodwin (1982:15) has reminded us,

> compliance is as much a mental as a physical act:
> the ideas supporting and validating advanced
> industrial society must be propagated and
> internalised. The study of political theory should
> make us more defensive and sceptical of the
> justifications of the systems which nourish our
> compliance, and more willing to contemplate
> alternative political and social forms.

Above all, the literature of political philosophy

raises and tackles the profound and primordial questions of what is good and right. There is a sound case for extending the geographical imagination by transcending empirical studies of <u>what is</u> and broaching the deeper question of <u>what ought to be</u>. As Wittgenstein warned, "... when all possible scientific questions have been answered, the problems of life remain completely untouched" (cited in Sayer, 1981:51).

REFERENCES

Ackerman, B. A. (1980) <u>Social Justice in the Liberal State</u>, University Press, New Haven
Barry, N. P. (1980) <u>An Introduction to Modern Political Theory</u>, St. Martins, New York
Berlin, I. (1962) 'Does political theory still exist? in P. Laslett and W. G. Runciman (eds.), <u>Philosophy, Politics and Society</u>, Blackwells, Oxford, 1-33
Buchanan, A. E. (1982) <u>Marx and Justice</u>, Methuen, London
Busteed, M. A. (1983) 'The developing nature of political geography', in M. A. Busteed (ed.), <u>Developments in Political Geography</u>, Academic, London, 1-68
Buttimer, A. (1974) <u>Values in Geography</u>, Association of American Geographers, Washington D.C.
Claval, P. (1983) 'Equity and freedom in political geography' in N. Kliot and S. Waterman (eds.), <u>Pluralism in Political Geography</u>, Croom Helm, London, 36-46
Cohen, M., Nagel, T. and Scanlon, T. (1980) <u>Marx, Justice and History</u>, Princeton University Press, Princeton, N.J.
Cohen, G. A. (1981) 'Freedom, justice and capitalism', <u>New Left Review</u>, 126, 3-16
Editorial Board (1982) 'Editorial essay: Political geography - research agendas for the nineteen eighties', <u>Political Geography Quarterly</u>, 1, 1-18
Feinberg, J. (1980) <u>Rights, Justice and the Bounds of Liberty</u>, Princeton University Press, Princeton, N.J.
Flathman, R. E. (1973) <u>Concepts in Social and Political Philosophy</u>, MacMillan, London
Flathman, R. E. (1976) <u>The Practice of Rights</u>, Cambridge University Press, Cambridge
Goodwin, B. (1982) <u>Using Political Ideas</u>, Wiley, Chichester, U.K.
Gottmann, J. (1982) 'The basic problem of political geography: the organisation of space and the search for stability', <u>Tijdschrift voor Sociale en Economische Geografie</u>, 73, 340-9
Gould, P. (1983) 'Things that worry me: 1. Peer review and correcting error', <u>Environment and Planning A</u>, 15, 432-4
Graham, K. (1982) <u>Contemporary Political Philosophy: Radical Studies</u>, Cambridge University Press, Cambridge

Kliot, N. (1982) 'Recent themes in political geography - a review', Tijdschrift voor Economische en Sociale Geografie, 73, 270-9

Laslett, P. and Runciman, W. G. (1956) 'Introduction', in P. Laslett and W. G. Runciman (eds.), Philosophy, Politics and Society, Blackwells, Oxford, vii-x

Laslett, P. and Fishkin, J. (1979) 'Introduction', in P. Laslett and J. Fishkin (eds.), Philosophy, Politics and Society, Blackwells, Oxford, 1-5

Lukes, S. (1974) Power: A Radical View, MacMillan, London

MacPherson, C. B. (1978) Property: Mainstream and Critical Positions, Toronto University Press, Toronto

Nozick, R. (1974) Anarchy, State and Utopia, Basic Books, New York

Parekh, B. (1982) Contemporary Political Thinkers, Martin Robertson, Oxford

Partridge, P. H. (1961) 'Politics, philosophy, ideology', Political Studies, 9, 217-35

Partridge, P. H. (1965) 'Political philosophy and political sociology', Australian and New Zealand Journal of Sociology, 1, 3-20

Pennock, J. R. and Chapman, J. W. (1980) Property, New York University Press, New York

Pirie, G. H. (1983) 'On spatial justice', Environment and Planning A, 15, 465-73

Pirie, G. H. (1984) 'Race zoning in South Africa: board, court, parliament, public', Political Geography Quarterly, 3

Plamenatz, J. (1960) 'The use of political theory', Political Studies, 8, 37-47

Petit, J. (1980) Judging Justice, Routledge and Kegan Paul, London

Quinton, A. M. (1967) 'Introduction', in A. Quinton (ed.), Political Philosophy, Oxford University Press, London, 1-18

Rawls, J. (1972) A Theory of Justice, Harvard, Cambridge, Ma.

Runciman, W. G. (1965) Social Science and Political Theory, Cambridge University Press, Cambridge

Ryan, A. (1979) The Idea of Freedom, Oxford University Press, London

Sandel, M. J. (1982) Liberalism and the Limits of Justice, Cambridge University Press, Cambridge

Sayer, R. A. (1981) 'Defensible values in geography: can values be science-free?' in D. T. Herbert and R. J. Johnston (eds.), Geography and the Urban Environment, Wiley, Chichester, U.K. 29-56

Smith, D. M. (1977) Human Geography: A Welfare Approach, Arnold, London

Strauss, L. (1949) 'Political philosophy and history', Journal of the History of Ideas, 10, 30-50

Taylor, P. J. (1983) 'The question of theory in political geography', in N. Kliot and S. Waterman (eds.), <u>Pluralism in Political Geography</u>, Croom Helm, London 9-18

Tuan, Yi Fu (1974) 'Commentary', in A. Buttimer (ed.), <u>Values in Geography</u>, Association of American Geographers, Washington, D.C., 54-8